GREATNESS
Revealed

by Andy Purvis

From One to Another !
Go Wolf pack 1974
Andy Purvis

Foreword by Dr. Manuel Flores

XULON PRESS

Xulon Press
2301 Lucien Way #415
Maitland, FL 32751
407.339.4217
www.xulonpress.com

Paperback ISBN-13: 978-1-6628-5276-3
Hard Cover ISBN-13: 978-1-6628-5277-0

Also by Andy Purvis
"The Greatness Series"

In the Company of Greatness
Copyright © 2010

Remembered Greatness
Copyright © 2012

Greatness Continued
Copyright © 2014

Secrets of Greatness
Copyright @ 2016

This Close to Greatness
Copyright © 2017

Greatness Above the Noise
Copyright © 2018

Shadows of Greatness
Copyright © 2019

Legends of Greatness
Copyright © 2021

purvisbooks.com

ABOUT THE AUTHOR

Andy Purvis is a long time sports enthusiast. He lives in Corpus Christi, Texas, with his wife Jan and one cat. He has four grandchildren and six great grandchildren. They are also in his Hall of Fame! He has been in restaurant management for over 37 years and has retired. Andy has always had an acute interest in and knowledge of sports history and has been blessed to meet and interview many of his childhood heroes. Andy writes for the *Island Moon*. He has also co-hosted several sports talk radio shows with a couple of different partners for 26 years and continues on SportRadioCC 1230 KSIX. He maintains contact with many sports "greats" and other sports friends. Feel free to visit www. purvisbooks.com, and leave a comment in the review section.

Praise for the "Greatness Series"

"Andy, I enjoyed the warm memories of Pepper Rogers, among others in your book Legends of Greatness. I was at KU during his final years there. I appreciate the biographical detail that you use as a foundation for the stories and the lively details you supply. How do you remember them all and keep them straight? It's a lifetime of colorful tidbits for each sports figure, and then multiply it over all your books and it's an overwhelming amount of information you're sharing. It's a sport fan's dream come true."

Kris Bair
Pastor for Island Presbyterian Church

"Got your book Legends of Greatness, and the first story I read after my daughter checked it out was about Chip Williams, phenomenal. As always you are amazing, but this one hit me harder, especially after losing my father-in-law whom I loved like he was my dad. Thank you. He was my Chip. You do that to more people than you will ever know. What a blessing you are."

Everett Bush
Sports Fan and Fan of Yours!

"I received your book <u>Shadows of Greatness</u>, today. I won the book on the radio show you guest appear on and am looking forward to diving into the stories. I am new to Corpus Christi and I make a point to tune into KSIX Radio on Tuesday mornings and Thursday evenings to catch your shows with "Pudge" and Dennis. You are a breath of fresh air to listen to. You have a gift of being knowledgeable and entertaining without being negative or disrespectful. I wanted to take a moment to thank you for your generosity and for the note you include with the book. Best regards and I look forward to the book, your other books, and hearing you on the radio."

Scott Schuler
Postmaster, Refugio Post Office

"Only Andy Purvis could redeem irredeemable longtime Arkansas basketball coach, Eddie Sutton, in the eyes of a Texas Longhorns fan like me. That's just one example from one of Andy's previous books of his gift for seeing and showing the best in people. If you're a kid age nine to ninety, Andy's stories about sports heroes will captivate you. You'll eat up what you already knew and you'll find out plenty you didn't – like I did about that damned Eddie Sutton!"

Tom Whitehurst
Tom is a Multiple Award Winner for Editorial and Column Writing with the Corpus Christi Caller Times. He is also a Charter Member of the CC Songwriters Hall of Fame

"Andy, I have been reading your last book entitled <u>Legends of Greatness</u>. Your book about these untold stories is absolutely superb. You did an outstanding job. It took me back in time and I caught myself dreaming of these legends and all about sports folklore and the events they participated in. Love you, brother!"

Bobby Purvis
Cousin on my Father's Side

"The Greatness Series by Andy Purvis is a collection of sports stories that enables the reader to experience sports from the perspective of the athletes and fans from a different era. The research-based narratives place the reader deep into the struggles, challenges and successes of the individuals involved in reporting, coaching and competing in the world of sports. These books are a true gift to families, legacies and memories of our heroes from the past. Thank you, Andy, for the opportunity to be able to read these books with my grandchildren. The experience of sharing these books is a tribute to your legacy."

Raul R. Prezas, Ed. D.
Retired Professor of Educational Leadership
Texas A&M University-Corpus Christi

"Good afternoon Mr. Purvis. I simply wanted to reach out to you today to thank you for your weekly contributions to the *Island Moon*. I enjoy reading your articles. I am a born and raised Corpus Christian, but I only started working on the island about a year and a half ago. I work at the Fire Station on Commodore. I look forward to each issue and typically read it from cover to cover. Continue the good work sir."

David Amaro III
Fireman

"Over the years I have enjoyed reading Andy Purvis' Greatness Series of books. The research that Andy puts into each of his heroes jumps off the page, as he reveals one golden nugget after another. What makes reading the stories that Andy has shared with us even more enjoyable is that we're able to hear the stories too. As each story unfolds, we're able to HEAR Uncle Andy's voice come through the charm of his prose. It's impossible to put Andy Purvis' books down because as you finish one story, you're ready to be enriched with the glorious story of another sports hero."

Michael "Pudge" Aradillas
Radio Show Host: The Halftime Report with Pudge

DEDICATION

This book is dedicated to my two newest teammates, my great grandkids Miss Etta Bennett and Master Judge James. These two were both born during the writing of this book. We look forward to laughing out loud, finding out about new things together and learning about each other.

Andy Purvis

Greatness Revealed
CONTENTS

Legends of Greatness
CONTENTS

FOREWORD

IS THIS SPORTS HEAVEN?

With apologies to the Righteous Brothers, if there is a "Sports Heaven," there must be some hellacious teams up there. Imagine all the great athletes who have left us. From "Babe" Ruth to Muhammad Ali, Bart Starr and Mickey Mantle, they were the epitome of "Greatness." This Corpus Christi writer and sports enthusiast has made it his life's project to document the accomplishments and deeds of more than 450 athletes, coaches, owners and broadcasters, rekindling memories of greatness with each page he writes about these men and women, who thrilled us with their athleticism and enthralled us with their careers. These were not mere humans. They were like Greek gods who descended upon the Earth and for a brief moment became legends. They were "Greatness" personified. Andy's books – nine of them now with the printing of Greatness Revealed this year – pay tribute to those great athletes who have passed on. He is like the gate keeper at the "Pearly Gates" interviewing them one last time to write the ultimate story about them before they see St. Peter and gain admission to an eternity of greatness. That greatness and ultimate ticket to sports eternity is granted by Purvis as he pens one last sports story, one final definitive obituary and one more eloquent eulogy to the memories of these man and women who have left us.

So, imagine Mickey Mantle, the greatest switch-hitter ever in baseball stepping up to be interviewed by Andy. Behind Andy stands a bearded man flipping a baseball bat into the air and catching it with his left hand. St. Peter, who throws a pretty mean curveball, is reviewing a set of books and watching videos on a large screen. He is looking into

Mantle's life and marveling at his exploits on and off the field. Mickey is distracted by St. Peter's activities, but first he must talk to Andy for that final interview. "Mickey, Mr. Mantle," Andy says to the startled Hall of Fame player. "You're not lost. You're in the right place, Sports Heaven.... but first, an interview. Sit down, please." Mickey lets out a sigh and murmurs below his breath, "Another one? Not again. I did enough of those interviews with you sports guys down on Earth. Now, I have to do another one?" Andy responds, "Don't worry. It's just that St. Peter up there wants a brief bio and reflection of what you've done." Andy flips through some pages of material while Mickey keeps looking anxiously at St. Peter, who has the final decision on Mickey's fate. He's wearing a jersey with the No. 42 on it and a bright blue baseball cap with an Old English "B" on it. "Mickey you were a great baseball player," Andy tells him. "Those monstrous homers were impressive, and your awards and records certainly point to greatness." "Thank you," Mickey responds to Andy, doing his best "Aw Shucks" impression that only a country boy from Oklahoma could muster. "I think you have the credentials, but I'm not sure how ol' Pete feels. You know, he's wearing Jackie Robinson's jersey number now. He heard I was going to interview a baseball great and he dressed for the occasion." Mickey looks up at St. Peter again. He didn't bring a pinstriped New York Yankee's jersey with his No. 7 on the back and he is worried. "Give me a second," he pleads with Andy, "and I'll go back down for awhile and bring him a Yankee cap and jersey." "Too late for that," Andy shoots back. "Jackie was special. Because of the troubles he had breaking into baseball because of his color; St. Peter fixed it so that everyone now must wear a jersey with Jackie's number on it – 42 – at least once a year. Besides, he's not always impressed by that. You should see the number of jerseys, caps, and balls of all kind and even shoes he has up there in Heaven. It's like a sports museum." "Shoes?" Mickey asks. "Yes, they're from Shoeless Joe Jackson of the Chicago White Sox betting scandal in 1919. He brought them with him. I don't think that worked, Poor Joe." "Gee, say it ain't so, Mr. Purvis," Mickey, now in deep thought, responds. "What about Pete, how will he do?" "Ol' Rosey? Well he's still being judged. There's time," replies Andy. "And don't call me Mister. That's for guys with suits. I wear jeans, a t-shirt and tennis shoes, sometimes just comfortable enough to watch a baseball game....oh, and cap." Andy is running out of time. Behind Mickey are nearly 50 other sports greats who have made the journey for their last interview. He has work to do. The deadline for his next book is approaching. "Okay Mickey, let's get to it," Andy remarks. "Mickey you were kind of a rascal down there. You drank a little too much and partied as if it was going to be your last day on Earth, every day since you were a 20-something phenom. And, some of the escapades you and your pal Billy Martin, and others, got into around New York City; well, people are still talking about them. Why there's even a story of you two shooting some rancher's mule, his cows and chickens down in Texas. Mickey stood up. "Now wait a minute, that's only a story. That didn't happen," he said. Andy replied, "Mickey there's almost as many pluses and minuses in your story to pretty much even things out. You're a tough one." "So, am I safe at home?" Mickey asks. "Yes, you're safe at home Mickey," Andy replies. "That's going to be my recommendation. St. Peter will see you now." Andy puts down his pen and turns off his recorder. He realizes he's talking to "The Mick." He understands he has been blessed in pursuing a sports writing career. Yes, Mickey you gave us thrills to last a lifetime and beyond. And, so many little kids of that era adored you. You gave them hope. You made them understand that life is not easy, no matter how talented you are. You were their hero, and you will live forever in their minds and in the minds of their children and grandchildren, who will yearn to own a baseball card with your image. Mickey thinks about that a while. "It'll be my privilege," The Mick said. "I signed a few extra before I left Texas so that there would be some authentic Mickey Mantle signed cards available after I leave. You know how those imposters are. And, if you want to make sure, just look at how I signed the "M's." "Yes Mickey, they have to be as authentic as you," Andy responds. "Now I have some interviews to do and stories to write. Go see St. Peter now." The interview ends.

Mickey thanks Andy and tells him it's the best interview he ever had, as he climbs up the Heavenly stairs lined with baseball bats, gloves and balls. Andy tells him, "You know the stairs are different for each sport the athlete represents. And, Mickey, baseball tryouts are tomorrow up there. Let's see which team chooses you." Mickey keeps walking, turns around and pulls something from his pants' pocket. It's an autographed baseball which he will give to St. Peter. "Hey, just in case," he remarks. Andy just smirks as the next athlete steps up for an interview. Beside, there are several games tonight and The Mick makes his Heavenly debut tomorrow. Mickey Mantle was greatness and he is part of the legends of "Uncle Andy's" "Greatness Series." Mantle was in Purvis's first book entitled, In the Company of Greatness. Now he has new company to challenge as he meets the new group of athletes enshrined into Andy Purvis' "Greatness Series." Uncle Andy, by the way, is the moniker he earned for his radio personality on a Corpus Christi sports talk radio show entitled "Halftime Report with Pudge," hosted by a sports jock nicknamed "Pudge." The title is well-deserved and his stories are even better when heard live on the radio.

But enjoy the book. The stories are marvelous. Two of the best ones are the articles on Tommy Lasorda, former Los Angeles Dodgers manager, and Houston Astros pitcher J.R.

Richard. They were friends of Andy as were many of the athletes he wrote about in his books. But it was Andy Purvis who got the last word, the last and lasting reflection of these great athletes enshrined in Uncle Andy's prose and Hall of Greatness. Thank You, Andy Purvis, for keeping greatness alive.

> Dr. Manual C. Flores
> Award Winning Sports Columnist
> Professor of Communications / Journalism
> Texas A&M University Kingsville

INTRODUCTION

Satchel Paige once asked, "How old would you be if you didn't know how old you were?" I would like to think 18, but now that I'm rounding third base and heading for home, I find it fulfilling to share my thoughts about some of our favorite sports heroes with others. We must learn to embrace the blessings when they come. So, Greatness Revealed, the ninth book of the Greatness Series is just another way of saying thanks for the memories. Sometimes silence is the loudest noise.

This book is a bit different as it is filled with some of the best of the best from the world of sports. So, let me fill you in on a little secret. No athlete is a super hero. They are all just human beings like you and me. But sometimes the game puts these athletes in extraordinary circumstances where things happen during a game that requires them to step up. It's those things they don't choose to happen that make them who they really are. These people eventually become great. Names like Hank Aaron, K.C. Jones, John Chaney, Curley Culp, John Madden, Don Sutton, Bobby Bowden, Floyd Little, and Elgin Baylor jump off these pages. Add stars like Bobby Unser, Sam Huff, Lee Elder, Phil Niekro, Tommy Lasorda, Jerry Remy, Dick Allen, Marvin Hagler, Sam Jones, and you begin to understand that during the year 2021, where Covid 19, variants and vaccines were front page news, we lost a significant group of icons from the sports world.

My friends all tease me that they don't want to be in my next book because everyone I have written about has now left us for a better place. But for me passing away is not an ending. As far as I'm concerned, they are all still here and I carry them inside of me for as long as I am here. Hopefully, these words and thoughts of mine that you are reading will allow you to do the same. We can search and search for the answer to why, but sometimes we just have to be still and be ready to receive the answer that's coming.

I started off writing about things that I saw when younger. Now, I write more about the times that I miss. Why do we miss these people so much? We can't turn back time. When things happen in real time, it's final, and those moments never come again. Maybe that's the secret.

Andy Purvis

PREFACE

Have you ever noticed that we count time with stories? It may be one of the best ways to measure our lives. So often, we find meaning for our lives through stories. I've spent the last 12 years sharing others' stories through my words, not so much for me, but for them. I give them a voice. The spectacle of sports is real and unrehearsed. Sports can help us heal and move forward. I love sharing their stories and the moments with all of you. The 48 stories you are about to read in my newest book, <u>Greatness Revealed</u>, are not just sports stories, they are also life stories. Sometimes life feels like a long series of losing people and things that you love, but I'm not going to lose this one. Some folks can't come to terms that their family, friends, companions, and sports heroes are no longer here, but some of my sports heroes are and some of yours are, too. I carry all of their memories within me every day; they give me strength to forge ahead. They never go away. These legends don't die just because the person does. As long as people talk about them, they are still relevant.

These players bring our memories back to life. They bring our grandfathers, uncles, brothers, and dads back to life. They connect these games and the players to our lives. Maybe that's why we care so much. Sometimes the folks I write about get a bad rap. This is my way of sticking up for some of these guys. I can't right the wrongs that have been done to them, but I can help their families deal with the hurt. That is part of the power of kindness and the written word. When people allow you into their lives through the written word, the radio or TV, what greater compliment could you ask for? That's powerful. How lucky am I? When I go to work, I know I'm going to help others have fun, smile and laugh out loud.

Ever wonder what our life's purpose really is? We all have our roles. Most of what I set out to do, I did against great odds. We are all who we are, and it takes all of us to make a family. We can't explain miracles; we can only give thanks for them. I never really knew what was in store for me in my life, but I have always been surprised and grateful. Finding God has been my biggest find. I have always believed that if you give something all you've got, everything you have; then it doesn't really matter whether you win or lose, as long as you risk everything by putting all your eggs in one basket. I've tried to do that with my faith, my marriage and family. I also did that with my work in the restaurant business, my sports-talk radio career, and my writing. There's no halfway with me. It's all or nothing and that's why I feel so blessed to have lived a charmed life.

It's tough when we start seeing our sports heroes' age. Then I look in the mirror and go "Oh yeah, me too." I do believe that one of God's greatest gifts to mankind is old age. I believe that one of the jobs of a great-grandparent is to help their offspring become great-grandparents. Maybe getting older is time's way of reminding us how great the best moments of our life really were.

So, who's going to remember us? That is a question all of us ask ourselves eventually. Who will remember our exploits after we're gone?

What happens 50 years from now when the name Andy Purvis comes up and folks respond, "Who was that guy?" and nobody knows. That would be a travesty. That's why I choose to keep these people relevant with my books. It's hard to write about others without sharing with the reader some of yourself. Some of these people became my friends and most are Hall of Fame athletes. They were smart and funny and kind. They were also unselfish and loyal. So, I wanted to reveal to you what kind of persons they were. That way, I bring this book to life; for they will be with me and now you, for always.

In the movie *A River Runs Through It*, there's great line that goes like this. "Now nearly all those that I loved and did not understand in my youth are dead, but I still reach out to them." It's true that these folks I write about are no longer with us. I choose not to mourn their deaths, but celebrate their lives. They may have even suffered at the end, but they were some of the strongest men and women I have ever known. Some of them even changed the fate of those who watched them perform. There are three things you have to consider to be a good writer. What you know to be true, what you think you know, and what you don't know. When I write about these folks, I don't see athletes, owners, announcers, or coaches; I see mothers and fathers and sons and daughters. My job is to show you how they made a difference. That is the true reason for what I do. Enjoy!

Andy Purvis

THE REAL SAINT

Have you ever noticed how players start to sway side-to-side when standing on the sidelines before a game and listening to the National Anthem? Some have both hands behind their back and others place their right hand over their heart. That's what athletes do when they're getting ready to go into battle. See that sway? See the look on their faces, that faraway stare? That means they are focused. It's personal now. They've been thinking and preparing for this moment and now is the time to empty their tank. The atmosphere is crazy. Now it's on.

All linebackers are incredibly gifted athletically. They have a high threshold for pain, and they are willing to put a lot of time into the sport. They also have a mean streak. Most of them come across as the nicest guys in the world, but they all have something dark inside of them to draw their strength from. The media nicknamed him "Super Collider," but his teammates called him "Meat."

He was strong and stout, just a powerful man. This guy was as mean as the entire 1990 Detroit Pistons basketball team, and he was always looking for someone to hit. The man loved football like a kid loves cake. He had the instinct of a cheetah, owned the eyes of an assassin and showed no emotion, like a surgeon. His neck was so big it reminded me of a telephone pole. The best way to describe this guy was "Yikes." This fellow was the kind of guy who thought nothing of being the bully and kicking sand in your face. He had sweet feet, and when he got to a ball carrier, it was not a

1

pretty sight. Some believed he collected and kept opposing running backs' body parts in his bathtub. This guy was as good as two players; it was like lining up against Starsky and Hutch. No doubt he was a train wreck waiting to happen, and his fans loved him like a child loves Christmas. The man was always all in and hit so hard, his opponents went down like they had been a part of a drive-by-shooting.

Some of the best defensive players in the NFL were born in North Carolina. You will recognize the names of Carl Eller, Bobby Bell, Jethro Pugh, Jack Tatum, Chris Hanburger, and Julius Peppers. Now you can add Vaughan Johnson, the real saint.

Vaughan Monroe Johnson was born on March 24, 1962, in Morehead City, North Carolina, to Monroe and Valerie Johnson. His father worked in the marine construction business, building docks, seawalls and bridges. Vaughan was recruited by many different programs out of West Carteret High School in Morehead City, N.C. He played running back and linebacker for Head Coach Robbie Barrow's Patriots. Vaughan led his West Carteret High School team to a 17-3 win-loss record in his final two seasons. Head Coach, Bo Rein of the N. C. State Wolfpack, made an impression on him, and Vaughan signed with the Wolfpack in 1980. Besides, he wanted to stay in state so his family could see him play. By the time he arrived on campus, Coach Rein had been replaced by Monte Kiffen. Johnson was given #33 to wear. Vaughan sported a clean-shaven head, stood 6-feet-two inches tall and weighed 180 pounds, as a freshman. He played mostly on special teams during his first season. As a sophomore, he was a backup linebacker, but by his junior year he had added one inch to his height and 55 pounds of muscle to his frame. He became a starting linebacker for the next two years under Pete Carroll, the defensive coordinator for the Wolfpack. In 1982, a kid named Andy Hendel walked onto the football team and became a standout linebacker. These two would become known as the "Blitz Brothers." Johnson and Handel combined for 328 tackles during their junior year. Vaughan Johnson was selected an All-American in 1983. He also earned first-team honors from The Sporting News and second-team honors from the Associated Press. Johnson led the team in tackles in 1982, with 167, and again in 1983 with, 144. His career total for tackles stands at 384, which ranks him sixth all-time in the Wolfpack record books, against other linebackers like Chuck Amato, Bill Cowher and Stephen Tulloch. No doubt, Johnson was one of the scariest linebackers to ever suit up for the Wolfpack. Vaughan once said about the opposing players, "When I hit them, I like to see their eyes glaze over and roll back."

Johnson and Handel also spent two years together after graduation from N. C. State, with the Jacksonville Bulls of the United States Football League, (USFL). This league folded at the end of the 1985 season, and Vaughan joined the New Orleans Saints, who had drafted him 15th overall in 1984 supplemental draft of USFL players. He joined Head Coach, Jim Mora, and the Saints in 1986 and played in all 16 games, as a rookie. In 1987, he was moved to a starter and played every game for the next four years.

On November 29, 1987, the Saints traveled to Pittsburgh to take on the Steelers. It was a cold day and the Saints had won five games in a row. Pittsburgh, trailing 20-14, had the ball first-and-goal on the Saints' four-yard line, with less than four minutes to play. On first down, Vaughan Johnson stopped Rodney Carter at the two-yard line. On second-and-goal, Merrill Hoge was stopped by Johnson at the one-yard line. On third down, quarterback Mark Malone had running back, Frank Pollard, open in the end zone for a touchdown, but the pass was deflected by Johnson. On fourth and goal from the one, Johnson took out the lead blocker, allowing

Sam Mills and Brett Maxie to tackle Pollard, short of the goal line. The Saints held on to win that day, 20-16, and clinched their first winning season in franchise history, along with a spot in their first playoffs. This game reminded me of a series of car crashes, like racing at Talladega in shoulder pads. It had been Vaughan Johnson's finest hour.

They were called the "Dome Patrol." Sam Mills, Pat Swilling, Ricky Jackson and Vaughan Johnson were the line-backing core of the New Orleans Saints under Head Coach Jim Mora, in the late 1980's and early 1990's. These four played together for seven years for defensive coordinator, Steve Sidwell, in his 3-4 defense. Vaughan and Mills were the inside linebackers, while Swilling and Jackson played on the outside. These guys left more bodies lying around on the field than Freddie Kruger. Together they were as nasty as anyone you have ever seen in your nightmares. They combined to play in 18 Pro Bowls and received 10 first-team All-Pro selections. The "Dome Patrol" led the Saints to the playoffs four times in six years, 1987, 1990, 1991 and 1992. In 1992, they made NFL history, as all four linebackers from the same team made the Pro Bowl together. All four players are in the Saints' Hall of Fame and the Louisiana Sports Hall of Fame. Ricky Jackson was inducted into the Pro Football Hall of Fame in 2010.

Johnson became one of the hardest hitters to ever wear the black and gold. Vaughan played eight seasons with the Saints (1986-1993), and finished his career with the Philadelphia Eagles in 1994. After football, Johnson returned to North Carolina and started his own concrete construction business. During his pro career, he recorded 669 tackles, five fumble recoveries, 12 sacks, four interceptions and 11 forced fumbles. Johnson totaled over 100 tackles in three different seasons; including a career best 114 in 1988, to go with two sacks and an interception. Johnson earned six All-Pro mentions and four Pro-Bowls trips. He was inducted into the Saints' Hall of Fame in 2000 and the Louisiana Sports Hall of Fame in 2011. Johnson is also a part of the Greater New Orleans Sports Hall of Fame and the Allstate Sugar Bowl Hall of Fame.

Famed philosopher and author, Ayn Rand, once wrote, "The question isn't who is going to let me, it's who is going to stop me." That was the very essence of Vaughan Johnson.

Vaughan Johnson left us on a Thursday, December 12, 2019. He died at Duke University Medical Center, from kidney disease. He was 57 years old. Johnson is survived by his wife Shirley, three sons Brandon, Bryan, Michael, and a daughter Vonda. Vaughan and Shirley also had three grandchildren.

In a conversation with Tim Peeler after retirement, Johnson said. "God has been good to me," said Vaughan. "I loved coming back to work with my father during college breaks and during the off-season. I love working with my hands and building things, and I loved working for myself. God blessed me. I was fortunate to play as long as I did and get out of the sport in good health. I was able to make a smooth transition and return home to do what I always wanted to do."

CLASS ACT

There is an old saying about baseball: "When you figure it out, you can't play anymore." This is not true about umpires. With time, they continue to get better and better. Let me tell you about this fellow. He was a positive person who was extremely likeable. This guy could put the good in good morning. A fun guy, baldheaded and smart, he was as straightforward as a bayonet. He loved Notre Dame Football and could be seen wearing their gear in the umpire's dressing room. He wasn't born with tremendous speed or the ability to leap tall buildings in a single bound. I don't think he could even skip. But what he was born with was a love for the game of baseball, a lot of patience, determination, "guts," will power and nerves of steel. You can't be a Major League Umpire without all five of those. After graduating from college, he attended the Joe Brinkman Umpire School and spent nine years in the Minor Leagues. This guy watched kids pitch who couldn't find the mound, much less home plate. Most baseball umpires are like elephants, they never forget. He was taught that umpires must be quick to think and slow to anger and that a good umpire umpires the ball, not the player. Umpires behind home plate may make as many as 275 to 300 calls per game. This man had fantastic strike-zone awareness.

Most umpires are loners. It has to be that way. Umpires very rarely stay in same hotels as the teams. They are never seen in the same restaurants. Chances are if you're a regular fan, you would not recognize an umpire off the field. He is usually with a fellow umpire or an old friend outside of baseball.

In case you're wondering, the three toughest plays for the home plate umpire to call are number one, stealing home: he has to call a ball or strike, make sure the pitcher didn't balk, determine if there was interference on the batter or the catcher, and call the runner out or safe, all in three seconds; number two, the half-swing: because the umpire's sight is usually blocked by the catcher; and number three, the foul tip in the dirt.

Legendary sportswriter, Grantland Rice, once wrote, "Class is a very hard thing to define. It could be the swing of a slugger's bat. It could be the lift of a thoroughbred's hoof. It could be the flick of a quarterback's arm, but once you see it, you never forget. Eric Cooper was a class act!" This wasn't just a paycheck for Eric, being a Major League umpire was a dream. If your kid wants to grow up to be a baseball umpire, just show him Eric Cooper highlights.

Eric Richard "Coop" Cooper was born on December 18, 1966, in Des Moines, Iowa, to Bill and Beth Cooper. Eric played baseball with Hoover High School. He attended and graduated from Iowa State University in 1989, with a degree in Transportation Logistics. In 1990, you could find Eric in Florida at umpire school. He had grown to 5 feet 10 inches tall and weighed about 215 pounds. For the next nine years, Cooper honed his skills in the Appalachian League (1990), Midwest League (1991), Florida State League (1992), Eastern League (1993-1994), American Association (1995-1997) and the Pacific Coast League (1998).

On June 17, 1996, Coop made his debut in the Majors as a Minor League fill-in. He wore #56 and joined a Major League Umpire staff in 1999 until his recent death. He would spend the next 21 years doing what he loved the most besides his family. Coop became a part of "crew chief" Joe

Wests umpiring crew that also included Will Little and Andy Fletcher. Interestingly, I went to college with Joe West and his roommate, Drew Coble, now a former National League Umpire. West and Coble were my suitemates for two semesters. "Country Joe" West was a fine quarterback in college and pitcher for the baseball team. You know umpires are funny guys, too. One time, West and some of his fellow umpires including Cooper gave legendary baseball announcer, Vin Scully, a gift. It was a book entitled <u>Everything I Know about Broadcasting</u> by Vin Scully. "When you open the book," laughs Scully, "every page is completely blank. I keep it out on display at my home in the living room for all to see."

During his 21 years, Eric Cooper umpired 2,684 games, 672 of those behind home plate. Coop has been credited with 70 ejections over his career, with seven being the most, in 2001. He has ejected mostly managers for arguing balls and strikes. Those managers included Bobby Valentine, Terry Collins, Mike Hargrove, Charlie Manuel, Clint Hurdle, Bob Brenly, Ron Gardenhire, Tony LaRussa, Bobby Cox, Dusty Baker, Jim Leyland and A. J. Hinch. Hall-of-Famers Frank Thomas and Mike Piazza also made the list. Eric Cooper was inducted into the Hover High School Hall of Fame.

Cooper's last game as a Major League umpire occurred on October 7, 2019, during the American League Division Series between the New York Yankees and Minnesota Twins. He umpired second base during Game 3 at Target Field in Minnesota.

Eric Cooper was a rising star. Before interleague play the All-Star Game was the crown jewel of baseball. It was the only time fans could see players from other teams, besides at the World Series. He was selected to work the All-Star Game in 2005. He worked three Wild Card Games in 2015, 2016 and 2017. Coop also worked nine Division Series' in 2003, 2005, 2008, 2009, 2011, 2012, 2013, 2014 and 2019. He was part

of the umpiring crew for four League Championships Series'
in 2004, 2015, 2016 and 2017. Eric Cooper was picked to
work the 2014 World Series between the Kansas City Royals
and the San Francisco Giants, because of his success rate on
replay challenges. Eric Cooper had only three calls reversed
all season. Cooper also worked the World Baseball Classic
games in 2009 and 2013.

Cooper was also present during some historic games, as
part of the umpiring crew. On October 6, 2001, he worked
home plate in Cal Ripken Jr.'s final game. He was the third-
base umpire in the last game played in old Yankee Stadium in
2008. Eric was behind home plate on September 11, 2008,
when Francisco Rodriquez tied the Major League single-
season record for saves. Cooper was also behind home plate
during three no-hitters. Hideo Nomo threw a no-hitter in
2001, and two no-hitters were thrown by Mark Buehrle in
2007 and 2009, the second one a perfect game.

Players' Union Chief Tony Clark said upon hearing the
news of his passing, "Eric Cooper's friendly and familiar
presence in the baseball community will be missed by all of
us. He was a professional and a gentleman whose passion for
our game, the players, and his fellow umpires was evident in
the way he went about his work and life."

Here is an example shared with me by former Baltimore
Orioles' manager, "Buck" Showalter. Cooper once spoke
to Showalter after working an Oriole's game behind Caleb
Joseph, a young catcher. "This kid can catch," said Eric. "It
may have been the difference in me making the team or not,"
said Joseph.

They all stood at attention for Eric Cooper that night in
Houston, Texas. The date will read October 22, 2019, and
it was Game One of the 115th Fall Classic. Life had thrown
"Coop" a Major League curveball. Eric Cooper died on
October 20, 2019. He was but 52. Cooper had had knee

surgery earlier in the week and was recuperating at his father, Bill's home. The surgery was successful, and Eric phoned his fellow umpires on Saturday. Eric suffered a pulmonary embolism (blood clot) on Sunday and passed away. Eric Cooper made his home in Citrus Park, Florida, with his wife Tara, and two stepsons, Chaz and Colt. Eric Cooper thought he was lucky to be an umpire. I thought it was the other way around.

THE BEAST

All linebackers are a little bit crazy, but this guy may have been the Dracula of the bunch. A large man, he stood 6 feet 4 inches tall and weighed 240 pounds. He looked more like a prizefighter than a football player. This guy controlled the line of scrimmage the way he used to run the neighborhood, by sheer force. The man was all Texan and spoke with a gravelly voice. He wore a cowboy hat and loved horses. He creaked when he walked and his knees wore the scars of ten years of smash-mouth professional football. The first time I saw him, he was wearing a Kansas City Police Department cap. I wanted to ask him if he got that before or after he was booked. "He was a bad boy," said my pal Bobby Smith, former running back for the Buffalo Bills. "He would pick you up and throw you down like a guy throwing mail bags off a train." Linebackers see their careers as one long walk through enemy territory, armed with only a helmet, shoulder pads and a nasty temper. As long as he was in the huddle, his teammates felt like they had a chance to win. When he lined up at outside linebacker, the Kansas City Chiefs' defense reminded you of a shark frenzy. This team was terrific and played punch-you-in-the-mouth defense. He was also as good at stealing footballs out of the air as John Dillinger was at robbing banks, and he left his impression on every running back in the league. Otherwise, he was very much a Southern gentleman, but underneath all that gentleman stuff there was pure steel. E. J. Holub played football like Jeb Stuart attacked a flank.

Emil Joseph (E. J.) Holub, Jr., was born on January 5,

1938, to Emil and Theresa Holub in Schulenburg, Texas, population less than 2,500.

The running joke was that the town was so small they didn't have a town drunk so they all took turns. His family later moved to Lubbock, Texas, and he graduated from Lubbock High School in 1957. He lettered in football and track and field where he threw the shot put and discus. He was offered and accepted a football scholarship to attend Texas Tech University. He became a two-way player at offensive center and linebacker. His teammates nicknamed him "The Beast." As a senior, E. J. recorded 15 unassisted tackles and 8 assisted tackles against the University of Baylor. He also had 18 unassisted tackles, 10 assisted tackles, and returned an interception 40 yards, for a touchdown against the University of Arkansas. He was some kind of player. From 1958 to 1960, Texas Tech was transitioning from the Border Conference to the Southwest Conference. Under Head Football Coach, DeWitt Weaver, Holub became a two-time All-American offensive center (1959, 1960) and was First Team All-SWC twice (1959, 1960). He finished tenth in the 1960 Heisman Trophy voting.

Holub was chosen by the Dallas Texans in the 1st round (6th overall) of the 1961 AFL Draft and the Dallas Cowboys in the 2nd round (16th overall) of the same draft. He signed with the Dallas Texans. During his rookie season, Holub once played for 58 minutes during one game at offensive center and outside left linebacker. He only left the field during kickoffs. He would later play for 54 minutes during a game. Having a player play on both sides of the ball in the same game was not very common in the 1960s. I can only think of one other player, who was named Chuck Bednarik, of the Philadelphia Eagles, that did that and his nickname was "Concrete Charlie." Obviously, it took a tough guy to play both ways. In 1963, the Dallas Texans became the Kansas City Chiefs. They were not associated with the NFL

Dallas Cowboys.

E. J. wore #55 both in college and in the pros. He played in 127 games in ten professional seasons for the Texans and Chiefs. He recorded nine interceptions for a total of 76 yards in returns. In 1963, he tied the record for the most interceptions in a season, with five. He also recovered one fumble. He did not score a touchdown. During his ten seasons, he underwent over 20 surgeries. Eleven of those surgeries were on his knees (six on his left and five on his right). His teammates were amazed at his ability to have his knees drained of blood and fluid before game time.

Holub was a five-time Pro Bowler (1961, 1962, 1964, 1965, and 1966) and a two-time All-Pro (1962, 1963). He was a three-time AFL Champion (1962, 1966, and 1969) and the only player to start in two Super Bowls (I and IV) at two different positions. He was a starting linebacker for the Chiefs during Super Bowl I. Remarkably, in Super Bowl I, Holub would face another fine Texas Tech player, in Donny Anderson of the Packers. Green Bay won 35-10. Holub started at offensive center in Super Bowl VI and helped Kansas City beat the Minnesota Vikings 23-7. E. J. retired from football after suffering another left knee injury during the 1971 training camp. In 1976, Holub was inducted into the Kansas City Chiefs' Hall of Fame.

Interestingly, the photo used for the cover of Sports Illustrated for Super Bowl IV is a picture of Holub snapping the ball to the Chiefs' quarterback Len Dawson. I purchased a copy of that magazine and placed it in a stamped self-addressed return envelope along with a $25 check and sent it to the Kansas City Chiefs. I requested an autograph from Len Dawson on the cover. All that needed to be done was Len sign the cover, place it back in the envelope and mail. I never got the magazine back but guess what? The check got cashed. So, I have Len Dawson's autograph on the back of my check.

Besides all his athletic accolades, E. J. Holub will be remembered for two things: his ability to impact the game of football on both sides of the ball and his dedication to Texas Tech University. Holub was placed in the Texas Tech Hall of Fame in 1977. In 1986, E. J. Holub became the very first College Football Hall-of-Famer from Texas Tech. In 1989, his #55 became this very first number retired by the University as a Red Raider. In 2012, he was named a Texas Tech Big 12 Legend and was also enshrined into the charter class of Texas Tech's Ring of Honor.

After his career, Holub became a professional cowboy. He loved horses and managing ranches. In fact, he even had a horse named "Cowboy." He also spent lots of his time and effort raising money for student-athlete scholarships as a member of the Red Raiders' Club. He stayed close to the football team and could be seen on the sidelines for most games. During the final game of the 1999 season, Holub gave an incredible speech during halftime of the Texas Tech-Oklahoma game. The Red Raiders stormed out of the locker room at AT&T Stadium and beat the Sooners 38-28. It was Red Raiders' Head Coach "Spike" Dykes' final game. Holub was one of the many that picked up Dykes and carried him off the field.

E. J. Holub died on a Saturday, September 21, 2019. He was 81. E. J. is survived by his wife Sandi, and their two daughters, Jana Hill and Joell Doyle, and two step-children, Shannon and Jeff Ireland. He had eight grandchildren and one great grandson. E. J. Holub represented old-time values and he had a heart for people. He was just a tough guy who loved football and being a cowboy. He will be well-remembered.

Four Quarters of the Truth

There he sat coiled like a snake. He looked like a guy who might have a price on his head somewhere north of Georgia. This man loved contact. This guy was out there and would punish you at the drop of a hat. The man was a cyclone, tornado and typhoon all rolled into one. It was like someone dropped him out of the rafters. He played the game of football all his life with his teeth and fist clinched. His intensity and drive were unparalleled. He wasn't the most popular guy on the team. If this guy had wanted to make friends, he would have become a birthday clown. Everyone was his enemy, and he took out his aggression on the playing field. FBI agent Melvin Purvis would have gotten nervous if this fellow flew into town. This man was known for his blue collar, hardnosed, punch-you-in-the-mouth defense. He was the kind of kid that would dance on the television when he was younger, but his mother would scream, "Get off the TV; you're going to break it." As long as he was in the huddle, you felt like you had a chance to win. He was the type of player who could bring a play to an end in a flash. Stealing passes was his game. He was silly, and said he didn't mean to interrupt people. He explained that he just randomly remembered things and got really excited. When you asked him what he was doing today and he said "Nothing," it did not mean he was free. It meant he was doing nothing. They should have named a satellite after him; and after a game, he always looked like he had just come home from a bar fight.

Somewhere along the line, every bad guy does something good, but it doesn't mean he gets a pass on the bad stuff.

This man believed that whatever God puts in your heart, whatever dreams he gives you, you can do this. Regardless of his personality and funny quirks, the man never lied about anything. You always got four quarters of the truth from Jake Scott. He was the right guy at the right time, and would become the standard for NFL free safeties. It was like Scott was armed with an extra sense when he played safety. Ever see a cat playing with a mouse? The idea is not to kill the mouse, but just to keep the game going. This guy could anticipate, and he mirrored receivers. He studied their step count and releases. He was never into self-promotion. The only thing dirty about Jake Scott was his uniform.

Jacob E. Scott, III, was born on July 20, 1945, in Greenwood, South Carolina, but grew up in Athens, Georgia. As a young man, Scott played football at Washington-Lee High School, located in Arlington, Virginia. Scott was recruited by former Bulldog, Fran Tarkenton, and enrolled at the University of Georgia to play college football. Georgia head coach, Vince Dooley, started him as a receiver, but then moved Scott to the safety position. While at Georgia, Scott led the Bulldogs with six interceptions in 1967 and 10 in 1968. He was named First-team All-SEC Defensive Back by the Associated Press (AP) in 1967, and again in 1968 by the AP and United Press International (UPI). Scott returned his 10 interceptions for 175 yards in 1968. Scott's college career total of 315 return yards on interceptions is still the most in Georgia school history, and he also holds the current Georgia record for career interceptions.

In 1969, Scott left Georgia after his junior year to play professional football for the BC Lions of the Canadian Football League. He played flanker and returned punts for one year, before bring drafted by the Dolphins.

Scott was drafted in the seventh round, with the 159th pick of the 1970 NFL Draft, by the Miami Dolphins. Scott became the NFL's first $100,000-a-year defensive back. During his rookie season, Jake had five interceptions and returned one punt for a touchdown, while playing with a separated shoulder. He also had seven interceptions for 138 yards during his second year (1971), while playing with a broken left hand and right wrist. Both injuries required a cast. Still, he helped his team reach Super Bowl VI, but the Dolphins lost to the Cowboys 24-3.

There is no doubt that Jake Scott was an integral part of the 1972 Miami Dolphins' undefeated team (17-0). He was teamed up with Dick Anderson to form one of the top safety duos in NFL history. Two interceptions in a Super Bowl game against quarterback Billy Kilmer of the Washington Redskins was just another day at the office for Jake Scott. The Dolphins won that day 14-7, and Scott was chosen the MVP of Super Bowl VII. After receiving a brand new automobile for the MVP Award, Scott said, "I think I'll give Bill Kilmer an extra set of keys." Jake also helped the Dolphins win Super Bowl VIII 24-7 over the Minnesota Vikings by recovering two fumbles, and recording 20 punt return yards and 47 kickoff return yards in a Super Bowl game. Jake set the record for most career fumble recoveries in the Super Bowl with two and he is still the only player to have recovered one of his own team's fumbles and one of his opponent's fumbles in a single Super Bowl. In 1976, after six seasons in Miami, Jake had a "falling out" with head coach Don Shula and was traded to the Washington Redskins for Bryant Salter.

From 1970 to 1978, Jake Scott, a free spirit if there ever was one, played free safety and returned punts for the Miami Dolphins and the Washington Redskins. During his six seasons with Miami, he never missed a game. If you needed a Blue Collar guy, he was it. Standing 6 feet tall and weighing 188 pounds, Jake Scott played in 126 games during his nine seasons. He intercepted 49 passes and returned them 551 yards during his career, 35 in six seasons as a Dolphin, and 14 in his final three years as a Redskin. Scott also had 13 fumble recoveries during his NFL career. Jake recorded 1,357 special team yards by returning punts and he scored one touchdown. He also added 137 yards on six kickoff returns. Scott played in three consecutive Super Bowls, winning back-to-back championship rings during the last two.

In 1974, Scott became the *Football Digest* Defensive Back of the Year. He was a five time Pro-Bowler from 1971-1975 and a two-time First-Team All-Pro in 1973 and 1974. Jake Scott was inducted into the Georgia Sports Hall of Fame in 1986. He joined the Florida-Georgia Hall of Fame in 1998 and the Athens Athletic Hall of Fame in 2000. On November 18, 2010, Jake Scott and his roommate, Bill Stanfill, were inducted into the Miami Dolphins' Honor Roll. And last but not least, Jake Scott joined the College Football Hall of Fame on May 17, 2011.

During Super Bowl XL, all the living Super Bowl MVPs were invited back to be introduced before the game. Scott was one of only three who chose not to attend, along with Terry Bradshaw and Joe Montana. He did attend Super Bowl L.

Jake Scott was somewhat of a recluse; he never married and shunned the spotlight. He also harbored ill feelings for his Georgia head coach, Vince Dooley, and Dolphins' head coach, Don Shula. After football, Scott and Shula did not speak with each other for 28 years. Jake very rarely attended team reunions. Scott was one of only two living players who skipped the 1972 Dolphins' 25th celebration in 1997. They finally met at a memorabilia show in 2010. Don Shula died in May of 2020. As for Coach Dooley, Vince said, "Jake Scott was the greatest player I ever coached" and ranked him ahead of Heisman Trophy winner, Herschel Walker. It's funny, but now that I think about it, Scott wore the #13. I find it interesting that a decade later, Dan Marino would wear the #13 for the Dolphins during his career. That would not have happened if the Dolphins had retired Scott's number. After football, Scott lived in the Colorado Mountains, the Florida Keys and Hawaii. He invested wisely in rental property, and loved to hunt, fish, play golf and travel.

Jake Scott died on November 19, 2020, in an Atlanta hospital. He suffered a severe head injury when he fell down a flight of stairs. The fall left him in a coma. The doctors were unable to stop the bleeding in his brain. He was 75 years old.

I believe that the moral of Jake Scott's story is what we make of our life and what we leave behind. That's our legacy.

PIONEER

Lou Holtz once said, "Ability is what you are capable of doing, motivation determines what you do, and attitude determines how well you do it." This guy had all three in spades. There was something different about him. Tall and strong, he looked like a racehorse. Faster than an F-15, he was as dependable as tomorrow and as quiet as a forest. This man had the knack of making the dramatic look easy. The man never took a day off. On the field he was a wild mustang that could not be captured. He was all gas, no brakes, and poetry in motion at track and field. He was a one-man show. It has been said that you can't teach toughness. You're either born a willow or an oak tree. The bigger the moment the better he performed, and most agreed that he performed like he was possessed. For Rafer Johnson, running was freedom. He never looked to his left or his right, for that would only slow him down. Look at the way horses run, straight ahead at all times.

Pioneer is a word that is seldom used when describing athletes. Rafer Johnson used his amateur athletics career in the Olympics, to pioneer a formable career in acting. He understood that we never know when today will be our last day. We never know when we will play our last play. So, while you have the chance, appreciate it.

Made of sand and grit, Rafer Lewis Johnson was born In Hillsboro, Texas, on August 18, 1934. His father, Lewis, worked in the cannery business and his mom, Alma, was a housekeeper. At 18 months old, he and his family moved to Dallas. Rafer then moved with his family to Kingsburg,

California, at the age of nine, where they lived in a railroad car and suffered from poverty. It turned out that the Johnson clan was the only African-American family in town. Rafer attended Kingsburg High School where he participated in football, baseball, basketball, and track and field. He was also elected the class president in both junior high and high school. At the age of 16, between his sophomore and junior years in high school, Rafer's coach, Murl Dodson, drove Johnson 24 miles to Tulare, California, to watch Bob Mathias compete in the 1952 U. S. Olympic decathlon trials. After the event, Johnson mentioned to Dodson that he thought he could have beaten most of the athletes he had just watched compete.

The decathlon consists of ten events over the course of two days. Those events are as follows: 100 meter dash, running broad jump, shot put, high jump, 400 meter dash, 110 meter hurdles, discus throw, pole vault, javelin throw and 1500 meter run. A month later, Coach Dodson drove Rafer back to Tulare to watch Mathias's victory parade. A few weeks later, Johnson competed in a high school invitational decathlon and won the event. Rafer Johnson won both the 1953 and 1954 California State high school decathlon meets. Johnson would top out at 6 feet 3 inches tall and weighed 201 pounds. He attended the University of California, at Los Angeles (UCLA). You couldn't find an athlete who worked harder than he did. He would proceed to break the world record in total points scored, in his fourth competition. In 1955, Johnson won the decathlon and a Gold Medal in the Pan American Games held in Mexico City, Mexico. He also qualified for both the long jump and decathlon for the 1956 Summer Olympics, to be held in Melbourne, Australia. Rafer was unable to compete in the long jump due to an injury, but he did finish second and also won the Silver Medal in the decathlon behind teammate Milt Campbell, of the U.S. It would be the last time Rafer did not win in any competition.

Rafer Johnson was a complete athlete. He played basketball under legendary coach John Wooden, at UCLA. He was a starter for the 1958-59 team and was considered by Wooden to be a great defensive player. Can you imagine Rafer Johnson on a fast break? He was chosen Sports Illustrated Sportsman of the Year in 1958. In 1959, Johnson was also drafted in the 28th round by the Los Angeles Rams of the NFL, as a running back. Johnson studied and trained under UCLA track coach, Elvin C, "Ducky" Drake. Johnson missed competing in 1957 and 1959 because of injury and a car wreck, but broke the world record in the decathlon in 1958 and again in 1960, at the Olympic Summer Games held in Rome. Also in 1960, Johnson won the James E. Sullivan Award as the top amateur athlete in the U. S., and he was chosen as the first African-American to carry the American Flag during the Opening Olympic Ceremonies in Rome. Coach Drake also mentored Yang Chuan-Kwang of Taiwan, who attended UCLA. Rafer and Yang trained together and became friends. During the competition, the lead in points swung back and forth between Rafer and Yang, with Rafer holding the lead by a small margin after nine events. Johnson would run his personal best time at 4:49.7 in the 1500 meter and finished just 1.2 seconds slower than Yang, winning the Gold Medal by 58 points with a new Olympic record total of 8,392 points. Exhausted and drained afterwards, Johnson ended his athletic track and field career. His personal best in the 100 meter stands at 10.3 seconds.

It seems that while Rafer was training for the 1960 Olympics, his friend Kirk Douglas told him about a part in the movie, *Spartacus*. It was the part of an Ethiopian gladiator named Draba, who refuses to kill Spartacus after defeating Douglas in a duel. Johnson read for the role and received the part, but was forced to turn it down, because being paid for the part would make him a professional and that would ruin his amateur athletic status and he would not be able to compete in the Olympics. The role would eventually go to another UCLA athlete known as Woody Strode.

In 1960, after the Olympics, Johnson worked as a sportscaster and in

motion pictures. After making several films he found himself the weekend sports anchor on the local NBC affiliate in Los Angeles, KNBC. Johnson married Elizabeth Thorsen in 1971 and they had two children together, as well as four grandchildren. His movie career would last from 1961 to 1990. Rafer made appearances in, *The Sins of Rachel Cade*, and *Wild in the Country*, with Elvis Presley. Also *Pirates of Tortuga*, *None but the Brave*, *The Last Grenade* and *Soul Soldier* preceded his James Bond film, *License to Kill*.

In 1968, Rafer Johnson served on the organizing committee for the very first Special Olympics competition to be held in Chicago, Illinois. The following year (1969) he founded the California Special Olympics. Rafer also worked on United States Senator Robert F. Kennedy's 1968 presidential election campaign. On June 5, 1968, with the help of NFL tackle, Rosey Grier, they apprehended Sirhan Sirhan immediately after Sirhan had assassinated Kennedy at the Ambassador Hotel in Los Angeles. Kennedy died the following day at the Good Samaritan Hospital. Johnson served as a pallbearer for Robert Kennedy and would later discuss the details in his autobiography entitled <u>The Best I Can Be</u>, published in 1999.

In 1998, Johnson was named one of ESPN's 100 greatest North American Athletes of the 20th Century. In 2005, Johnson was awarded an honorary Doctor of Humane Letters degree from Whittier College. In 2006, the NCAA named him one of the 100 Most Influential Student Athletes of the past 100 years. On August 25, 2009, Governor

Schwarzenegger and Maria Shriver announced that Johnson would be one of 13 California Hall of Fame inductees in the California Museum. Rafer Johnson was a member of the Pigskin Club of Washington D.C. and the National Intercollegiate All-American Football Players' Honor Roll. The Junior High School Rafer attended in Kingsburg is now named after Johnson, as are the Rafer Johnson Community Day School and the Rafer Johnson Children's Center, both located in Bakersfield, California. In 2016, Johnson was inducted into the Texas Track and Field Coaches' Hall of Fame.

Rafer Johnson died after suffering a stroke on Wednesday, December 2, 2020. He was 86 and living in Sherman Oaks, California. He is survived by his wife Elizabeth. His brother, Jimmy Johnson, was a cornerback for the San Francisco 49ers and is a member of the Pro Football Hall of Fame; and his daughter, Jennifer, competed in beach volleyball at the 2000 Olympics in Sydney, Australia, after she graduated from UCLA. His son, Joshua Johnson, followed his father's footsteps and won a medal in the javelin throw, during the USA Outdoor Track and Field Championships.

In 1984, at the age of 50, Rafer Johnson climbed the 99 steps in the Los Angeles Memorial Coliseum to light the caldron at the start of the Summer Olympics. There were 92,516 in attendance. Johnson reminisced: "Was I concerned about making it to the top of the stairs? Yes! Was I thinking about whether I might trip or fall? Yes! Did I have any doubt that I would come through? No!"

DEEP, FAR AND GONE

Albert Einstein once wrote, "Force equals mass times acceleration." I wondered if Albert had seen this guy hit a baseball. This man loved to put his bat in motion and he owned a beautiful swing. He was the home run kid, the kind of guy who gave his team breathing room with his bat. Watching this man play baseball was like eating Jell-O, there was always room for more. He wasn't shy, outspoken, and carried a chip on his shoulder the size of the national debt. I hope this guy had a good lawyer because he murdered baseballs. He could hit a baseball farther than most. Some of the balls he hit stayed up in the air longer than astronaut Allen Sheppard. He was such a dangerous hitter; the man was even walked intentionally during batting practice. When a well-timed swing connects with a pitch, the ball leaves the neighborhood. He knew the instant he hit the baseball that it would take a guy with a ticket in the stands to catch it. To call him just a hitter was like saying Secretariat was just a horse or John Wayne was just an actor. This man was put on this planet to hit with runners in scoring position, and he was so active he wore out the dirt around third base. As a pitcher you wanted this guy guarding the third-base line when you went to the mound. His swing was so powerful; he could knock the air out of the park. The man could hit anywhere. He was so strong; his home runs left the park at the blink of an eye.

His true love was hitting; all the rest was just work. His ability to spray line drives and home runs with one swing was incredible. Hitters like him couldn't be replaced, because there weren't many like him. He perfected the baseball swing and there was serious thunder in his bat. The man could hit .350 in the dark or 20 home runs, by accident. I'm not so sure the balls he hits 450 plus feet were still round when they found them. When Dick Allen hit the ball, it made a different sound. There is nothing in sports that compares to the home run in baseball. It's the Big Bam, the punctuation, the Bambino, the Sultan of Swat. It's Mickey Mantle, Willie Mays, Hank Aaron and Frank Howard. It's Robert Redford in *The Natural*. It's all of those things. He loved putting on a show and when this guy hit a home run, you would talk about it. Dick Allen had a quick bat. The faster the ball arrived at home plate, the harder he hit it back. "Deep, far and gone" was Dick Allen's mantra.

Richard Anthony Allen showed up on March 8, 1942, in Wampum, Pennsylvania. Allen would later become know as the "Wampum Walloper" for his ability to hit a baseball, but he grew up in Chewton, Pennsylvania, a town of 488 people located just outside of Wampum. Dick was one of nine raised by his mother, Era, who kept houses for a living. She called him Dickie. His favorite team was the Brooklyn Dodgers, and he remembered spending hours each day hitting rocks and announcing every hitter in their lineup. "I was always paying for new window panes all over the neighborhood," said his mom. Dick became a great athlete at Wampum High School and started at guard for the basketball team. In 1958, Dick and his older brothers, Hank and Ronnie, all played for coach L. Butler Hennon on the same basketball team. In 1960, as a senior, Dick was a strong physical man who stood 5-feet-11 inches tall and weighed 187 pounds, yet he captained his high school basketball team to the Division B State championship. That year, Dick Allen was selected an All-American. All three brothers were selected All-State in basketball and all three were also signed to play baseball by the Philadelphia Phillies. Although Dick loved basketball, he put the game of baseball ahead of basketball, because the pay was better. Dick and his brothers wanted to buy a new home for their mother. Allen was signed by Phillies scout, John Ogden, upon graduation from high school, for an estimated $70,000. The first thing he did was buy his family a new house.

Interestingly, Allen was signed as a shortstop, in 1960. He and his brother Hank started their careers in Elmira in the New York-Pennsylvania League. During his physical, he was told that he needed glasses and was soon switched to playing in the outfield. His batting averaged went up and he spent 1961 with the Magic Valley team located in Twin Falls, Idaho, in the Pioneer League. In 1962, Dick played in the Double-A Eastern League located in Williamsport. John Ogden had been right. Dick Allen was one of the crown jewels of the Phillies organization. During his first three seasons in the Minor Leagues, Dick hit 49 home runs and drove in 245 runs.

The Philadelphia Phillies were a terrible baseball team and the club finished in last place from 1958 to 1961. They even managed to lose 23 straight games during the 1961 season. In 1962, the Phillies improved a bit and enjoyed their first winning season since 1953. No doubt, Philly was a tough town for any sports figure, especially if you were a player of color. Who could forget how disgraceful their treatment was of Brooklyn's Jackie Robinson in 1947? In fact, the last team in the National League to integrate was the 1957 Philadelphia Phillies. By then, every other team in the National League had an established black star on their team. Most of the early players of color on the Phillies were Cuban, Mexican or Panamanian. Their first African-American star was Wes Covington, acquired in a trade with the Kansas City Athletics in 1961. In 1963, the Phillies Triple-A Minor

League club moved from Buffalo to Little Rock, Arkansas. Dick Allen was the first black player to play there. Allen was shocked at the response he received from the fans. "I didn't know anything about the racial issues in the Deep South and didn't really care," said Allen. "Maybe if the Phillies had called me in, man to man, like the Dodgers had done with Jackie Robinson, at least I would have been prepared. Instead, I was on my own." Allen promptly dropped the very first routine fly ball hit to the outfield. The crowd went nuts, and it frightened Allen. Dick was raised in small town where blacks and whites got along. But here, he was chastised by racial taunts, threatening notes left on his car windshield and stuff thrown at him from the bleachers. He was harassed by the local cops and was afraid to walk around town alone. Allen considered quitting the team. His older brother Coy came to see him and convinced him to stick it out. In his autobiography entitled <u>CRASH</u>, Allen talks about how fans would yell names at him and call him "chocolate drop" as he came off the field between innings. "I would have loved to have gone a round or two with those racist cowards," said Allen. "Black players learned to not look up."

Interestingly, Allen finished the season hitting .289 with 33 home runs and 97 RBIs. Even with all the hardship, he was voted the MVP of the International League. As a result, Allen was called up to the Phillies and made his Major League debut on September 3, 1963, in Milwaukee, Wisconsin. Initially, Allen wore #32 before switching to #15.

By 1964, you could find Allen at third base instead of the outfield. Phillies' Manager, Gene Mauch, insisted on calling him "Richie". Mauch's decision was simple. The Phillies were a left-handed hitting team and they needed a right-handed hitter with power in their lineup. Richie would become the talk of baseball in 1964. On April 19, 1964, at Wrigley Field he hit two home runs against the Cubs and raised his average to .429. But, there was trouble on the horizon, because he did not like being called Richie. Yet, he was listed as Richie on all the scorecards, rosters and team info. "To be truthful with you, I'd like to be called Dick. I don't know how Richie got started. My name is Richard and they called me Dick in the Minor Leagues. He continued, it makes me sound like I'm ten years old. I'm 22. Anyone who knows me well calls me Dick. I don't know why as soon as I put on a uniform, it's Richie." The Philadelphia sportswriters continued to call him Richie until 1966, and then they began to refer to him as Rich Allen.

With Allen hitting .313 in August of 1964, pennant fever had engulfed the city of Brotherly Love. While his bat continued to talk the talk, his fielding was a sore spot with 41 errors committed at third base. Yep, he was booed unmercifully. At the end of the season, the Phillies had a 6½ game lead with 12 games to be played. The Phillies had a complete collapse and proceeded to lose 10 games in a row. Still, Allen had done his part by hitting .400 during those ten games. Both the Cardinals and Reds caught the Phillies, and St. Louis would go on the beat the New York Mets and clinch the National League pennant.

Allen won the 1964 Rookie of the Year Award with a .318 batting average, 29 home runs, and 91 RBI's. He also led the league with 125 runs scored and was the only one on his team to start all 162 games. In 1965, Allen held out for a raise and refused to attend Spring Training. He asked for $25,000, but was offered $20,000 a year and he accepted. The team started slowly again in 1965, but not Allen. On April 12th, he hit the first regular season home run ever hit in the new Astrodome in Houston. One of his most impressive moments occurred on May 29th at Connie Mack Stadium, against the Cubs. Allen took a first inning pitch from Chicago's pitcher, Larry Jackson, and drove the ball an estimated 510 feet. This blast sailed over a 15-foot high billboard located on the roof in left-center field and the ball landed in a tree some 50 feet up on Woodstock Street, a block away from the ballpark. It may have been the longest home run ever hit at Connie Mack Stadium. Allen seemed unimpressed. Dick was selected the starting third baseman for the All-Star team.

On July 3rd, Allen and teammate Frank Thomas had words while taking their hacks in the batting cage. Words and blows were exchanged and after the game, Thomas was placed on waivers. Thomas was a popular player and the fans booed Allen and blamed him for Thomas's release. The 1965 season ended with the Phillies in sixth place, but Allen still batted .302 with 20 homers and 85 RBIs. He had also cut down on his errors from 41 to 26 and led all National League third basemen with 29 double plays turned.

In retaliation to the fans that booed, Allen wrote messages to them and himself in the dirt around third base with his cleats, until the commissioner made him stop. Allen also began wearing a batting helmet at all times for protection from items being thrown at him by the fans and had his best year with the bat in 1966. He swatted 40 home runs while hitting .317 and drove in 110 RBIs. He was also voted to his second All-Star Game and finished fourth in the National League MVP vote. Teammate and funny man, Bob Uecker started calling him "Crash," as in crash helmet. His play rewarded him with an $85,000 a year contract in 1967. Allen started again for the All-Star Team and hit a home run to give the NL an early 1-0 lead. On July 8, 1967, he showed up late for a night game and was benched by manager Gene Mauch. He was back in the lineup the next day and hit a huge home run. Still the fans booed. There were many controversies during Dick Allen's career. Eventually, he wanted out of Philadelphia. On August 24, 1967, Allen was pushing a car he was rebuilding up his driveway when his right hand slipped and went through the headlight. Two tendons were severed and a nerve was damaged. After a five-hour operation, the doctors gave him a 50-50 chance of ever playing baseball again. By the end of the 1967 season, Dick Allen had been labeled an outlaw by the local media. Despite leading the team in every offensive category, Allen remained the nemesis. His hand healed enough for him to attend Spring Training in 1968. He was moved to right field. Dick showed up late again on June 1st and was fined and sent home. By now, manager Gene Mauch had experienced enough and gave the Phillies a "him or me" ultimatum. The Phillies fired Mauch on June 15, 1968, and replaced him with Bob Skinner. Still, the Phillies finished the year in seventh place. They tried to trade Allen that winter but were unsuccessful.

The 1969 season would be Dick Allen's last in Philadelphia. Dick continued to miss airplanes and show up late at home games. On June 24th, he learned of his suspension by Skinner on the car radio while trying to get too a game whose starting time had been moved up because of a doubleheader. At the time of his suspension, Dick was hitting .318 with 19 home runs and 45 RBIs. Allen stayed away for 26 days until meeting with Phillies owner, Bob Carpenter, on July 19th. Allen agreed to come back to the team and Carpenter promised to trade him at the end of the year. Bob Skinner eventually became fed up and resigned. On October 7, 1969, the Phillies traded Dick Allen, "Cookie" Rojas and pitcher Jerry Johnson to the Cardinals for Curt Flood, catcher Tim McCarver, outfielder Byron Brown and pitcher Joe Hoerner. Allen arrived in St. Petersburg, Florida, for Spring Training in 1970. He continued to wear the #15. On opening day, Allen hit a home run and two doubles in five at-bats to help St. Louis beat the Montreal Expos 7-2. On April 10, 1970, the Cardinal fans gave Allen a standing ovation before his first home game in St. Louis. Allen was excited about being in St. Louis. "No wonder they win over here. I feel like I made the big leagues," said Allen. "This is the best ballclub I ever played with, and I'm not kidding. This team has a lot of talent and a lot of speed." He would be voted to his fourth All-Star Team as the starter at first base. In Mid-August of 1970, Allen led the team in home runs and RBIs, but tore his hamstring sliding into second base against the Giants on August 14th. He only played in five more games that season. Unfortunately, the Cardinals were a little disappointed on how long it had taken Allen to heal and traded him to the Los Angeles Dodgers on October 5th, four days after the 1970 season had ended. The Cardinals received second baseman Ted Sizemore and catcher Bob Stinson for Allen. Dick was a large part of the 1971 Dodgers' success. Wearing his usual #15, Allen hit .295 with 23 home runs and 90 RBIs in 155 games. Still, the Dodgers finished second to the Giants in the National League West.

Allen was then traded on December 2, 1971, for the third time in three years to the Chicago White Sox for pitcher Tommy John and infielder Steve Huntz. Allen continued to wear #15. The 1972 White Sox were managed by Chuck Tanner, a native of New Castle, Pennsylvania, and a long time friend of Dick Allen's family. Dick was far and away the most talented player on the team. Chicago fans flocked to see him play, and the White Sox drew well over one million fans during each of the three years he played there. In 1972, he led the league in home runs with 37 and 113 RBIs. He was also chosen the starting first baseman on the American League All-Star Team. Chicago finished the season with an 87-67 record; in second place behind the Oakland A's. Allen was voted overwhelmingly the 1972 American League MVP. Allen received a three-year contract worth $700,000 in 1973. He continued to hit the ball all over the field until suffering a fractured bone on his right leg on June 13th. He was out for a month and returned to the lineup on July 31st. He still had a noticeable limp and was shut down for the remainder of the season, on August 2nd. With his leg fully healed, the 1974 season was another good one for Allen. He led the league in home runs for most of the summer and started again on the All-Star Team. But, there was trouble on the horizon; he was still playing in pain. His shoulder hurt, and the pain spread to his back. Dick called a team meeting on September 14th before a game with the California Angels and tearfully announced his retirement. Interestingly, Allen never filled out the proper paperwork for retirement, and the White Sox tried to trade him to the Atlanta Braves in December of 1974. Allen said "No Thanks." He wanted no part of the Deep South. On May 7, 1975, the Phillies sent several Minor League players and an undisclosed amount of cash to the Braves for the rights to Dick Allen and catcher Johnny Oates. After six years, Dick Allen was going home. Philadelphia now played in Veterans' Stadium, nicknamed The Vet. Only two of his teammates were still on the team. On May 14, 1975, Allen played in his first game with the Phillies since 1969. He struggled most of the 1975 season and promised to be better in 1976. But, he ended up on the disabled list in late April. He was out of the lineup for a few weeks as the team played well and moved into first place in their division. On July 25th, Allen reinjured his shoulder in a collision at first base. Allen played cat and mouse with the team for the next few weeks. He claimed he took some time to consult his own doctor instead of the team doctor. Allen was activated on September 4, 1976. Allen played poorly and was benched by manager, Danny Ozark. The Phillies clinched the National League East Division in Montreal on September 26th. After the game, Allen remained in the dugout, as the team celebrated on the field. The Phillies were swept in three games by the Big Red Machine from

Cincinnati. Allen went 2-for-9. On November 5, 1976, Allen was released by the Phillies. His return to Philadelphia had been a disappointment. On March 10, 1977, Allen traded his #15 for #60 with the Oakland A's. Dick hit his final home run on May 17, 1977. June 19, 1977, would be the date of his last at-bat in the Major Leagues. He did try and return to the A's 1978 Spring Training camp, but was released on March 28th.

Dick Allen finished his 15-year career with a .292 batting average, 351 home runs and 1,119 RBIs. He played in 1,749 games, had 1,848 hits, scored 1,099 runs, and stole 133 bases. He played three positions, first base, third base and outfield. He was selected the 1964 NL ROY, the 1972 AL MVP and was a seven-time All-Star. Allen did spend some time with the 1982 Texas Rangers as a coach in Spring Training. He also appeared at baseball card shows and played in several Cracker Jack Old-Timers' Games. He wrote his 1989 autobiography entitled CRASH, co-written with Tim Whitaker. In 1994, Allen was inducted into the Phillies' Wall of Fame. In July of 2010, Allen was selected to the Philadelphia Sports' Hall of Fame. His #15 has also been retired by the Phillies.

Two of Allen's favorite pastimes were riding horses and music. He spent hours riding his horse named "Old Blaze." Dick had dreamed of being a jockey when he was a kid. He also loved to sing and formed a doo-wop group called the "Ebonistics". They recorded a song entitled "Echoes of November," which became an R&B hit in the Philadelphia area. In January of 1969, Allen and the Ebonistics performed this song during halftime of a Philadelphia 76ers game at the Spectrum.

"Cookie" Rojas tells a story of Allen arriving about 40 minutes before a game was to start. Allen asked, "Who's pitching?" Rojas answered, "Tom Seaver." Allen smiled and said "I'm gonna hit three home runs off Seaver today." Rojas continued, "He hit the first homerun to right field, then hit the second home run to left-center. Seaver was removed from the game and Allen hit his third home run off the reliever. He was some kind of hitter." There is no doubt in my mind that Dick Allen's name belongs with Hank Aaron, Willie McCovey, Frank Robinson, Willie Stargell, Roberto Clemente, Willie Mays, Billy Williams, and Reggie Jackson. Between 1964 and 1974, these gentlemen of color not only integrated the Major Leagues, but they were some of the top hitters in an era where pitching dominated.

Dick Allen died on a Monday, December 7, 2020. He was 78 and living at his home with his wife Willa, in Wampum, Pennsylvania, and Los Angeles, California.

Dick Allen fell just one vote short of a Hall-of-Fame induction six years ago, the last time his name appeared on the Golden Days committee ballot. The baseball writers had rejected him 14 times on their ballot, never giving Allen even 20 percent of their support. So, I will go ahead and say it. I believe their vote was colored by bias. Some of the voters do not understand the application of greatness. The sad note is when his day finally comes, and it will, now that he has passed it will be too late. But leave it to Dick Allen to sum up his final thoughts. "I never played the game to get into the Hall-of-Fame," said Dick. "I played to prove that I was good enough and could play with the best in the Major Leagues."

Doing This Interview

"Bear" Bryant once said, "Most coaches study the game film when they lose. I study them when we win, to see if I can figure out what we did right." This coach watched more film then Roger Ebert. He was a good-looking guy. If he could have winked at himself, he would. College football is about being a part of the community. It's about being a part of something that's larger than one's self; the games have meaning; the fans become one with one another. He was as good a coach as has ever managed a game and could spot a phony before they said their first words. With a button-down shirt and a tie, he could also be a man of mystery; some said he could have worked for the CIA. He was a stickler for details, hated clutter and unpolished shoes. The man could also be cranky and irritable, "a might prickly," as my dad would say. He thought the trouble with most coaches was that they wanted to make the game too darn complicated. This man was a tough little guy, the kind of fellow who would have fought at the O K Corral, fought at Gettysburg or Iwo Jima. He was a man's man. Most all successful coaches learned long ago that the leaders must always expect to face the opposition's best, but he never thought the opposition would include his own fans. There are football jobs, and then there's coaching the Texas Longhorns. For ten years, no matter how well his teams played, he would be compared to Darrell Royal, one the legends of Texas football. Darrell Royal and Fred Akers were completely different. Coach Royal was funny, down-home, media friendly and recruited like crazy. Darrell could have published a book of one-liners that would have become a bestseller. Akers, on the other hand, was not known for his Xs and Os, but for his defense, special teams, and he beat Oklahoma. There was a quiet swagger about him. They say down in Texas that when you find yourself standing on the wall of the Alamo, you realize that the outcome has already been decided. So, you take with you as many of them as you can before they take you.

Fred Akers defined success as having a chance to win every game. He got the most out of his players that he could, and used Earl Campbell like a bar of soap, until there was nothing left. Akers took the Longhorns to a bowl game in nine of his ten years at Texas, only to lose seven of those contests. Two of those losses, in the 1978 and the 1984 Cotton Bowls, played on New Year's Day, were to Notre Dame and Georgia. Both of those losses kept him and his Longhorns from being placed in the elite group of college football coaches and teams being ranked #1 in the nation. A reporter once asked Fred Akers what was the worst call he ever made; his answer, "Doing this interview."

On March 17, 1938, Fred Akers was born in an out-of-the-way town known as Blytheville, Arkansas, in a house untouched by progress. Fred spent his early days as a kid picking cotton. When he turned four, Fred received his first football from his father, who had found the football in a torn down Air Force barracks. He would eventually become a four-sport star in high school and chose a football scholarship at the University of Arkansas over a basketball full-ride at the University of Kentucky. Fred wanted to shake the dust of that small town off his feet. Akers starred at Arkansas as a halfback, punter and kicker, and graduated from Arkansas in 1960. His choice in life was to become a coach.

Akers started his coaching career in high school as an assistant at Port Arthur High School in Texas. In 1963, at the age of 24, Fred became one of the youngest high school head football coaches in the state of Texas, when he was hired to coach football at Edinburg High School. Akers compiled a 19-9-1 record at Edinburg in three years, before becoming the head football coach at Lubbock High School, in 1965. Akers finished his high school coaching career with a 26-12-1 record.

In 1966, Akers joined Darrell Royal's staff as an assistant offensive backfield coordinator and secondary coach at the University of Texas. Interestingly, it had been Mike Campbell, Royals' defensive coordinator, who had discovered Akers, while Fred was coaching at Lubbock High School. Fred would serve the Longhorns for nine seasons before receiving his first head-coaching job at the college level in 1975, with the University of Wyoming Cowboys.

Akers spent two years at Wyoming and posted a 2-9 record in 1975, during his first year. In 1976, with a team that started eight freshmen, Akers followed his first season with an 8-4 record and took his Cowboys team to the Fiesta Bowl. People took notice, especially, the University of Texas President Lorene Rogers and System Board of Regents' Chairman, Allan Shivers.

In 1977, Darrell Royal retired and Fred Akers became the Head Football Coach of the Texas Longhorns. Fred was 38. The Longhorn faithful were stunned. They expected Mike Campbell to inherit the head coaching job. Akers turned away from the popular wishbone offense and installed the I-formation offense, along with a young but strong defense and a future star running back by the name of Earl Campbell. Texas finished the 1977 season with a 57-28 win over Texas A&M. Before that game, it has been said that Akers whispered to Campbell, "If you give me 120 yards, I guarantee you'll win the Heisman Trophy." Campbell rushed for 222 yards. Akers would lead the #1 nationally-ranked Longhorns to an undefeated regular season, 11-0, with eight sophomores starting on defense, and a berth in the Cotton Bowl. Even though the Horns took a beating that day, losing to fifth-ranked Notre Dame, 38-10, Earl Campbell was selected the Longhorns' first Heisman Trophy winner.

Texas would come close to the national championship again in 1981, with a 10-1-1 record and finished #2 in the Associated Press poll. In 1983, the Longhorns ran the table with an undefeated regular season record, but lost to #7 Georgia, 10-9, in the 1984 Cotton Bowl. Eighteen players from Texas were drafted from that 1983 team to play in the NFL. After finishing 5-6 in 1986, Fred Akers was fired from his position as head football coach of the Texas Longhorns. It was the Longhorn's first losing season in 30 years. Akers spent a total of ten years in Austin and his win-loss record at Texas stands at 86-31-2. He had initially beaten Oklahoma and Barry Switzer, but lost his last three games against the Texas A&M Aggies. The fans voiced their displeasure for Akers whose Longhorns also lost four bowl games in a row, from 1982-1985. Fred would later accept the head coach's job at the University of Purdue. The Akers hiring caused the Boilermakers' starting quarterback, Jeff George, to transfer due to Akers' desire to run first and pass second. Akers posted a 12-31-1 record at Purdue, before being asked to resign. His 16-year career win-loss record stands at 108-75-3. In 1999, Akers coached the Shreveport Knights of the Regional Football League. The Knights finished the year, 3-5.

Darrell Royal's and Fred Akers' coaching styles were drastically different. I reached out to my friend Dotson Lewis who worked with and knew Fred Akers well. "I will say this," said Dotson. "During my tenure as Supervisor of Southwest Conference Officials, he was the second biggest pain in the neck. Number one was the President of my fan club (Lou Holtz)."

It has been said, "A good coach can change a game. A great coach can change a life." Fred Akers' players felt his honesty. Just ask Donnie Little, the first African-American quarterback to start at Texas. Little told the *Houston Chronicle*: "You could feel his honesty when he was sitting in our living room with my parents. He was preaching how he wanted to make change and make history at UT, and he was a man of his word." Donnie Little played at Texas from 1978 to 1980 and started at quarterback in 1978. There is no doubt that Little's play opened the door for other African-American quarterbacks like James Brown and Vince Young at UT. Akers knew in his heart he was a pretty darn good football coach. He did win a Western Athletic Conference Championship and two Southwest Conference Championships, while posting four top-ten finishes in the Associated Press poll. Just think, if he had won those two Cotton Bowls—heck, he may have coached at Texas forever. At least he'd have a highway named after him or a statue erected in his honor. Let's face it, in the last 127 years, only Darrell Royal and Mack Brown have won a National Championship in football, at Texas. Akers' 86 career wins at Texas rank third behind Royals' (167) and Browns' (158). He returned to Austin after his time at Purdue was over and he worked on his tennis game.

Fred Akers coached his last game of life on Monday, December 7, 2020. Fred coached the game of life until the final whistle. He was 82 and died at his home located in Horseshoe Bay, Texas, from complications of dementia. Akers was survived by his wife Diane, daughters Stacey and Lesli, six grandchildren and three great grandchildren. Danny, his son, preceded Fred in death.

No matter how much success Akers had as a coach, he never forgot how poor he was growing up. He always remembered what it was like being on the outside looking in. He believed in finding the good in people and in giving others a second chance. For him, coaching was always about respect; respect for your position, your state, the university, the fans and his players.

Tough Act to Follow

For most young football players, their fathers displayed reverence for the game. Playing football had value and meaning to people. The world seemed smaller when I was a kid. Being a Southerner meant hard work, great food, good times and football. The game of football carried our dreams on its shoulders. We never forgot who we were or who were our favorite players or teams. I remember sitting outside with my dad on Saturdays as he barbequed, while listening to the game on his transistor radio; and if the game happened to be on TV, the anticipation was unreal. My brother Cliff and I would live for those few days a year when we would actually go to the game in person. But in the world of football, quarterbacks and head coaches get judged on one thing, wins.

Lou Holtz once said, "I never coached football, I coached life." This fellow I'm going to tell you about didn't just ride into town on a bale of hay. He could be as serious as a heart attack, and became known as a system coach. The man could pull guys off a Greyhound Bus and score touchdowns. Whatever happened, he could fix it. He was the guy who could put Humpty Dumpty back together again. He was much more intense as a coach then he was as a player. He earned the reputation as a workhorse, studying film of practices at all hours of the night. He once told a reporter from *The New York Times* in 1979, "I don't remember taking a vacation." This fellow played with, worked for, hired, and replaced some of the best athletes and coaches the game of football has ever heard of or seen. His secret for success could be said this way: As a coach, for him it really was about the players. He spoke to all of his players differently, in a way to insure that everyone understood. This coach appeared so undone when his team was behind on the scoreboard. He looked like he had been washed on hot, several times in a row. His face told the story and had a line in it for every goal line stand, every blocked punt or every fit he ever threw. Sometimes you have to lose something to love it. Coaching is more than a job, more than an occupation. For him it was all about purpose. This guy could spot coaching talent from a moving car and hired some of the best in the business. Part of a coach's job is to deliver the hard truth to his assistants and athletes. A taskmaster, he asked his assistants for 16-18 hours a day.

As a player on the field, Ray Perkins could catch anything. He had the attention span of a gnat. Perkins didn't just play wide receiver; he was wide open most of the time. It wasn't that Ray was so much faster than everyone else; his opponents were just slower thinking. As a receiver, he'd put you to sleep and then take you deep. It was amazing how open Ray could get. When running with the football, Ray spent most of his time looking downfield, because there was no one close to him. Perkins was so open, he was lonely. Johnny Unitas' spirals were so crisp, Ray Perkins thought to himself, I can't drop this, they'll cut me. They called Ray Perkins "Grease." He did not accidently get that nickname. "My nickname was 'Grease' back then, because I worked as a mechanic before and after school," said Perkins. Ray always figured he could continue as a mechanic if football didn't work out for him. "I have to tell you," said Ray in an interview. "I think it all worked out O.K. for ol' 'Grease.'"

Walter Ray Perkins was born on November 6, 1941, in the small town of Mount Olive, Mississippi. Ray was the second of three children born to Woodrow and Emogene Lingle Perkins. Woodrow made a living as a carpenter, and his mom was a homemaker. At the age of three, the family moved to Petal, Mississippi, a suburb of Hattiesburg. Ray became the star running back for the Petal High School football team and, after graduating in 1963, he ended up receiving an athletic scholarship to attend the University of Alabama. Besides football, Ray also lettered in basketball, baseball and track at Petal High School. He enrolled at Alabama in 1963. After Ray suffered a serious head injury during his freshman year at Alabama, which required surgery, Coach "Bear" Bryant moved Perkins from the running back position to wide receiver. His surgery required the doctors to drill three holes into his skull, to relieve the pressure. After he recovered, Perkins became one of the lightning bolts of the Crimson Tide offense. Perkins wore #88 at Alabama and fit the wide-receiver profile, while standing 6 feet 3 inches tall and weighing 183 pounds. From 1964 to 1966, with the help of Ray Perkins, Alabama won the Southeastern Conference title in football all three years, and was crowned National Champion in 1964 and 1965. Two of Perkins' teammates, at that time, were future Hall-of-Fame quarterbacks, Joe Namath and Ken Stabler. In the days of three-yards-and-a-cloud-of-dust, Perkins caught 63 passes for 908 yards and nine touchdowns. In 1966, during his senior year, Perkins served as the Crimson Tide team captain, was chosen the Southeastern Conference (SEC) Player of the Year and was also selected a First-Team All-American split end.

Ray Perkins was selected by the Baltimore Colts with the 110th pick of the 7th round of the 1966 NFL Draft. The Colts were guided by the legendary Don Shula and quarterbacked by Johnny Unitas. For Perkins it was all about pleasing "Johnny U." Unitas had been accused of being too hard on young receivers, but took a liking to Ray right away, because of his speed and grasp of the passing game. Perkins wore #27 and spent five years in professional football (1967-1971). He played in 58 games, catching 93 passes for 1,538 yards, and scored 11 touchdowns. Ray also ran the football 10 times for 77 yards. Perkins appeared in eight playoff games, including two Super Bowls. The Colts lost Super Bowl III to the New York Jets, 16-7. Perkins' biggest catch came in the 1970 AFC Championship Game, where he caught a 68-yard pass from Johnny Unitas, for a touchdown. That touchdown helped lead the Colts to a 27-17 victory over the Oakland Raiders and insured the Colts that they would play in Super Bowl V. Baltimore won Super Bowl V, 16-13 over the Dallas Cowboys. There is no doubt that Ray would have played longer, but he suffered from several knee injuries that cut his playing career short.

In 1973, Perkins joined the Mississippi State coaching staff as an assistant for one year. From 1974-1977, Perkins coached in the NFL as an assistant for the New England Patriots. He then coached one season (1978) as an assistant for the San Diego Chargers, before being hired as the head coach of the New York Giants in 1979. Perkins was not the Giants fans' first choice; they wanted Dan Reeves. George Young did not really know Dan Reeves, but he knew Perkins from their days with the Baltimore Colts. Young had been the offensive line coach for the Colts. From 1979 to 1982, Ray only led the Giants to one winning season (1981), but he laid the groundwork for future success by hiring Bill Parcells, Bill Belichick and Romeo Crennel as assistants. Parcells had been an interesting choice. Parcells was an unknown linebacker coach for the Air Force Academy. "He's the only reason I was in pro football," said Parcells. "He's the one who brought me into the league. He was my friend." The New York Giants finished the 1981 season 9-7 and qualified for post-season play, the Giants' first since 1963. Part of Perkins' claim to fame was developing such fine players like Lawrence Taylor, Phil Simms and Harry Carson. While Parcells would replace Perkins and eventually lead the Giants to two Super Bowl wins in 1986 and 1990, Perkins returned to the University of Alabama in 1983 to coach the Crimson Tide. The New York Giants, led by Perkins, won 23 games and lost 34.

On January 26, 1983, one month after he retired, "Bear" Bryant suffered a heart attack and passed away. At the age of 42, Ray Perkins replaced shoes too big for one man to fill. It was a tough act to follow. The old saying in coaching is "Never replace a legend." As head coach at Alabama, Perkins inherited a good football team, but was still a stranger. Ray proceeded to change the offense, the announcer, he let go of several assistants, and removed Bryant's tower from the practice field. Perkins also served as the Athletic Director. Then there was Auburn and a kid named Bo Jackson. On December 3, 1983, the final score of the Iron Bowl was: Auburn 23, Alabama 20. Tide fans were not happy and spoke out after Perkins finished the 1984 season 5-6, Alabama's first losing season since 1957. In his four years as head coach, Perkins compiled a win-loss record of 32-15-1, while winning three bowl games. At Alabama, Ray averaged eight wins a season, but it was not enough. He never came close to a National Championship. At times, Perkins could be an arrogant guy, who ticked off all the Alabama fans. He was out of a job by 1986. They blamed him for everything, including global warming. Bill Curry took over for Perkins in 1987.

Ray Perkins landed on his feet by accepting his second NFL head coaching job with the Tampa Bay Buccaneers in 1987. Perkins stayed in Tampa for four years, but he never won more than five games in any one season. The Bucs won 19 games and lost 41. He was fired in the middle of the 1990 season. Perkins finished his NFL head-coaching career with a 42-75 record.

In 1992, Ray Perkins moved on to Arkansas State

University and posted a 2-9 record. From 1993 to 1996, Ray became the offensive coordinator for Bill Parcells of the New England Patriots. Ray moved on to the Oakland Raiders as an assistant, in 1997. In 1999, Ray joined the Cleveland Browns' staff as the tight-end coach and then running-backs coach in 2000. On December 20, 2011, at the age of 70, Ray became the head football coach at Jones County Junior College in Ellisville, Mississippi. His two year win-loss record there was 15-5. Ray also spent some time at Oak Grove High School, as their coach. Perkins finally called it quits and retired, in 2017. His overall college coaching record stands at 34-24-1, with three bowl wins.

There was no doubt that Ray Perkins played, coached and walked with giants of the game of football. A list of coaches who worked under Perkins is as follows: Bill Parcells, Bill Belichick, Mike Shula, Jim Stanley, Sylvester Croom, Mike DuBose, Joe Kines, John Bobo, Romeo Crennel and Marc Trestman. Perkins also worked for many great head coaches including Chuck Fairbanks, Tommy Prothro, Don Coryell, Bill Parcells, and Joe Bugel.

Ray Perkins was elected to the Alabama Sports Hall of Fame in 1990 and the Mississippi Sports Hall of Fame in 1998. In 2005, Perkins joined the Senior Bowl Hall of Fame.

Perkins never enjoyed the success as a coach that he did as a player, when he won championships with Alabama and later with the Baltimore Colts.

Ray Perkins departed on a Wednesday morning, December 9, 2020. He was 79. Perkins was living in Northport, located just outside of Tuscaloosa, Alabama. Ray had been suffering from a heart condition. Perkins' first marriage had ended in divorce. He is survived by his second wife, Lisa, two sons from his first marriage, Martin and Michael, and two daughters from his second marriage, Rachael and Shelby. He also had two grandchildren.

It has been said what you go though early in life is what forges you and helps make you who you are today. Perkins cared about each and every player. He had a heart for people, a love for people, and I believed he loved them all. Ray Perkins was a symbol of American old-time values.

I'M GETTING CLOSER

Knute Rockne once said, "It isn't necessary to see a good tackle. You can hear it." This man played a game that required you to punish your opponent in order to gain his respect. His teammates referred to him as "Pound for pound, inch for inch, the toughest football player they had ever met." He was so tough, he was darn near illegal. The man could go Li'l Abner on you in a heartbeat. This guy was known for being very physical at the point of attack; he just threw people out of his way. He loved closing fast from the blind side and could undress you with his collisions. This guy was one strong son-of-a-gun, and could hit you so hard it would knock the taste out of your mouth. He could have been a textbook Navy Seal. This fellow played football with that look of death in his eyes. He was not the kind of guy you would take literally. Calm was just not part of his DNA. His blood pressure was undetectable. I don't know if he really ever had a blood pressure. This fellow never did anything in slow motion; he was always at full speed. When he slid his helmet on, his eyes seemed to melt into one. He could be as dark as the inside of a football. Born hardnosed, a violent man on the field, he stood 6 feet 3 inches tall and weighed 249 pounds, but could run like a scat back. He owned long, flowing blonde hair, arms as hard as anvils and legs that looked like tree stumps. He had been described as "Hercules in a helmet," "Adonis in cleats." He was one of the few who could take more pain and punishment and still play, than any other player. This guy could keep the opposing teams' doctors busy. During the game, he would yell at the opposing quarterback, "I'm getting closer."

No doubt a villain, he was like a dose of poison to quarterbacks with big reputations. He spent his Sundays looking into the eyes of Joe Montana, the next weekend Dan Marino, the next weekend John Elway, Troy Aikman, Brett Favre, and then Steve Young. The list of Hall-of-Fame quarterbacks just went on and on. If you looked up the word "chaos" in the dictionary, you'd find a picture of Kevin Greene. He could roll quarterbacks like dice. The man was a kamikaze from the outside; he would come up the field, turn his body at a 45-degree angle to the ground, plant his helmet in the offensive tackle's chest and force him back on top of the quarterback. Kevin Greene had a ticket on a rocket ship to the Pro Football Hall of Fame. When talking about Greene, you heard the word "passion" far more then the word "football." Because of his passion, he could have been one of the best at anything he wanted to do.

Kevin Darwin Greene was born in Schenectady, New York, on July 31, 1962, to Patricia and Therman Green. His dad served in the U.S. Army for 30 years and retired as a colonel. The family moved to Illinois in 1976. As army brats, Kevin and his brother Keith grew up in Granite City, Illinois, after spending several years in Germany. They literally played football on military bases all over the world. His mom and dad were from Choccolocco, Alabama, and they grew up Auburn Tiger fans. "When you grow up in Alabama, you're either an Alabama Crimson Tide fan or an Auburn Tiger fan," said Kevin. Granite City High School was known for its soccer teams and not football. They were state champs in soccer four years in a row. Greene not only played football, but also basketball, and was a high jumper for the track team. Kevin graduated in 1980 and sent his high school football game films to Auburn, and they replied. They said, "We've filled the spots for linebacker. We'd like you to come down and walk on," said Kevin. "That's what I did." In 1998,

Kevin Greene was inducted into the Granite City Sports Hall of Fame.

There was a time when football was ingrained in the culture of the Southern community and it was not going to go away. Young men were destined to play football. In 1980, Greene attempted to walk on as a punter. In 1983, he tried again and made the team. Kevin Greene never earned a scholarship at Auburn and did not start a game until the Tigers' outside linebacker, Joe Robinson, was injured. Joe was a fine player and was later drafted by the Minnesota Vikings. Luckily, Kevin's parents could afford to pay his tuition to Auburn. In 1984, Greene started and ended up leading the Southeastern Conference with 69 unassisted tackles and 11 sacks, and he won the Zeke Smith Award as best Defensive Player of the Year. He was also selected the 1984 SEC Defensive Player of the Year. Kevin earned a degree in criminal justice and also enrolled into the Reserve Officers' Training Corps (ROTC). He would train with the National Guard at Fort McClellan in Anniston, Alabama, and earn the rank of captain, while completing airborne training at Fort Benning to become a paratrooper.

When asked about college, all Kevin could talk about was the great running backs at Auburn during Coach Pat Dye's reign. "We had Bo Jackson, Lionel James, Brent Fullwood, Tommie Agee and Tim Jessie. It was like 'Running Back University,'" said Greene. "Bo Jackson was a special cat. I knew that practicing against him at Auburn was going to make me a better player," said Greene. Kevin also befriended Charles Barkley while at Auburn. "He was such a good dude, always kind and nice to me as if I was a big time famous athlete like he was," said Kevin.

It was Coach Pat Dye that convinced Kevin that he could play football at the next level. "I think there's a place for you somewhere in the NFL," said Dye. "That's all I really needed," said Greene. With the 113th pick, Kevin Greene was the first player taken in the fifth round of the 1985 NFL Draft by the Los Angeles Rams. Greene was also selected by the Birmingham Stallions of the United States Football League, but chose to play in the NFL. He would wear the #91 for the rest of his NFL career.

From 1985 to 1987, Greene lined up at left defensive end in the Rams' 3-4 defense. The first sack he recorded in 1985 came against the Dallas Cowboys in a playoff game. Greene finished second in team sacks during his 1986 and 1987 seasons. In 1988, Greene was moved to the left outside linebacker position. That year, Kevin led the Rams with 16½ sacks and was second only to Reggie White in the entire league. That total included 4½ sacks against the great Joe Montana. Greene collected 16½ sacks the following year, too. He then made the All-Pro Team in 1989 and was also named to his first Pro Bowl.

In 1988 and 1989, Greene earned $225,000 for each season. In 1990, Kevin wanted a new contract worth $1 million a year. After a 39-day holdout, Greene signed a new three-year contract worth $2.5 million. His 13 sacks in 1990 gave Greene a total of 46 sacks, the most ever recorded in the NFL in a three-year span. But things changed. In 1991, Jeff Fisher became the Rams' new defensive coordinator and installed a 4-3 defense, one that Greene had never played. Greene started at three different positions during the season and only recorded three sacks. The entire Rams' coaching staff was let go after the 1991 season. In 1992, "Chuck" Knox became the head coach, but the Rams remained in a 4-3 defense and Greene was asked to play left outside linebacker. Still, he led the team in tackles and sacks.

In 1993, Kevin Greene became a free agent and he went looking for a team that played the 3-4 defense. He visited the Green Bay Packers first before joining defensive coordinator,

Dom Capers, and the Pittsburgh Steelers. Green signed a three-year $5.35 million free-agent contract with Pittsburgh. He returned to the left outside linebacker position and posted 12 ½ sacks. Greene led the league with 14 sacks in 1994 and led the team to Super Bowl XXX in 1995. During Greene's three years with Pittsburgh, their defense only allowed 3.48 yards per rush, best in the NFL. Kevin Greene spent eight seasons with the Rams before joining the Pittsburgh Steelers. Kevin had an immediate impact in Pittsburgh. Greene along with Greg Lloyd led a Steelers' defense that became known as "Blitzburgh," and played in Super Bowl XXX. I was there that day in Phoenix with my cousin Bill Osborne, to see the Dallas Cowboys outlast Kevin Greene and the Steelers. Greene was not re-signed by the Steelers due to salary cap problems. Although disappointed, Greene continued to hold the Steelers in high regard.

In May of 1996, Kevin signed with the Carolina Panthers. Kevin set an NFL record with five consecutive multi-sack games and led the NFL again, in sacks. He would finish the season named as the NFC Linebacker of the Year. Greene also received the NFL Alumni Linebacker of the Year Award. While in Carolina, Greene helped the Panthers reach the NFC title game in 1996. Remarkable, after one season and a dispute with the front office, Greene was cut by the Panthers. On August 26, 1997, Greene signed a six-year $13 million contract with the San Francisco 49ers that also included a $750,000 signing bonus. Greene had 10½ of the 54 total sacks by the 49ers. His time in San Francisco was not to be. At the start of the 1998 season, Kevin left the 49ers and signed again with the Carolina Panthers. In December of 1998, Greene got into a scuffle with Panthers' linebacker coach Kevin Steele, during a game, and was suspended for one game. Nevertheless, Greene was named to the Pro Bowl for the fifth time in his career after recording 15 sacks during the season. After 12 sacks in 1999, Greene retired from the game he loved. Kevin chose to retire while still playing at a high level rather than becoming a "designated pass rusher".

From June 16, 1996 to July 12, 1998, during the off season, Kevin Greene participated in five professional wrestling matches for World Championship Wrestling (WCW). Four of these events appeared on pay-per-view. He shared the ring with former Chicago Bear NFL alumnus, Steve Michael, and some of the biggest names in the sport. Hulk Hogan, Randy Savage, Ric flair and Roddy Piper were just some of the stars who shared the ring with Greene. In Greene's 1997 contract with the 49ers, a stipulation was included that prohibited him from wrestling. His contact with the Panthers the following season included the same. As a result of the danger involved, his professional wrestling career came to an end in 1998.

During his career, Greene played in six conference championships games and one Super Bowl. He led his club in sacks for 11 out of 15 years. Interestingly, despite playing only three of his 15 years with the Steelers, Greene decided to receive his Hall of Fame ring from the Pittsburgh Steelers instead of the Rams. "I had the time of my life playing for the Steelers," said Greene.

On January 26, 2009, Kevin Greene was hired by the Green Bay Packers as their outside linebacker coach, by Dom Capers. The Packers decided to change their defense to the 3-4 instead of their traditional, 4-3. Kevin served in this position from 2009 until 2013. On February 6, 2011, Greene became a Super Bowl champion as a coach with Green Bay. The Packers beat his favorite team, the Pittsburgh Steelers, 31-25, in Super Bowl XLV. Greene left the Packers in 2013 to coach high school football and his son, Gavin. He eventually stepped away from coaching in 2014 to spend more time with his family.

In January of 2017, Greene was hired by the New York Jets

as their outside linebacker coach. After Adam Gase was hired as the Jets' head coach in 2019, Greene was not retained.

Kevin Green played in 228 NFL games and recorded 773 tackles during his 15-year career. Only four linebackers (Clay Mathews, Bill Romanowski, Ray Lewis and James Harrison) played in more games. Sixty-two and a half of those tackles occurred behind the line of scrimmage. Greene also forced 23 fumbles. Greene was named to the Pro Bowl five times and chosen as part of the NFL's All-Decade Team of the 1990s. He led the NFL in sacks in 1994 and 1996, and recorded the third most sacks in NFL history with 160, behind only Bruce Smith (200) and Reggie White (198). Greene also owns the NFL record for sacks recorded by a linebacker, ahead of players like Lawrence Taylor and Derrick Thomas. Greene is tied for second in the NFL in career safeties, with three, and third in fumbles recovered, with 26. He returned two of those fumbles and one of his five interceptions for touchdowns. Greene averaged over ten sacks a season for 15 years.

"I loved getting a sack," said Greene. "My teammates depended on me to do that. I contributed. I didn't want to let my teammates down." After being a finalist for five years, Kevin Greene was finally inducted into the Pro Football Hall of Fame in 2016. Kevin Greene gave one of the best Pro Football Hall-of-Fame speeches ever. Look it up. Greene was joined by Brett Favre, Marvin Harrison, Orlando Pace, Kenny Stabler, Dick Stanfel, Tony Dungy and Edward DeBartolo, Jr.

Kevin Greene died on Monday morning, December 21, 2020. He was surrounded by his family at his home in Destin, Florida. Greene was 58. No cause of death was given. He is survived by his wife Tara, his son Gavin, and his daughter Gabrielle.

Gone to soon, Kevin Greene once said in an interview, "I believed in my heart that I was unblockable." He may have been right.

WHO'S GOT NEXT?

John Wooden once said, "Talent is God-given; be humble. Fame is man-given; be grateful. Conceit is self-given; be careful." This man never worried about what others thought about him. He was okay with who he was and what he stood for. He was low-key, never one to seek credit and found that his personal glory came from just being on a winning team. Not everybody needs fame. Some of us are just looking for direction. Whether he was making a wish or a swish, he was invested. Someone once said, "No man is a failure who has friends." This fellow meant something special to so many people. Talking with this guy gave you the ammunition you needed to accomplish whatever you wanted to do. No doubt, he made his teammates better. You did not need to watch a lot of film to know that he was good at the pick-and-roll. Rather small in size, he didn't strike fear into opposing defenders, until he started dribbling the basketball. This guy owned a killer crossover dribble, a voice as soft as Church music, and the man was never careless with the rock. This fellow was all gas and no brakes. He was Houdini with a round ball. This guy always played under control; he was never going to snap, and the man may have had the ugliest knees in the NBA. Have you ever noticed that bad shooters are always open? When needed, Jones had that touch from deep. He was clever, swift and could shoot the ball. He could beat you up like you had stolen something.

K.C. Jones once said, "You don't work at basketball, you play it." I had always wanted to kid with him and ask if he had received more frequent flyer miles, for all the traveling he had done? Jones was also great at concentration and I'm not talking about the board game. He understood that the free throw line is the only place in the game of basketball where it's okay to be greedy. On defense, he could get in your way faster than a speeding bullet. As a defender, he could scramble, close and was always active with his hands. Hall-of-Fame guard and Coach, Lenny Wilkins once said, "K.C. stuck to you like glue. He was with you, right on you, every step. He'd bump you, hold you, and get in your way." One could look long and far and not find anyone else who has won as much as K.C. Jones. Who's got next, takes on a whole new meaning in Heaven with K.C. Jones there.

K. C. Jones not only became a Hall-of-Fame basketball player, but also one of the most respected coaches in the NBA. This man was a leader, who positively shaped the destiny of this team. He didn't see color out there on the floor, he saw movement. Sometimes being in charge is not any fun. Everyone looks to you for guidance and answers, when you sometimes have none to give. The true test of a leader is when he is as frightened and confused as those who look up to him. In that moment when you can't find it in yourself, you will find the answer in them. That's leadership.

K.C. Jones was born May 25, 1932, in Taylor, Texas. K.C., the oldest of five children, spent some time living in Corpus Christi and Dallas, before moving with his family to California. He was named after his father, K.C., who in turn was named after the legendary railroad engineer, Casey Jones. His dad was a factory worker who also worked in an oil field and was a part-time cook. His mother, Eula Mae, became the lion of his soul, as his parents divorced and his dad left the family, when he was but nine. It was Eula Mae, who moved the family to San Francisco, California. They settled in a housing project located in an area that would eventually become Candlestick Park. They ended up living on welfare.

K.C. learned to play the game of basketball in a yard made up of gravel. Standing only 5 feet 9 inches tall, K.C. played football and basketball in high school. He became a fairly good shooter, but a below-average student. He was an All-Regional selection, and graduated from Commerce High School in 1950. One of his teachers, Mildred Smith called the University of San Francisco basketball coach, Phil Woolpert, and asked that he take a chance on K.C. Remarkably, Jones passed the college entrance exam. Was he lucky, good or both? K.C. Jones enrolled at the University of San Francisco in 1952 and played with the great Bill Russell on the Dons' NCAA Championship teams of 1954-55 and 1955-56. Woolpert also went the extra mile and found Eula Mae a job at the St. Francis Hotel, as a chambermaid. While in college, K.C. grew four inches, but lost his shooting touch. Defense now became important to him. Bill Russell showed up in 1953, and these two became college roommates. During the 1953-54 season, K.C. only played in one game before having emergency appendectomy surgery. Jones lost 25 pounds and consciousness for four days, and he was not expected to live. After recovery, Jones rejoined Russell and the Dons, and the team lost only one game the next two years and won two NCAA titles in 1955 and 1956. A lob pass from Jones to Russell, underneath the basket, would later become known as the "alley-oop" pass. In his book Red and Me, written by Bill Russell with Alan Steinberg, Russell wrote about his teammate in college, K.C. Jones. "K.C. had a way different attitude. When rude or insensitive people confronted him, K.C. just said, 'That's ignorant' and deliberately walked away. He was a good man, who gracefully avoided confrontation, although he could have easily beaten the hell out of any of his antagonists if he had wanted to. I must have heard a hundred times during my freshman year, 'Why can't you be more like K.C.?'" Russell and Jones also played together on the 1956 United States Olympic team, which won the Gold Medal in Melbourne, Australia. This U.S. team set the record for defeating their opponents by an unsurpassed margin of 53.6 points per game.

Bill Russell was obtained by the Boston Celtics in the first round of the 1956 NBA Draft in a trade with the St. Louis Hawks. K.C. Jones grew four inches in college and now stood 6 feet 1 inch tall and weighed 200 pounds. He was drafted by Boston with the 13th pick of the second round, the same year as Russell; but he didn't think he was good enough to make the team, so he joined the Army. While stationed at Fort Leonard Wood in Missouri, K.C. turned some heads playing football. Jones was offered a tryout with the Los Angeles Rams and actually started three exhibition games at defensive back, before developing a large calcium deposit on his thigh. After a conversation with Red Auerbach, Jones left the Rams camp and flew to Boston to join the Celtics. Jones joined the Celtics for the 1958-59 season. By then, Bill Russell was playing in his third season with Boston and had won the first of his 11 titles in 13 years. K.C. married his first wife, Beverly Cain, in 1960 and together they had five children. Playing behind Bob Cousy and Sam Jones, K.C. came off the bench as a reserve during his first five seasons and then became a regular in 1963, after Bob Cousy retired. That Celtics team became one of the first teams besides the Philadelphia 76ers to start five African-American players: K.C. Jones, Sam Jones, Willie Naulls, Tom Sanders and Bill Russell. From 1959 to 1966, Jones was a part of eight NBA Championship teams with the Celtics. K.C. retired at the end of the 1966-67 season. He now tried his hand at selling insurance, before coaching.

K.C. Jones spent three years (1967-1970) as the head coach at Brandeis University, a year at Harvard as an assistant from (1970-1971), and then joined former teammate, Bill

Sharman's staff as an assistant on the Los Angeles Lakers' bench, during the 1971-72 season. The Lakers won 33 straight games, finished 69-13, and then won the NBA Championship. On August 8, 1972, Jones was offered and accepted the first-ever head coaching job of the San Diego team of the ABA, known as the Conquistadors. He stayed for one year before becoming the head coach of the Capitol's Washington Bullets. During his three years in Washington (1973-1976), his teams never finished worse than second place. Jones was fired after the 1976 season, his marriage began to fall apart and his life was a mess. Before the beginning of the 1976 season, he got another coaching job in Milwaukee as an assistant under Don Nelson, but was released after one season. In 1978, Jones left his wife, moved back to Boston and joined Tom Sanders as an assistant for the Celtics. Jones outlasted Sanders and Bill Fitch, and had no idea he would be the next in line to become the Celtics' head coach. Jones found his second wife, Ellen, in Boston and the two were married in 1980. They had one son. Fitch was fired after the 1982-83 season, and Jones took his place.

During the 1984-85 season, K.C. Jones wanted desperately to win back-to-back NBA titles in Boston. It had not been done since 1969. But it was not to be. The Celtics lost that year to the L.A. Lakers, even though they had won 63 games and had an imposing frontline and a terrific backcourt. Larry Bird, Kevin McHale, Robert Parish, Dennis Johnson and Danny Ainge were considered the best starting five in the NBA. It was the bench that would be their undoing. In Game Six of the Finals, the bench only contributed 26 minutes, and K.C. Jones never used M.L. Carr, Quinn Buckner, Cedric Maxwell, Carlos Clark or Ray Williams. All five of these players would be somewhere else by the end of the 1985 season. Clark would be the last released.

K.C. led the Celtics to NBA titles, in 1984 and 1986.

He retired after the 1987-88 season, having led Boston to the NBA Finals in four of his five seasons. Jimmy Rogers took his place. Jones became vice president for the Celtics' basketball operations for one season, before moving on to coach the (1989-90) Seattle Supersonics, as an assistant. Jones was later named head coach in Seattle, from 1990 to 1992. K.C. continued to chase the dream by joining Don Chaney and the Detroit Pistons as an assistant, in 1994. He returned to Boston as an assistant in 1996 and spent his last year in coaching with the 1997 New England Blizzard, an up-and-coming women's team associated with the American Basketball League. K.C. Jones coached the game he loved from 1967 to 1998. Jones' win-loss record as an NBA head coach stands at 552-306. He also won 30 games and lost 54, in the ABA.

K.C. Jones #4 was retired by the San Francisco Dons. Jones #25 was retired by the Boston Celtics on February 12, 1967. In 1986, Jones was inducted into the Bay Area Hall of Fame and also became a member of the U.S. Olympic Hall of Fame that same year. In 1989, K.C. Jones was joined by Lenny Wilkens in the Naismith Basketball Hall of Fame. Jones played for the Celtics from 1958 to 1967. During his nine years with Boston, Jones played an average of 25.9 minutes per game, in 676 games. He scored 5,011 points (7.4 ppg), pulled down 2,399 rebounds per game (3.5 rpg) and handed out 2,908 assists per game (4.3 apg). K.C. was also elected to the College Basketball Hall of Fame in 2006. In 2016, Jones won the Chuck Daly Lifetime Achievement Award.

K.C. Jones is only one of eight players in basketball history to have won an NCAA Championship, NBA Championship and a Gold Medal, joining Bill Russell, "Magic" Johnson, Michael Jordan, Jerry Lucas, Clyde Lovellette, Quinn Buckner and Anthony Davis. Only Bill Russell (11) and Sam Jones (10) have won more NBA Championships during their playing career than K.C. Jones.

I was very fortunate to meet K.C. Jones when he was the head coach for the Seattle Supersonics. The Sonics were in town playing the San Antonio Spurs. I had a chance to shake his hand and say "hello." I also took a photo of him after the game.

Red Auerbach once said, "The biggest thing you can say about K.C. is that he's a winner." K.C. Jones' greatest assets were the respect he received from his players, and his lack of ego.

K. C. Jones died on Friday, Christmas day, December 25, 2020. Jones had been staying at an assisted living center in Connecticut. At 88 years old, he had been built to last. Jones had suffered from Alzheimer's disease for several years. He is survived by his wife Ellen of 39 years, six children and many grandchildren.

As a player, K.C. Jones won NBA titles in 8 of his 9 years, all with the Celtics. As a coach, he was a five-time NBA All-Star Game head coach (1975 and 1984-1987). He won two NBA titles as head coach (1984 and 1986) and two NBA titles as an assistant coach (1972 and 1981). He won so many rings, he ran out of fingers. After hearing about the passing of K.C. Jones, Larry Bird said, "K.C. was the nicest man I ever met."

Anyone who has ever met this man would agree.

MAGIC ON THE MOUND

It was like trying to hit a butterfly. His knuckleball was one of the best ever seen. He talked about the knuckleball like it was a family heirloom, and in many ways it was. The hitter didn't know where it was going. The catcher didn't know how to stop it, and the umpire had a hard time seeing it. He always seemed to be able to relax. The man never seemed to be in a hurry and could go to sleep in a bus or plane with ease. But, on the mound, he became an intense competitor. It has been said that the hardest part of pitching is what happens between the ears. This guy pitched so effortlessly that I was convinced he could throw a doubleheader and still have plenty to spare. A good-looking man, this guy had a face that God handed out like candy, and he once said, "You can never practice too much." It was written that his knuckleball was allergic to wood, and his pickoff move to first base was one of the best in baseball.

"It's like watching Mario Andretti park a car," said Ralph Kiner. "It giggles when it goes by," laughed Rick Monday. "Trying to hit it was like trying to eat Jell-O with chopsticks," stated Bobby Murcer. What are these guys talking about? Phil Niekro's knuckleball, that's what. What kind of pitch did you expect from a guy who was born on April Fool's Day? Phil and his younger brother, Joe, learned how to master the knuckleball, in their backyard, from their dad, Phil Sr. To this day, Phil's 318 career wins are the most ever recorded by a knuckleball pitcher. Add his brother Joe's victories and they have a total of 539 wins together, the most combined wins by brothers in Major League baseball.

Only twenty-four pitchers have reached the 300-win milestone and all are in the Hall of Fame except Roger Clemens. Phil Niekro was known by his teammates and fans as "Knucksie" and his career had been as up, down and sideways as his knuckleball. Phil Niekro provided the magic from the mound and strolled into baseball history.

My pal, broadcaster Milo Hamilton, wrote the introduction to Phil Niekro's book entitled Knuckler, written by Wilfrid Binette. "He had a knuckler that truly danced, darted and jumped, and he was the first to admit that he didn't know where it was going," wrote Milo.

Philip Henry Niekro, Jr., was born on April 1, 1939, in Blaine, Ohio, a town of about 1,000 people. He was raised in Lansing, Ohio. His father Phil, Sr., was a coalminer and his mom, Henrietta, who went by "Ivy," was a homemaker. Born in 1937, Phyllis was the oldest followed by brother Phil, and then Joe, who was five years younger than Phil. The family attended church every Sunday and barely made ends meet. They did not own a television or car. So what did they do? They played baseball. Phil grew up loving hunting, fishing and chocolate milk. Phil never played Little League, Colt League or Pony League baseball, but learned the game and how to throw the knuckleball from his dad, when he was in the sixth or seventh grade. Phil was fascinated. Phil Sr. played semipro baseball in the 1930s, and his nickname was "Primo." Phil played high school baseball at Bridgeport High School. It was here that Phil made two lifelong friends, John Havlicek (Boston Celtic Hall-of-Famer) and Bill Mazeroski (Pittsburgh Pirates Hall-of-Famer). Phil played football, basketball and baseball with John Havlicek for three years, and Havlicek became his catcher in high school. Niekro averaged 20 points a game on the basketball court as a senior. During his freshman year at Bridgeport, Phil went 17-1 as a pitcher, with his only loss coming from Warren Consolidated

High School located in Titonsville, Ohio. The score was 4-3. "Maz" pitched and played shortstop for Warren Consolidated and later hit a home run off Niekro. "He never let me forget that," said Niekro. With Phil on the mound, Bridgeport High School won three straight Eastern Ohio High School Baseball League titles. He was also named to the All-Ohio All-Star Team in 1957. Phil graduated in 1957 and passed up a chance to play college baseball at West Virginia or Detroit University. Growing up poor, Phil never thought about college as an option. He eventually attended Fairmont State College for several semesters in 1957 and 1958.

Phil attended a Milwaukee Braves' tryout camp in 1958, in Bellaire, Ohio, and was signed in July by their scout, Bill Maughin, for $250 a month and a $500 signing bonus. He was sent to Eau Claire, Wisconsin. In 1959, before Spring Training, Phil signed a Class-C contract. He was then sent to Wellsville, New York, the Braves' Class-D League. He did not pitch well and the Braves thought about releasing him. Eventually they gave him another chance and sent Phil to their Rookie League team located in McCook, Nebraska. Niekro pitched well and went 7-1 with a 3.12 ERA and lead his team to the Nebraska State League Championship. In 1960, Niekro jumped to the Class-A Jacksonville, Florida team. It was here that he met one of his favorite managers, "Red" Murff. Red convinced him to throw the knuckleball more often. From 1960 to 1964, Phil Niekro would bounce back and forth between several different Minor League teams located in Louisville, to Austin, back to Louisville and then Puerto Rico. He also spent some time at Fort Knox, Kentucky, serving in the U.S. Army and pitching for the camp team. In 1964, Phil was brought up to the Milwaukee Braves to play for Manager, Bobby Bragan. In 1965, Phil started his first Major League game and won. By 1966, Phil had married a stewardess he met on a plane, and her name was Nancy.

Phil Niekro would become one of the best pitchers in the game in 1967. Up until this time, Phil had been used as a relief pitcher, until the Braves traded for catcher, Bob Uecker. Because he threw the knuckleball, some catchers did not want to catch Phil. Joe Torre was one of those. In fact, the Braves hired Bob Uecker to catch Niekro when he became a starter, because Torre refused. Before every game, Uecker went through a ritual to catch Niekro. "I took four aspirin before the game for the headache I knew I would have after it ended," said Bob. With Uecker behind home plate, passed balls became fewer. Even Astros' catcher Alan Ashby had his issues in Houston, catching Phil's brother, Joe.

Meanwhile, the big news in the Niekro family was that his brother Joe Niekro had been signed by the Chicago Cubs. On July 4, 1967, these two toed the mound against each other. Because of their age, they had never before faced each other in a baseball game. Phil was 28 and Joe had turned 22. The Braves won 8-3 that day. In 1968, Phil started the season by hitting a home run in his first game and ended up winning 14 times that season. His brother Joe got even by beating Phil and the Braves 10-4, on April 23, 1968.

Phil Niekro called the 1969 season one of his best. In the July issue of *The Sporting News*, he was referred to as "Knucksie" for the first time. Phil won 23 games that year, lost 13, but led the Braves to the Western Davison title. The Braves then lost the National League Championship Series to the New York Mets. He later admitted to throwing 99 knuckleballs in 105 pitches, during one game. He finished second, in the National League, Cy Young Award voting, to none other than Tom Seaver. Phil also pitched and starred in the All-Star Game in Washington D.C.

From 1970 to 1977, the Braves only had two winning seasons, and their play was lackluster at best. There were two things they could count on: 30 home runs from Hank Aaron and 30 starts from Phil Niekro. From 1978 to 1980, Phil led the league in games started and went 19-18 in 1978. In 1983, after 20 seasons with the Milwaukee-Atlanta Braves, Phil Niekro was released. He was 44 years old and 32 wins shy of 300 victories for his career. George Steinbrenner, the New York Yankees owner, always recognized opportunity when it reared its head and signed Phil Niekro to a player's contract on August 6, 1984. Niekro won 16 games in 1984 and 16 games in 1985, therefore becoming the first Yankee to amass 300 wins while wearing the New York pinstripes.

But this story is not so much about wins as it is about the things that really matter: love, faith, family, and fate. All the truly good stories begin and end in the heart. You see, as Phil moved closer to the magic 300-win plateau, Steinbrenner saw an opportunity to magnify the event. The "Boss" loved nothing more than touting his Yankees. In September of 1985, the Yankees traded for Phil's brother, Houston Astros' pitcher, Joe Niekro.

During this time, their father, Phil Sr., was sick and had been placed in a hospital in West Virginia and had slipped into a coma. Joe and Phil spent every off day traveling back and forth to be with their dad. During one of these visits, Joe mentioned to Phil that he had heard that even patients in a coma can sometimes be aware of their surroundings and what is being said. So, the Niekros asked their dad to blink if he could hear them and to their amazement, he blinked. Then he raised his arm and brought it back down. The boys scrambled to find a pencil and paper. Remarkably with time, their dad scribbled these two words, "Win happy." Phil automatically takes this to mean he needs to return to New York and make history by collecting his 300th win and therefore make his father happy.

On the last game of the season, with 299 wins, Joe and Phil

made a deal. Phil would start the game and Joe would come in and save the game, so both would be associated with Phil Niekro's milestone. The Yankees jumped out to a 7-0 lead through eight innings and Phil's 300th win looked to be "in the bag." In the top of the ninth inning, the Yankees score again. In the bottom of the ninth, Phil recorded the first two outs, and in trots Joe Niekro to close it out. But it's not to be. Joe comes out as the pitching coach and refuses to take the ball from Phil, and then he informs him that if he gets another out, he will be the oldest pitcher in Major League history to throw a complete game shutout. Joe then suggests in jest that Phil give the batter an intentional walk, as he heads to the dugout. Phil Niekro used his famed knuckleball on the final pitch, for the win.

While walking off the field after the game was over, Joe ran into his brother's arms with a message about their dad. The hospital had allowed George Steinbrenner and the Yankees to broadcast the game through the telephone lines and into their father's hospital room. Their mother listened to the broadcast by Phil Rizzuto and Bill White, and then she relayed the events as they happened to their father. During the seventh inning, Phil Sr. had awakened from his coma, turned to his wife and said, "Sonny" (Phil) is pitching a pretty good game." Their father continued to get better and lived two more years, including being able to watch Joe pitch in the 1987 World Series with the Minnesota Twins.

Phil Niekro's 300th win was a complete game shutout over the Toronto Blue Jays, on October 6, 1985. At age 46 years, 188 days, Phil became the oldest pitcher to pitch a complete game shutout in the Major Leagues. Niekro's record stood for 25 years until Jamie Moyer (age 47 years, 170 days) moved past him in May of 2010. Interestingly, Niekro did not use his knuckleball until the last batter, the former American League MVP, Jeff Burroughs. Burroughs struck out to end the game on a Phil Niekro knuckleball. Sometimes the healing powers of this great game shine through the lost stories of our heroes.

Phil and Joe ended their careers with a combined 539 wins. Phil's last appearance in a game occurred on September 27, 1987. He was 48 and had started in 716 games. Phil pitched for four clubs: Milwaukee/Atlanta Braves, New York Yankees, Cleveland Indians and Toronto Blue Jays. His win-loss record stands at 318-274, over 24 seasons. Phil recorded 5,404 innings pitched and gave up 482 home runs. His career ERA was 3.35 and he recorded 3,342 strikeouts. He hit 123 batters. Phil won the Gold Glove Award five times and also appeared in five All-Star Games. Phil recorded his only no-hitter against the Padres on August 5, 1973. Phil Niekro's #35 was retired in 1984, by the Atlanta Braves, and he has been inducted into the Atlanta Braves' Hall of Fame. His statue has been placed in front of Turner Field and Truist Park. He received the Lou Gehrig Memorial Award in 1979 and the Roberto Clemente Award for outstanding community service in 1980. Phil Niekro was elected, in his fifth year of eligibility, to the Baseball Hall of Fame, in 1997. He was joined by Tommy Lasorda, Nellie Fox and Negro League legend, Willie Wells. He has served on the Hall's Board of Directors and as a member of the Veterans' Committee.

Phil would be the first to tell you about longevity in sports, especially baseball. Playing baseball in the Major Leagues requires long days and short nights to be successful. A baseball player's day is often every bit as long as a doctor's or lawyers. They arrive at the ballpark on game day about four hours early, and then spend as many as seven or eight hours there before going home. Add 2-3 hour plane trips from coast to coast and personal appearances at local church groups, PTA events or clubs, and it all adds up to long hours. Baseball players are lucky to get a day or two off once a month, instead of every Saturday and Sunday. Players put up with the hours because the money is good and for their love of the game. And of course, those long hours cause a strain on their family life.

Phil Niekro left us on a Saturday. The date will read December 26, 2020. He was 81. Phil had been suffering from cancer and died in his sleep. Phil and Nancy were living in their retirement home in Flowery Branch, north of Atlanta on Lake Lanier, with their three sons, Philip, John and Michael, and two grandchildren, Chase and Emma. Phil lost his brother Joe Niekro on October 27, 2006. Joe was 61 and died from a brain aneurysm. Joe pitched for the Houston Astros for 11 seasons (1975-1985) and won a franchise record 144 games, before being traded to the New York Yankees in 1985.

After his retirement, Phil continued to mentor other pitchers like Tim Wakefield, Steve Sparks and R.A. Dickey, in the finer points of throwing the knuckleball. I was not only privileged to meet Phil at a memorabilia show in Houston, but also met and took pictures of his brother Joe, at an Astros' Old-timers Game. These two were special when together. Phil's only regret in life may have been that he couldn't sit in the stands and watch himself pitch.

THE FRANCHISE

LSU football coach Paul Dietzel once said, "You can learn more about a person's character on the two-yard line than anywhere else in life." The guy I'm going to tell you about had a future was so bright that he had to wear shades. Scolding this man in front of his teammates was like feeding spinach to Popeye. It only made him stronger. He was a linebacker at heart in a running back's body. He was enormously disciplined and was so bowlegged a pig could run between his legs. This guy started out as a powerful, straight-ahead runner. He was always in motion; only the lens of a camera could stop him. Watching this guy run was like a drug for football. You could not stop watching him. This guy could change your mind about him with one carry. He either made you miss or just simply ran by you. Every time this guy took the handoff from the quarterback, you edged up to the front of your seat, because he was a threat to score. When he got the ball in his hands, it took the whole team to bring him down. He was seldom tackled by one player.

Academy Award winning producer Brian Grazer once said, "I get moved by greatness, just human greatness. Greatness can be small things or big things or small things leading to big things, but just human greatness."

Cool under fire, Floyd Little was clean cut, good looking, and a class act. Don't be mistaken by his shy, coy look. Little could play football like a junkyard dog. Floyd was instant offense and became his team's first star. He loved the game of football. He lived it, breathed it and brought it every single game. Little wasn't just a star; he was a game changer.

71

Floyd Little became known in Denver as "The Franchise;" a human highlight film, but in life, unlike in chess, the game continues after checkmate. Even though their win/loss record during the 1960s and 1970s was not all that great, this Denver Bronco team was tough to beat. Little made all those mediocre seasons worthwhile. The team colors of the 1967 Denver Broncos (orange, blue and white) reminded me of what a bruise looks like. Floyd Little owned a football heart.

Floyd Douglas Little was given to us on Independence Day, July 4, 1942.   He was born in New Haven, Connecticut. Little played halfback and attended both Hillhouse High School and the Bordentown Military Institute, located in Bordentown, New Jersey.   Interestingly, Floyd Little, standing only 5 feet 10 inches tall and weighing 196 pounds, was recruited by Notre Dame and none other than General Douglas MacArthur, to play football at the United States Military Academy. MacArthur told Floyd that if he enrolled at West Point he would ascend to the rank of general. Ernie Davis, the first African-American to win the Heisman Trophy, persuaded Little to play for the Orangemen of Syracuse University. Floyd Little played for the Orangemen for three seasons. He wore the iconic #44 that had been worn by the legendary players, Jim Brown and Ernie Davis. In 1964, Floyd had 157 carries for 874 yards and scored nine touchdowns. He also caught 17 passes for 257 yards and scored one touchdown. In 1965, Little carried the ball 193 times for 1,065 yards, scored 14 touchdowns and caught 21 balls for 248 yards and one touchdown. In 1966, he carried the ball 162 times for 811 yards and scored 12 times. He also caught 13 passes for 86 yards and scored twice. Little was chosen first-team All-American all three years (1964-1966), but finished 5th in the Heisman Trophy voting in both 1965 and 1966. His career total for rushing the football totaled 2,750 yards and 39 total touchdowns. On November 12,

2005, Syracuse retired the #44 to honor Brown, Davis and Little.

Floyd Little was drafted by the Denver Broncos with the 6th pick of the first round of the 1967 AFL-NFL Draft. The Denver Broncos were one of the original AFL teams in 1960. He would continue to wear the #44 and was chosen team captain as a rookie. During his nine seasons in Denver, Little became one of the NFL's best running backs and helped the Broncos become a contender. At first he was used more as a return man. During his rookie season, Little returned 35 kickoffs for 942 yards, but in week 12 of the 1968 season, Little caught four passes out of the backfield against the Buffalo Bills for 165 yards and scored a 66-yard touchdown, setting the Broncos' franchise record of 41.25 yards per catch. That record still stands today.

During his career, Floyd Little rushed for 6,323 yards, while catching passes for an additional 2,418 yards. He scored 52 touchdowns (43 rushing and 9 receiving) while playing in 117 games. Little earned five Pro Bowl selections and led the entire NFL in rushing yards (1,133) during the 1971 season. He earned first-team All-Pro honors in 1969 and made second-team All-Pro twice, in 1970 and 1971. He also led the league in rushing touchdowns with 12 in 1973. Floyd was the first Bronco to win a rushing title, leading the AFC in 1970 with 901 yards. In 1971, Floyd became the 13th player ever in the history of professional football and the first Bronco to rush for more than 1,000 yards (1,133) in a single season. Little totaled 893 yards on 81 career punt-returns and scored twice. He also ran back 104 kickoffs for 2,523 yards. He is also the only player in the NFL to return punts for touchdowns in both the 1967 and 1968 seasons. From 1968 to 1973, Little totaled more yards rushing and receiving than any running back in the NFL. In 1975, the Broncos retired his #44 for all-time. On October 1, 1984, Denver placed Little into their team's inaugural "Ring of Honor" along with Rich Jackson, Lionel Taylor and "Goose" Gonsoulin.

In 1975, after football, Little attended the University of Denver Law School. He received his master's degree in legal administration. Little owned and operated several car dealerships in the Denver, Seattle and Santa Barbara areas. Floyd Little was inducted into the College Football Hall of Fame in 1983 and the Pro Football Hall of Fame on August 7, 2010, along with Jerry Rice, Emmitt Smith, Russ Grimm, Rickey Jackson, John Randle and Dick LeBeau. Little was always in attendance at the Pro Football Hall-of-Fame inductions held in Canton, Ohio.

In 2008, actor Chadwick Boseman portrayed Floyd Little in a Universal Picture entitled *The Express: The Ernie Davis Story.*

From 2011 to 2016, Little worked at the University of Syracuse in the athletic department, as a special assistant. He would receive an honorary doctorate degree in Humane Letters on May 16, 2016, from the university. On May 17, 2019, Little was awarded the University of Denver's Distinguished Alumni Award, and on May 18, 2019, Little was awarded an Honorary Doctorate of Laws, as speaker at Denver University Strum College of Laws Commencement Ceremonies. Interestingly, of all the awards that Little received, and there were many, the one he loved the most occurred on September 15, 2011, when the New Haven Athletic Center was renamed in his honor, The Floyd Little Athletic Center. "Wow," said Floyd. "Just think. There are 267 members of the Pro Football Hall of Fame. How many of them have a building named after them?" Last but not least, the Syracuse football practice facility is the home of three bronze statues: Jim Brown, Ernie Davis and Floyd Little.

Floyd Little passed away at the age of 78 on Friday night,

January 1, 2021, while living in Las Vegas, Nevada. He had fought a losing battle with a rare cell cancer. His cancer had been discovered in June of 2020 and was diagnosed as a Stage 2 Neuroendocrine tumor. He was placed in hospice care in November. Floyd Little suffered and died from the same disease that his father had suffered and died with, when Floyd was six years old. His wife DeBorah, his son Marc Little, and his daughters Christy Jones and Kyra DaCosta, were by his side.

Floyd Little was once asked about his running style. "I can't explain my moves," said Little. "I don't think any good runner can. I can't copy anyone. I don't know what I'm doing until I do it, then I can never repeat it. It's some kind of instinct. I look at me on film and say, 'Jeez that guy made a helluva move. What was that?'"

That, my friend, was Floyd Little.

PACING THE HARDWOOD

Longtime Lakers announcer, Chick Hearn once said, "If that shot goes in, I'm walking home." Hearn may have been watching this guy play. The man played hard and dreamed big. He was a Christian, just a nice guy; the kind of fellow that if he went to an animal shelter, he would leave with a new pet. This man was so mentally-prepared come game time. Standing 6 feet 4 inches tall and weighing 195 pounds, his body was built for the game of basketball. Being concerned about his performance was like worrying about Jim Bowie in a knife fight, a waste of time. He was a great playmaker and a strong defensive player. The man wore #44 and jumped for rebounds like a cat leaping for butterflies. As a guard, he could shoot the basketball with both hands. What you need to understand is that the locker room is one of the funniest places on earth. This guy could be fun to be around. Some said he thought an assist was passing a glass of milk to his friend without taking a sip.

After 12 years in the NBA, he still wanted to be a coach. So, he became one. He consistently built winners. The man was a proven winner, a great innovator and motivator. If you couldn't play for Paul Westphal, you couldn't play for anybody. Most coaches worry about making the wrong choice when they should be worried about not making a decision at all. Westphal understood that if you never make a decision, you never learn anything. Pacing the hardwood as a basketball coach was all Paul Westphal ever wanted to do.

Paul Douglas Westphal was born on November 30, 1950,

in Torrance, California, to Armin and Ruth Westphal. His dad was an aeronautical engineer. Paul spent day and nights with his brother Bill, shooting hoops in the family driveway. From 1966 to 1969, Paul would star at Aviation High School located in Redondo Beach and worked his way toward a basketball scholarship at the University of Southern California. In 1968, Paul was chosen "Mr. Basketball USA." While playing guard with USC, Paul averaged 16.9 points per game and was voted First-team All-PAC-8 twice, in 1970 and 1971, and second-team All-American by the Associated Press poll in 1971. In 1972, Paul was selected team captain and graduated from USC at the end of that year. His #25 has been retired by the USC Trojans.

Paul Westphal was selected with the 10th pick in the first round of the 1972 NBA Draft by the Boston Celtics. His teammates called him "Westy." Because he played behind Jo Jo White and Don Chaney, Westphal spend most of his time coming off the bench as a reserve during his first three years in the league. Westphal really made his presence felt during the 1974 NBA Championship Finals against the Milwaukee Bucks. Westphal not only scored 12 points against the Bucks, but played shutdown defense against one the best ever, guard Oscar Robertson. The "Big O" only made 2 of his 13 shots taken. The Celtics won, 96-87, and captured the 1974 NBA title, four games to three.

In May of 1975, Paul was traded to the Phoenix Suns for another great guard, Charlie Scott. Interestingly, Westphal returned to the NBA Finals in 1976 with the Suns and their opponents were none other than the Celtics. Even though Paul scored 25 points in Game Five, the Suns were beaten 128-126, in triple overtime in what has been called "The greatest game ever played." The Suns lost the series to Boston, four games to two.

Paul played for the Phoenix Suns from 1975 to 1980 and later returned to Phoenix for his final NBA season as a player, in

1984. Westphal finished the 1977-78 season, sixth in scoring in the NBA with 25.2 ppg. He also became the first player to win the NBA All-Star Weekend H-O-R-S-E Competition Championship. Paul had been a four-time All-Star for the Suns. He also played with the Seattle Supersonics during the 1980-81 season. Paul was traded for Dennis Johnson. While in Seattle, he gained his fifth All-Star selection, but later suffered a stress fracture in his right foot. After healing, Paul signed with the New York Knicks in the middle of the 1981-82 season. It would be his 12th and last season as a player. Westphal scored 12,809 points or 15.6 points per game. Not bad for a guy who came off the bench early in his career. He recorded 3,591 assists and pulled down 1,580 rebounds. His #44 has been retired by the Phoenix Suns, and his name has been placed in the Suns' Ring of Honor.

Westphal's first coaching job was for Southwestern Baptist Bible College (now known as Arizona Christian University), in 1985. His team finished 21-9 in his first season as head coach. He later coached at Grand Canyon University from 1986 to 1988, where he led his team to the NAIA Championship in 1988. At the end of 1988, he became an assistant coach for the Phoenix Suns and by 1992, he had been promoted to their head coaching position. Paul Westphal was their Moses, the guy who would lead the Suns team to the promise land. With great players like Charles Barkley, Kevin Johnson, Dan Majerle and Danny Ainge, the Suns made it to the NBA Finals, but lost to the Chicago Bulls in six games. Phoenix would make the playoffs under Westphal every year he was there, but they never returned to the Finals.

In 1995, Westphal was fired from the Suns, and he decided to coach some high school basketball in Arizona for a couple of years. In 1998, the Seattle Supersonics called, and he became their new head coach until 2000. He was let go after the 2000-01 season. The following year, 2001, Paul took the job of head coach at Pepperdine University for the next six years. He coached his Pepperdine Waves to a 22-9 record and a berth in the NCAA Tournament, in his first year as head coach. He was dismissed at the end of the 2006 season.

In 2006, Paul worked as a studio analyst for Fox Sports Net West, with the Los Angeles Clippers and Los Angeles Lakers.

On June 28, 2007, Westphal was hired as an assistant for the Dallas Mavericks, under Avery Johnson. By June 10, 2009, you could find him leading the Sacramento Kings from courtside. Paul was fired by the Kings on January 5, 2012. From 2014 until 2016, Westphal served as an assistant for the Brooklyn Nets. Westphal served as an NBA head coach for all or part of ten seasons. Paul Westphal coached basketball in some form from 1985 to 2016, 31 years. Brooklyn would be his last stop. His win-loss record for NBA games coahced rest at 318-279.

Paul Westphal even dabbled in the world of television. In 1982, he got a taste of TV when he was hired for a small role as a police officer on ABC's daytime drama, "The Edge of Night."

In 2018, Westphal received his call from the College Basketball Hall of Fame. Paul Westphal joined the Naismith Basketball Hall of Fame as a player, on September 6, 2019. His presenters were Elgin Baylor and Charles Barkley. Westphal joined Bill Fitch, Bobby Jones, Sidney Moncrief, Jack Sikma and Teresa Weatherspoon.

Paul Westphal died on a Saturday, January 2, 2021. He was 70 and had suffered from brain cancer. He is survived by his wife Cindy, their daughter Victoria, and a son Michael.

Westphal had always felt he was destined to be a coach. Paul once said, "I hoped to be a player, but always planned on being a coach." While pacing the hardwood, Paul Westphal could never envision living life without basketball.

TRUE BLUE

He was short in stature, with a potbelly figure and sagging pouches under his eyes. The man was also loud in person, and feisty, kind of like Casey Stengel and Napoleon Bonaparte all rolled into one. He may have been the P. T. Barnum of baseball. When he was younger, he waked up every morning looking for a fight. He was an eternal optimist, a great storyteller at heart and, man, could this guy talk. The three things he loved to do: talk, fight and play baseball. For 14 Minor League seasons, he threw both his fist and left-handed fastballs with equal enthusiasm. He was in fights so often that his wife pleaded with him before a game, "Don't start any fights." Smart, seasoned and committed, he never accepted "no" for an answer. He was a reporter's dream. This guy has never said, "No comment" or "This is off the record." All you had to do was ask him a question and then be prepared to listen. I bet he could talk underwater. There is no doubt that he was a very interesting baseball man, Einstein in spikes. He had always said, "God is a Dodger and I'm taking an autographed baseball with me to Heaven, so I can get a good seat at the table." This man was very much a competitor and hated losing. He loved the game, his country, his teammates, and the fans. This fellow was a huge part of what baseball means to the fans of the game. He always claimed that he lived at 6-4-3 DP Lane. His heart was bigger than his talent. "This game does not belong to the players or the owners; it belongs to the fans," he would say. He was more of a motivator than a manager, a fine ambassador of the game, and his life story could not have been duplicated. This man was in a class by himself as a non-player. He has been a player, scout, coach, manager, international manager of our Olympic team, and a Baseball Hall-of-Famer. He also said once, "I love doubleheaders. That way I get to keep my uniform on longer." He's had seven doctorate degrees bestowed upon him and has been inducted into 16 different Halls of Fame. He even has an asteroid named after him along with the late news anchor, Walter Cronkite. He owned several World Series rings as a player and manager, and an Olympic Gold Medal. There is a difference in admiration, respect and love. Tommy Lasorda was loved.

Baseball to Tommy Lasorda was like oxygen for the rest of us. "The ballpark was my home!" said Tommy. He never charged anyone for his autograph. "It's my way of giving back to the game," he said. "Autographs mean a lot to these people." He was a Dodger for life. He played in Brooklyn, managed in Los Angeles, and made Chavez Ravine his home for 20 years. He owned an extraordinary personality, loved the attention and touched so many along the way. There was no grey area with Tommy Lasorda. He greeted every new rookie like this. "Hi, I'm Tommy Lasorda, and your life has changed forever. You will learn how to play for the name on the front of your jersey and not the back." He was the rock of the franchise. Tommy Lasorda was the very definition of "True Blue."

Thomas Charles "Tommy" Lasorda was born September 22, 1927, and grew up a devout Catholic in Norristown, Pennsylvania. Both his parents, Sabatino and Carmella, were Italian immigrants. His father drove a truck in a rock quarry and could barely speak English. With little or no money, as a young man, Tommy worked as a bellhop and laid railroad track for the Pennsylvania Railroad. He also took out his anger on his schoolmates. Tommy was the second oldest of five sons and graduated from Norristown High School in 1945. He had started out playing first base in high school, but could not hit, so he became a third-string pitcher as a senior. Lasorda signed his first baseball contract with the Philadelphia Phillies, before the 1945 season. He would spend two seasons with the Phillies, in 1945 and 1948. The two years in-between were served in the U. S. Army. Tommy was sent to the Phillies' Class-D team, the Concord Weavers, part of the North Carolina State League. On November 24, 1948, Tommy was chosen by the Brooklyn Dodgers in the Minor League draft and signed a new contract.

After six seasons with the Brooklyn Dodgers farm club, the Montreal Royals, Lasorda became the winningest pitcher for the team. There's a crazy story about Tommy Lasorda pitching in the Minor Leagues. After the team had given up a couple of runs, the manager came out to replace Lasorda, but Tommy did not want to leave, and the manager had to chase him around the mound to get the ball. While this was all happening, Lasorda was screaming, "Don't take me out. Take out the third baseman; he's the one who made the two errors." On February 21, 1953, he was purchased by the St. Louis Browns, but returned a month later to the Dodgers, on March 26, 1953. In 1954, Tommy went 14-5 for Montreal. Lasorda once recorded 25 strikeouts in a Class-C game for Montreal. Wearing #29, he was called up to the Brooklyn Dodgers and debuted on August 5, 1954. He was later sent back to the Minors to make room for a hotshot kid named Sandy Koufax. Tommy received the #23 when his contract was purchased by the Kansas City A's, on March 2, 1956.

On July 11, 1956, the Kansas City A's traded him to the New York Yankees and he was sent to their Triple-A team, the Denver Beavers. He was later sold back to the Dodgers on May 26, 1957. When Lasorda returned to the Dodgers in 1957, he was given the #27 to wear.

In 1957, you could find Lasorda pitching in the Minor Leagues for the Los Angeles Angels of the Pacific Coast League. It would be the year of "The Fight of 1957." Lasorda was upset that he had given up a home run to the Hollywood Stars' pitcher and the next Stars' batter was "Spook" Jacobs. Tommy threw at Jacobs intentionally. Jacobs was able to fall out of the way of the pitch but became mad. The next pitch Lasorda threw, Jacobs intended to bunt between first and second, so Tommy would have to cover first base and Jacobs would get a chance to spike Lasorda when he tried to cover the bag. Jacobs bunted, but the ball went back to Lasorda. As Jacobs headed to first base Tommy never even tried to field the bunt, instead he took off after Jacobs and caught him from behind. The fight lasted 33 minutes and made quite a stir as the game was being televised. Tommy continued to pitch in the Minors until 1960. Lasorda spent a total of 14 seasons pitching in the Minor Leagues.

Unfortunately, his Major League career only lasted 26 games, spread out over three seasons (1954-1956). His last game pitched occurred on July 8, 1956. During one of his starts, Lasorda tied a Major League record with three wild pitches thrown in one inning. Lasorda would finish his Major League career with a 0-4 win-loss record. He pitched 58.1 innings, struck out 37 batters and registered a 6.48 ERA. Tommy did not play in the 1955 World Series for Brooklyn against the Yankees, but he did receive a World Series ring for being part of the team.

In 1961, Lasorda became a scout for the Los Angeles Dodgers. By 1965, you could find Tommy managing Minor League clubs for the Dodgers in Pocatello, Idaho; Ogden, Utah; and Albuquerque, New Mexico. From 1969 to 1971, while wearing the #11, Tommy managed the Dodgers' Triple-A team in Spokane, Washington.

Bart Shirley and I have been friends for many years.

Bart played in the Dodger system as a second baseman and shortstop. He first met Tommy Lasorda in Spoken, Washington, while playing for the Dodgers' Triple-A team known as the Spokane Indians. Bart became a player-coach for Lasorda for two years and a part of the PCL (Pacific Coast League) champions. "That team was incredible," said Bart. Davey Lopes, Steve Garvey, Bill Russell, and Bobby Valentine were just some of the great players I played with." Bart continued, "He was my mentor. I'm sorry to hear he has passed away. He had to have had a strong heart to go through all the things he did." Bart Shirley eventually became a Minor League manager himself, with the Dodgers' organization. Lasorda's Minor League teams won five pennants in seven seasons, and 75 players that he managed would make it to the Major Leagues. In 1973, Tommy Lasorda became the third-base coach for Walter Alston and the Los Angeles Dodgers. He was given the #52.

Three years later, Walter Alston retired on September 29, 1976, and Tommy Lasorda was offered the job. Tommy Lasorda chose to wear the #2 as the Los Angeles Dodgers' manager in honor of Leo Durocher, who managed the Brooklyn Dodgers in the 1960's. During an interview with Dodger announcer, Vin Scully, Lasorda was asked, "You know you will be replacing a legend, and a future Hall-of-Fame manager. Are you worried about replacing Walter Alston?" Lasorda thought for a minute before speaking. "You know, I'm worried about the guy who has to replace me," said Tommy. Lasorda inherited a terrific infield with Steve Garvey at first base, Davey Lopes at second base, Bill Russell at shortstop and Ron Cey at third base. As mentioned above, all four had played for Lasorda in the Minors. In the sixties and seventies, one of the manager's greatest weapons to get his player to play their best was fear, fear of being released, fined, or sent down to the Minor Leagues. In today's game, fear is no longer an obstacle for multi-million dollar players with longer contracts and a strong union. Tommy understood that in order for his players to do their best they needed attention, support and someone on their side. The word love comes to the surface when speaking about Lasorda. Tommy used the next best weapon, love and the feeling of family. Like the manager of a fine dining restaurant, Lasorda ate with, played cards with, and learned about his players' families. By doing so, he instilled confidence.

A personal friend of Don Rickles, Ronald Reagan and other Hollywood stars, Tommy certainly moved in high circles. He asked another one of his pals, Frank Sinatra, to sing the National Anthem before the first game he managed at Dodger Stadium. Manager Tommy Lasorda was a hit. Not only did his team win, but Dodger home attendance surpassed 3 million for the first time in 1978. Attendance peaked at 3.6 million in 1982.

The first time I met Tommy Lasorda was in the fall of 1983 in Tulsa, Oklahoma. He was one of the guests of honor at a golf fundraiser for mentally retarded adults, chaired by one of his former players, Jim Brewer. Jim had been born and raised in Broken Arrow, a suburb right outside Tulsa, and had pitched for Tommy and the Los Angeles Dodgers for 12 seasons. Brewer had pitched on three World Series teams, winning a ring in 1965. Jim was now the Manager for the Oral Roberts University men's baseball team, located in Tulsa. Other guests included the great "Lefty" Gomez, Hall-of-Fame pitcher of the New York Yankees; Steve Rodgers, a University of Tulsa graduate and starting pitcher for the Montreal Expos; George Frazier, a University of Oklahoma graduate and a relief pitcher for the Yankees and Twins; the Dodgers' future Hall-of-Fame pitcher, Sandy Koufax; and Dodger second-baseman, Bill Russell. Also on hand was Roy Clark, a local Tulsa resident and a Country Music legend. It was quite a group. How I got involved is another story.

I was working at a local restaurant right outside of Oral Roberts University campus and was asked by Coach Brewer if I would like to sponsor a $10,000 hole-in-one contest to help raise awareness and money for the event. I don't know how many of you know this, but back then you could buy an insurance policy for as little as $300 to insure your company against the possibility of an actual hole-in-one being recorded. It was a heck of a deal, because for my part I got to hang out with these legends, play a round of golf, and attend a dinner with my wife that night. It was the best $300 I have ever spent on advertising. Koufax played in my foursome; I was in Heaven.

That night after dinner, each of the guests took their place at the podium to speak. Brewer saved the best for last, Lefty and Tommy. Gomez and Lasorda went back and forth at each other with stories and jabs from the good old days. Lasorda is a fascinating speaker. He's a guy who actually thinks baseball should be fun. Being Italian, he speaks with his hands. I thought I would never stop listening. Tommy can be flamboyant, bold and confident. His enthusiasm is contagious and all-consuming. It is hard not to listen to him when he speaks.

One of the stories Tommy Lasorda told that night has remained with me over the years, and I have retold this story a countless number of times on the radio during my show. "When I was a kid, I was a school patrol boy for the school system in Philadelphia," said Tommy. "I knew that every year they picked the best school patrol person and gave them tickets to a baseball game, free of charge. I wanted to go to a game. So, I did a great job, rain or shine, protecting the other kids crossing the street and I won the trip. We went to Shibe Park where the visiting team always had to walk a ways down the outside of the park to the visitor's entrance door.

The kids would stand there and ask for autographs from the visiting players. I asked this player from the New York Giants for an autograph, and he shoved me aside," exclaimed Tommy. "As he turned, I noticed the number on the back of his jersey. It said #12. After we got inside we bought a program and #12 was a fellow by the name of "Buster" Maynard. Well, several years later, I was pitching in the Dodger Minor League system with the Montreal Royals team and we were in Atlanta. I was the starting pitcher and retired the first two batters when I heard the P.A. announcer say over the loud speaker, 'Now batting, #12, Buster Maynard.' This is the guy who had shoved me out of the way when I was a kid," said Tommy. "So, with the first pitch, I threw right at his head. His cap goes one way and his body the other, as he hits the dirt. I threw the next pitch in the same place, and down he went again, only this time I hit him. Confused, he gets up and trots down to first base. After the game, I'm leaving the park and this guy comes up to me outside the locker room and says, 'I'm looking for Tommy Lasorda.' "I said, 'I'm him, who are you?' He answered, 'I'm Buster Maynard.' He continued, 'I have been in the Major Leagues for years and there are only two reasons a pitcher throws at a batter. Either he hit a home run off of him or he doesn't like him. Since I have never seen or heard for you before, I can only assume you don't like me. I want to know why?' Lasorda answered, 'I know you were in the Major Leagues and when I was a kid you wouldn't give me an autograph.' 'You're serious,' said Maynard, 'and he turned, shook his head in disbelief and walked away.' "Because of that," Tommy said smiling, "I have always told my players to sign those darn autographs; you never know who they may grow up to be." I'm telling you, this story brought the house down.

To his last day, Tommy Lasorda never charged anybody for

his autograph. He showed up every year at Spring Training and the Hall-of-Fame inductions and signed for hours every day he was there. He joked, "They lined up early, like they were boarding Southwest Airlines."

The second time I met Lasorda was at the 2004 Major League Baseball All-Star Game in Houston, Texas. It was July 13th and I was working for ESPN KSIX 1230 AM in Corpus Christi, Texas. With my press pass, I was able to visit all areas of the ballpark including the dugouts. My job was to interview some of the legends of the game and bring those taped interviews back to Corpus to be aired on our radio show, entitled "Dennis & Andy's Q & A Session." Lasorda looked great and, as usual, was willing to speak with me. He spoke about his days managing and coaching the National League All-Star teams and how important it was for them to win that game. He even told his players that many of them might not get to play, because he wanted to secure a victory. This was before the winner of the All-Star Game received home-field advantage for their league in the World Series. It was never an exhibition game as far as Tommy was concerned. We spoke for about six minutes and laughed for ten. I reminded him of our earlier meeting in Tulsa and I thanked him for his time. He has always been a great ambassador for the game of baseball.

Not only did I interview Lasorda, but also Ozzie Smith, Ernie Banks, and Harold Reynolds. I also got a chance to speak with "Buck" O'Neil and "Slick" Surratt at a baseball card memorabilia show held at the Convention Center, next door to Minute Maid Park. It was a great trip.

Vin Scully once said, "Tommy Lasorda, from the day I first met him, that enthusiastic kid from Vero Beach, Florida, even now as he turns 86 years old, he still loves the game almost with a ferocious appetite for it, and he loves to talk about it. He loves people and he loves to tell stories. You put it all together, and he's the perfect ambassador for baseball. He doesn't mind being on the road and as long as he is surrounded by people, the number one subject will be baseball." I can't write about Tommy Lasorda without sharing some of his stories. The following are some of my favorites.

One time, the 1955 Brooklyn Dodgers' team was being honored at Shea Stadium by the New York Mets, and they were all lined up side by side, being introduced to the fans. Tommy was standing next to "Pee Wee" Reese. Tommy leaned over and said to Pee Wee, "If I would have told you that one day one of us would be the Manager of the Los Angeles Dodgers, how would you have lined up the 25 of us, according to chance?" Pee Wee said, "I would have put you 24th." Lasarda asked, "Who would you put at 25?" "Sandy Amoros," said Pee Wee, "He couldn't speak English."

There is a wonderful story about an excited Tommy Lasorda sitting in the dugout with newly signed left-hander, Fernando Valenzuela. Most of the reporters did not know that Fernando spoke very little if any English. An interpreter had not arrived when a Hispanic reporter asked Valenzuela a question in Spanish and Fernando answered him in Spanish. Another reporter asked out loud what Fernando had said, and Tommy interrupted and said with a big wide smile on his face, "He said Tommy Lasorda is the best manager I have ever played for." It was typical Lasorda.

During the 1988 draft, Lasorda insisted that the Dodgers take a kid named Mike Piazza. The Dodgers' scouting director had not been impressed. Yes, it's true that Tommy was a childhood friend of Mike's father, but the young Piazza could also hit. Lasorda finally said, "I tell you what, if we brought a shortstop in here and he swung the bat like that, wouldn't you sign him?" The scout said, "Yeah, if he were a shortstop." Tommy said, "What if he was a catcher?" The scout responded, "I'd sign him if he were a catcher." Tommy said, "Okay, he's a catcher." The scout responded "He's not a catcher." Tommy, "He's a catcher now. Sign him. All he wants is a chance." Mike Piazza was drafted with the 1,390th overall pick in the 62nd round and became the National League Rookie of the Year in 1993. Mike went on to hit 427 home runs and became known as one of the best hitting catchers in baseball history. Piazza was inducted into the Baseball Hall of Fame in 2016. "Tommy Lasorda was always in my corner," said Pizza. "He believed when he watched me hit at the young age of 14, that I could play Major League baseball."

The 1988 Dodger team lacked enough elite players to be considered dangerous. One of their players was an outfielder named Danny Heep. Heep was never known for his speed and Lasorda once told him, "You're so darn slow, if you got into a race with a pregnant woman, you'd finish third."

After being chosen by Bud Selig as the manager for the 2000 U.S. Olympic Baseball team, a reporter said, "They said they gave you a bad team." Tommy responded, "Are they alive?" The reporter said, "Yes." Tommy exclaimed, "That's all I need,"

Joe Garagiola once said, "You feel like a starting pitcher when you have dinner with Tommy Lasorda, because afterwards you need three days' rest." Lasorda once tried to explain his problem with weight as only he could. "When we win, I'm so happy, I eat a lot. When we lose, I'm so depressed, I eat a lot. When we're rained out, I'm so disappointed, I eat a lot." In 1988 on a dare, Tommy lost 40 pounds and became the pitchman for a weight-loss program called Slim Fast. Tommy also pitched Glad garbage bags and lent his name to pasta sauces and Italian restaurants.

"Baseball is like driving. It's the one who gets home safely that counts," said Lasorda.

Tommy's wife Jo once said to him in frustration, "You love baseball more than you love me." Tommy responded, "Yeah, but I love you more than football and basketball."

Tommy Lasorda has served this great game since 1949, and he still made up to 100 appearances a year. "Thank God for making it all happen," said Tommy. "God gave me a wonderful family and country. I love competition. If we won 102 games during the season, I was miserable 60 times," said Lasorda. "Guys ask me, don't I get burned out? How can you get burned out doing something you love? I ask you, have you ever got tired of kissing a pretty girl?"

So, where did Lasorda learn all those curse words? His language could be as blue as his Dodger blood. Umpires most often were on the receiving end. And he used bad language to motivate his players. Most of the time, his bad language was used behind the scenes, and never in public. Wearing a microphone was not a good idea for Tommy or Major League baseball. He was caught several times spewing venomous language even though most of it never made it live on TV.

As Tommy got older, he began to use a golf cart to motor around the Dodgers' training facility at Vero Beach during Spring Training. One day Lasorda sees the 66-year-old ex-knuckleballer, Charlie Hough. Hough says, "Great to see you Tommy. I'll talk to you later. I've got to get to work." "Charlie," yells Lasorda. "If you love it, it's not work." Lasorda was the one who had extended Hough's career by teaching him how to throw the knuckleball. Hough had been released on five different occasions as a player. "We're playing the Marlins in 1993 and we're facing Hough," said Lasorda. "He's 45 years old and sticking it to us. My wife, Jo, is happy because Charlie is her favorite player. I almost threw her out of the car."

Tommy Lasorda spent parts of seven decades with the Dodgers' organization as a player, scout, coach, manager, interim general manager and advisor. He retained the title of advisor to the Dodgers' chairmen until his death. Tommy managed a total of 3,040 games, 22nd most in Major League history. He recorded 1,599 wins, 1,439 losses and two ties, for a .526 win percentage. A heart attack when Tommy was 68 ran him out of the dugout. He spent 20 years as the Los Angeles Dodgers' manager and won two World Series titles, in 1981 and 1988, four National League pennants, and eight National League Division titles. Lasorda was a two-time National League Manager of the Year, in 1983 and 1988. Lasorda managed four National League All-Star teams, in 1978, 1979, 1982 and 1989. He also managed nine National League Rookie-of-the-Year winners: Rick Sutcliffe, Steve Sax, Fernando Valenzuela, Steve Howe, Eric Karros, Mike Piazza, Hideo Nomo, Raul Mondesi and Todd Hollandsworth. Lasorda was chosen to manage the 2000 U.S. Olympic Baseball team that won the Gold medal in Sydney, Australia, against a Cuban team which had gone 25-1 during the tournament.

In 1997, Tommy Lasorda was voted into the Baseball Hall of Fame and Museum by the Veterans' Committee, in his first year of eligibility. He was joined by Nellie Fox, Willie Wells and Phil Niekro. The Dodgers soon retired his #2 for all time. Tommy cried the day he found out. Lasorda was the 14th manager to be so honored. Here is my favorite part of Tommy Lasorda's Hall-of-Fame speech. "When I was 15, I used to dream that I was pitching for the New York Yankees. Bill Dickey was my catcher and I'm pitching in Yankee Stadium. I am surrounded by Ruth, DiMaggio, Rizzuto, and the rest, when my mom says, 'Wake up Tommy, it's time to go to school.' I'm so mad that she woke me up from my dream. Now I'm standing here being inducted into the Baseball Hall of Fame and I'm afraid I'm gonna feel my mom shake me awake to get up and go to school."

In 1991, Tommy's only son, Tom Jr., known as "Spunky", died at the age of 33. The man who bragged that he had only missed seven games in all his years as a manager, began to slow down after his son's death. Old age began to creep up on Tommy. It took Tommy years to grieve his death. As Tommy got older, he began to suffer physical setbacks. He suffered from tendonitis in his left shoulder and was bothered by arthritis, an ulcer and a hernia. In June of 1996, Tommy had a heart attack and underwent an angioplasty. He spent a month at home expecting to return to the dugout, but it was not to be. Owner Peter O'Malley and club president Fred Claire urged him to retire. Tommy managed his final game on July 23, 1996. The Dodgers had beaten the Houston Astros, 4-3. On July 29, 1996, with tears in his eyes and his voice trembling, Tommy Lasorda retired from the job he loved so much. Tommy later said, "I found out that it's not good to talk about my troubles. Eighty percent of the people who hear them don't care, and the other twenty percent are glad you're having troubles." Lasorda accepted a job as the vice president of the Dodgers, which allowed him to become an ambassador for the team and the game. He was replaced as manager by Bill Russell. In 2012, Lasorda had a pacemaker installed.

Lasorda's last public appearance was made possible by Bobby Valentine, who made sure Tommy attended Game Six of the 2020 World Series in Arlington, Texas, between the Los Angeles Dodgers and Tampa Bay Rays. There, Lasorda sat in a private suite at Globe Life Stadium and witnessed another World Series title by his beloved Dodgers. As he always did after a big win, Tommy yelled out loud, "Oh Yeah!"

Tommy Lasorda died on Thursday, January 7, 2021. He was 93 and living at his home in Fullerton, California. He had spent a total of 71 years with the Dodgers. On that Thursday night, after a seven-week stay in the hospital, Tommy suffered another heart attack. Tommy had just returned to his Fullerton home on Tuesday. He was pronounced dead at 10:57 p.m. Tommy is survived by his wife Jo, of 70 years, a daughter Laura Lasorda, and a granddaughter Emily Tess Goldberg. "When I die," said Tommy. "I want it put on my tombstone: 'Dodger Stadium was his address, but every ballpark was his home.'"

This man loved being Tommy Lasorda. He led a remarkable baseball life. God doesn't make managers like him anymore. The good Lord's team just got better in Heaven.

CONTROL OVER SPEED

In the movie "Field of Dreams," Shoeless Joe Jackson said, "I wake up in the night with the smell of the ballpark in my nose and the cool of the grass on my feet." That's baseball. Baseball is a kid's game filled with big-boy moments. Baseball always finds a story and a place for all of us. The game fills a need for belonging. It's like being young again. How can you not like baseball?

He owned long arms, soft hands and a quiet toughness about him, and all he seemed to care about was winning. He was the very definition of "Blue Collar" and owned a body built for baseball. When watching him pitch, you could never tell if he was winning or losing, if he had given up a home run or gotten a strikeout. This man was always seen as a clean-cut guy, who never got in trouble. Not only was he a glass half-full kind of guy, he always seemed to be thirsty. This fellow had a great mind; he could out-think the hitters. He did what he had always done on the diamond, he made a difference. His fastball was nasty. He could sink it, cut it, change it or curve it; that's pitching. But for him, it was his curveball that became his most beautiful pitch. He often forced hitters to duck and back away before watching the ball cross the heart of the plate.

This ageless wonder was durable, showed up every day and pitched at a high level until he was 43 years old. No one does that anymore. He was the king of "Here it is, can you hit it?" His hair was made up of crazy golden-brown curls with a little gray above his ears, and he had a perm. He was not pitching against a left-handed hitter or a switch-hitter. He was pitching against time. The man rarely showed emotion, but when he did, it was joyous. For 23 years, he never missed a start due to injury or illness. He may have pitched with a sore shoulder, but he was never hurt. His 756 career starts rank third all-time behind only Cy Young and Nolan Ryan. This guy is the only pitcher in Major League history with 200 innings pitched for 20 seasons.

Hitters could never relax with Sutton on the mound. Stepping into the batter's box against Don Sutton was like getting an oil change. You didn't want to think about it until you absolutely had to. They watched Don touch his cap, wipe his glove against his chest, hold it against his leg, hitch his belt, rub his neck, and sometimes scratch his bottom. None of these indicated that he was doctoring the baseball, but it sure gave them a lot more to think about than hitting the ball.

The list of pitchers in the 1960s, who were suspected of "scuffing" or "loading up" a baseball is long, distinguished and included Hall-of-Famers. Gaylord Perry, Lew Burdette, Kevin Gross, Joe Niekro, Mike Scott, Don Drysdale and yes, Don Sutton were all a part of that list. After denying on several occasions, Don Sutton began to understand that he could use the accusations against him in his favor. If it kept the hitters guessing, then checking the baseball could be a good thing, not bad. The following are a few examples of what Don went through. Sutton was once ejected from a game by umpire Doug Harvey, for throwing a baseball with a small rip in the cover. In 1976, Sutton had a perfect game through seven and a third innings, when the Pittsburgh Pirates' manager asked the umpires to stop the game several times to determine if Sutton was doctoring the ball. The Pirates' right-fielder, Dave Parker, finally broke up the perfect game in the eighth inning with a home run. Sutton gave up only one more hit, and the Dodgers won 5-1. "Sparky" Anderson of the Reds claimed that Sutton used sandpaper to doctor the baseball. Nolan Ryan remembered losing to Sutton 1-0 and noticed in the 7th inning, that the rosin bag was greasy from Vaseline. Sutton tells a funny story about doctoring the baseball. During one game, after receiving complaints from the opposing manager, an umpire inspected Sutton's glove for sandpaper or some other foreign substance. The only thing the umpire found was a note that read, "You're getting warm, but it isn't here." Don Sutton concentrated on control over speed. "I would rather be dependable and consistent, instead of spectacular or flamboyant," said Sutton.

Donald Howard Sutton was born in a tarpaper shack on April 2, 1945, in Clio, Alabama. The town had more stop signs than people. His father, Charlie, was 18 when Don was born. Charlie started out as a sharecropper and later worked in construction and concrete. His mother, Lillian, was 15 and took care of their home and two more children born after Don. Their names were Ron and Glenda. In 1950, when Don turned five, the Suttons moved to Molino, located near the panhandle of Florida.

Sutton grew up in a strict Christian family and as a New York Yankee fan. He devoted every waking minute possible to listening to Yankee games on his transistor radio. "All I ever wanted to be was a pitcher growing up," said Sutton. "If you asked me where I wanted to play, I'd have said in the middle of the diamond. Whose diamond, I don't care." He learned to throw a curveball before he turned 13. When he wasn't helping his dad, he spent his days in the yard playing ball with his imaginary friends, Yogi, Mickey, Whitey or "Moose." His favorite pitchers were Dick Donovan, Camilo Pascual and Whitey Ford. Sutton always claimed that the best advice he had ever received was from his sixth-grade teacher, Henry Roper, who had once pitched in the New York Giants' organization. Roper said, "Change speeds and throw strikes.

As long as you're throwing the ball over the plate, everybody has to work. If you walk'em, you're the only one working." Sutton played football, basketball and baseball at Tate High School, but only focused on pitching, after his sophomore year. Don pitched well in high school and posted a 21-7 win-loss record while at Tate. In his junior year, Don led the Tate Aggies to the Class-A State championship.

Even though he was a Connie Mack All-Star, Sutton was disappointed that he received no professional offers, after he graduated from high school in 1963. He attended Gulf Coast Community College, located in Panama City, Florida. While there, Sutton made several national teams and pitched well enough to attract several professional teams. Sutton became very impressed with the honesty of the Los Angeles Dodgers' scouts, Leon Hamilton, Monty Basgall and Burt Wells. Sutton never realized that the game of baseball was supposed to be hard. His fastball was in the mid-eighties, just a little bit higher than the speed limit in some parts of the country. Nevertheless, he turned down several higher offers and signed a $15,000 contract with the Los Angeles Dodgers on September 11, 1964, as a 19-year-old amateur free agent. His contract also included a stipend for college, if he chose to return to school. From the beginning, Don Sutton saw himself as someone special. Standing still was never part of his plan. In 1965, he reported to Vero Beach, Florida, the home of the Dodgers' minor league camp. After recording a 23-7 win-loss record for the Dodgers' Class-A and Double-A Minor League teams, he was promoted to the Major League club, guided by Walter Alston, in 1966. When star pitchers Sandy Koufax and Don Drysdale decided to hold out at contract time, an opening was created for him. Sutton believed that when those two finally reported to camp that he would be demoted, but he quickly proved that he was big-league ready. On April 14, 1966, Sutton, wearing #20, went seven innings, but lost his first game 4-2 to the Houston Astros. He would receive his first win four days later against those same Astros, 6-3 in the Astrodome. As a rookie, Sutton went 12-12 with a 2.99 ERA, but did not pitch in the 1966 World Series, against the Baltimore Orioles. The Dodgers were swept by the Orioles in four games.

From 1967 to 1970, Sutton's results on the mound were up and down. He did marry the love of his life, Patti, at the end of the 1968 season, and together they had two children, Daron, born in 1969, and Staci in 1973. Sutton made several appearances on the game show *Match Game*, in the 1970's.

Don always considered 1972 to be his finest year. He was named Opening Day starter for the first of seven consecutive seasons. Don won his first eight starts and was also named to his first All-Star team. Don finished the year with five wins in a row and an overall record of 19-9 in 33 games pitched, with a 2.08 ERA. His only hiccup occurred against San Francisco. Giants' first baseman, Willie McCovey, made history on July 2, 1972, when he hit his 14th career grand-slam home run off Don Sutton. That grand slam tied Willie with Gil Hodges and Hank Aaron for the all-time National League record. "I knew it was gone as soon as I hit it," Willie said. "I hit the stuffing out of it."

For 15 seasons with Los Angeles, Sutton never failed to reach the 200-inning mark and appeared in three World Series for the Dodgers in 1974, 1977 and 1978. Unfortunately, Don Sutton and Tommy Lasorda never found themselves on the same page. Lasorda took over for Walter Alston as the Dodgers' manager, in 1977. Sutton had wanted his former catcher, Jeff Torborg, as the club's new skipper. Sutton disliked Lasorda's show-biz approach. "With Lasorda, the volume of your discussion got louder and louder, until it was like two people trying to see who could out-yell the other without listening," said Don. Interestingly, Tommy Lasorda died on January 7, 2021, just 11 days before Don Sutton. Tommy was 93 years old. The Dodgers' team wore patches this year on the right sleeves of their jerseys in their honor, #2 for Lasorda and #20 for Sutton.

"I'm the most loyal player money can buy," said Sutton. I thought that comment was funny, considering he played for the Los Angeles Dodgers, Houston Astros, Milwaukee Brewers, Oakland Athletes and California Angels.

After the 1980 season, Don Sutton left the Dodgers and was signed by the Houston Astros as a free agent, on December 4, 1980, for $875,000, after J. R. Richard was lost when he suffered a stroke from a blood clot that had gone undetected. Don would continue to wear #20. In 1981, the players and the union went on strike for the first time since 1972, and that wiped out one-third of that season. Sutton went 11-9, but later got hit on the knee while batting and missed the Division Series. As a result, the Astros lost to the Dodgers. The following season, 1982, Sutton went 13-8, but the team struggled and played under .500 baseball.

"Don Sutton could beat you with four different pitches," said Astros teammate, Nolan Ryan, "but he didn't have a great anything." Sutton and Ryan were teammates for two years with the Astros. "He may have been the best finesse pitcher I ever saw," said Ryan.

In 1982, Don asked to be traded to the Milwaukee Brewers in mid-season and helped pitch the Brewers to the 1982 World Series. Don was traded on August 30th for Kevin Bass, Frank DiPino and Mike Madden, and he received the #21 to wear. The 1982 World Series was a clash of styles, "Harvey Wallbanger's" power versus the speed of the St. Louis Cardinals. The Redbirds beat the Brewers in six games, to win their first World Series since 1967. Sutton went 22-25 during his two seasons in Milwaukee, but still claimed that

Milwaukee was the greatest place he had ever played.

On December 7, 1984, Don was traded to the Oakland A's. The 40-year-old Sutton was 20 wins short of 300. Wearing #20, Don won 13 games for the A's before being sent to the California Angels on September 10, 1985. There, he wore #27 and won his first two games that season. His 1986 season began poorly as he lost his first three contests. Win #299 came on June 9, 1984, against the great Tom Seaver. "Tom Terrific" had won 306 games at the time. Sutton emerged victorious. On June 18, 1984, Sutton became the 19th pitcher in major-league history to win 300 games, in a complete game against the Texas Rangers. Sutton finished the season with a 15-11 record, as the Angels cruised to the American League West title. The Angels lost to Red Sox in seven games. Sutton won 11 and lost 11 in 1987 with the Angels and was released on October 30, 1987. He returned to the Los Angeles Dodgers on January 5, 1988, for his 23rd season. Sutton struggled through 16 starts and later agreed that returning to the Dodgers had been a mistake and a depressing way to end his relationship with L.A. The last time he "toed the pitching rubber" for the Dodgers occurred on August 9, 1988. He was released on August 10, 1988, at age 43.

Sutton is still the Dodgers' all-time leader in games started (533), wins (233), shutouts (52), and strikeouts (2,696), home runs surrendered (309), and losses (181). His career totals were worthy of a Hall-of-Fame career. Don pitched in 774 games in 23 seasons. His win-loss record stands at 324-256 with a 3.26 ERA. Sutton struck out 3,574 batters, in 5,282.1 innings pitched, while giving up 4,692 hits and 472 home runs. He completed 178 games and threw 58 shutouts. Don also went to bat 1,354 times, but never hit a home run.

Don spent five years on the Hall-of-Fame ballot before getting voted in. Sutton was not expected to be a first-ballot

Hall-of-Famer and gathered only 56.8% of the writers' vote in 1994, his first year of eligibility. By 1998, Sutton received 81.6 % and joined the Baseball Hall of Fame. He was the only player elected that year, but was joined by Larry Doby who was elected by the veterans' committee. Sutton's #20 was retired by the Dodgers in 1998.

In 1989, Don made a smooth transition into the broadcasting booth, after baseball with the Dodgers. He would join the Atlanta Braves' broadcast team from 1990 to 2006. Sutton stepped away from the Braves for two years, in 2007 and 2008, to broadcast for the Washington Nationals, before returning to Atlanta in 2009 and staying through 2019. Don was inducted into the Atlanta Braves' Hall of Fame as a broadcaster in 2015. "With apologies to Lou Gehrig, I'm the luckiest man on the face of the earth," said Sutton when he was inducted into the Braves' team Hall of Fame. "I have everything in life I've ever wanted."

Interestingly, Sutton began his career with Sandy Koufax and Don Drysdale as his teammates, and ended it with Orel Hershiser and Fernando Valenzuela. Early in has career, Don relied on his fastball and a curve that he would throw at any time. He later added a slider, screwball and changeup. His secret was that he delivered all five pitches with the same delivery and motion, so the hitter could not guess. Most great players acquire a nickname or two during their career. Sutton was no different. In his beginning, the newspapers in L.A. referred to him as "Little D" with a nod to "Big D" (Don Drysdale.) He was later called "Black & Decker" and "The Mechanic" for the relentless and fierce command of five different pitches.

Don Sutton never led the league in strikeouts or wins, but he won 324 games and held the record of 20 straight seasons with 100 or more strikeouts. Sutton never took home a Cy Young Trophy, but he pitched 200 innings in each of his first

21 seasons. He only had one 20-win season. In 15 National League Championship Series and World Series games with the Dodgers, Brewers and Angels, Don had a 6-4 record and a 3.68 ERA. He was elected to the Baseball Hall of Fame on his fifth attempt.

I am very fortunate to have met Don Sutton and he was kind enough to autograph the Dodgers hat I was wearing at the time.

Don Sutton threw his last curveball on a Tuesday morning, January, 18, 2021. He was 75 and living at his home in Rancho Mirage, California, with his second wife, Mary. The cause of his death was cancer. Don had his left kidney removed in 2002 and also lost part of a lung, removed the following year. Sutton missed the 2019 season with a fractured left femur and did not return to the Atlanta Braves' broadcast booth. He had spent the last 60 years of his life going to the ballpark every day during the summer. The rest of his time was spent with family, tasting wine and playing golf. Don is also survived by his son Daron and two daughters, Staci and Jacquie, his only child by his second wife, Mary. It has been said that we are all just passing through time and we occupy our place in life very briefly. The time we had with Don Sutton was a gift, and we are all better that he spent his time here with us.

BAD HENRY

How do you begin to write about an icon? This quiet, skinny, little black kid had traveled the world, befriended Presidents and Heads of State, enjoyed wealth and fame, married twice, put all his kids through college, and he even has a place not only in sports history but also in American history. Still, he took nothing for granted. This guy hasn't played a baseball game since 1976, yet he was the right man at the right time and is still as relevant today as he was 45 years ago. Do not define this man on mere numbers. He may have been a better person than a baseball player, yet as a player, he will be remembered forever. As baseball fans and Americans, we all paused on January 22, 2020, when we heard the news. Don't mistake him for just any old ballplayer. This guy could hit anybody. He never begged for respect. The man refused to break and earned respect through his actions and the way he carried himself at all times. In spite of all the records he set, he focused on being humble instead of hitting home runs, becoming a role model rather than "Babe" Ruth, grace instead of greed, adversity verse anger, and mercy in the face of hatred. After baseball, opportunity became his opponent. His goal was to pick up where his idol, Jackie Robinson, had left off. He had "guts" and would say what he felt. He once said, "God gave me the gifts he did for a reason, to never be satisfied with the way things are."

This fellow was blessed with very strong wrists and hands. He used to use tongs to carry blocks of ice while working with his dad. This guy didn't have a particular style or a flair for the dramatic. The man was never about hitches in his swing, changing his batting stance or bat flips. He simply put the bat on the ball. This fellow was a terror at the plate and a professor of hitting. He once admitted to being a guess hitter, but he also claimed to have studied pitchers and their tendencies by watching them pitch through the little holes in his cap. He used a bat that was 34 inches long and weighed 33 ounces, during his entire career. His friends joked that he spoke three languages: Mobile, Alabama, and English, and could hit in any of them. He never seemed to hit a groundball to shortstop or third. It always went right in the hole between the two. Opposing pitchers always showed him respect. They didn't care how old he was. This guy could hit. Hall-of-Fame pitcher Don Drysdale surrendered more home runs (17) to him than any other pitcher. Drysdale therefore nicknamed him "Bad Henry." Don referred to him as "Bad Henry," because he could not get his fastball by him. The rest of us knew him as Hank Aaron. Before going to sleep at night, baseballs checked under their bed for Hank Aaron. The word "legend" is powerful. Standing 6 feet tall and weighing 180 pounds, Henry Aaron may have been more powerful. "Patience and quick wrist were the keys to my success," said Aaron. I wish all baseball fans remembered the Henry Aaron of the 1950's. The real story of Henry Aaron, in my opinion, is that he does not change who he is, while chasing Ruth's record. My goal in writing his story is to add to that memory.

There's a wonderful story about Walter Alston, Manager of the Los Angeles Dodgers, and his inability to fill out the lineup card for the National League All-Stars. Alston tells Willie Mays, "Here Willie, you know these players better then I do." Willie takes the card and says, "Well, I'll lead off because I can get on. Then I'll bat Clemente because he can get me over. Then I'll put in Aaron because he can drive me in. The rest of the lineup doesn't make any difference."

Then he hands the lineup card back to Alston.

Henry Louis "Hank" Aaron was born on February 5, 1934, and grew up poor in Mobile, Alabama, the deepest part of the South. Henry Aaron's father, Herbert, was a boilermaker assistant at the city dry docks and his mother had her hands full with kids. After being married, Herbert and Estella Aaron moved from Wilcox County, just south of Selma, Alabama, to Mobile. Henry's grandfather had been a minister. Henry was the third of eight children born into their family, and he always preferred to be called Henry instead of Hank. It wasn't until the early 1970s, as Henry closed in on Ruth's homerun record, that he received the nickname "Hammerin' Hank" from the press. Interestingly, Babe Ruth and Henry Aaron were born one calendar date apart; Aaron on February 5, 1934, and Ruth on February 6, 1895. Ruth turned 39 years old the day after Henry was born. Aaron attended Central High School and the school did not have a baseball team, so Aaron played softball. His friends nicknamed him "Snowshoes" in high school, because of the way he ran the bases. Aaron's friends talked about how they would use a broomstick and bottle caps to hit in the streets. Some said Aaron could hit a bottle cap a block and a half. Henry grew up hitting cross-handed and never wore batting gloves. Cubs' Hall-of-Famer, Billy Williams, later played football with Henry's brother, Tommy Aaron, at Central High School in Mobile.

I have always been amazed at what some folks have to overcome to be successful in life. In Henry's autobiography, I Had a Hammer, written by Aaron with the late Lonnie Wheeler, Henry describes his journey into professional baseball. In 1942, at the age of eight, Aaron's family moved to Toulminville, just outside of Mobile. They built a wooden house on two vacant lots. The house Henry grew up in was surrounded by farm animals, cornfields, a watermelon patch and blackberry thickets. The street was dirt and full of mud holes. They got their water from a well and used wood to heat and cook. There was no electricity, no windows, and a kerosene lamp was used to light the room. The bathroom was an outhouse in the backyard. "None of us ever had a bed to themselves," said Henry. Cornbread, butterbeans and collard greens were consumed at most meals. They did manage to slaughter a hog once a year for meat and grease, and everything else came from their garden. To supplement the family income, his dad also ran a small tavern next to their home, called "The Black Cat Inn." His sister Sarah helped run the tavern. Henry grew up shooting marbles, doing chores, reading comic books, catching snakes and playing baseball. He hated school, began to skip class, and eventually dropped out. In March of 1948, Jackie Robinson played in an exhibition game in Mobile. Jackie spoke of the importance of an education. It was quite a treat for the 14-year-old Henry Aaron. It was the beginning of his baseball dream.

In 1951, Ed Scott played and managed a semipro team known as the Mobile Black Bears. Although Henry was the youngest member of the team, he was paid ten dollars a game, but his mother refused to allow him to travel to away games. Therefore, every Sunday Henry Aaron played shortstop for the Bears at home.

In 1952, at the age of 17, his mother made him two sandwiches, stuffed two one-dollar bills in his pocket and cried as his father, his older brother Hubert, Jr., and his sister Sarah, along with scout Ed Scott drove him to the train station. Henry had never been on a train. He carried a knapsack with a pair of pants, a shirt, and a borrowed pair of shoes. Scott, who also scouted for potential talent, handed Henry an envelope to give to "Bunny" Downs, the business manager of the Indianapolis Clowns. He was on his way to

Winston-Salem, North Carolina, the home of the Clowns. At that time, only six of the sixteen clubs had broken the color line. "I never felt so scared and alone in my life," said Henry. "My mother said, 'If you don't do well in a month, you're coming back home and go to school,'" said Aaron. He had just turned 18 and was sure of only one thing in his life, he loved playing baseball. Did he do the right thing with his life? His mother had wanted him to be a teacher. No doubt, playing baseball gave him all that a man could have asked for.

That year, Dewey Griggs of the Boston Braves saw a 17-year-old hard-hitting shortstop named Henry Aaron play in Buffalo against the Memphis Red Sox. He suggested that Henry hold his bat with his right hand on top instead of cross-handed. Aaron hit a home run in his first at-bat and never hit cross-handed again. Griggs was also concerned that Aaron threw underhanded to first base and did not run the bases at full speed. So, Aaron bunted the next time up, beat the throw to first base and threw over-handed as hard as he could from shortstop position. Griggs sent a scouting report to John Mullin of the Braves. "I would love to have played for the Yankees," said Henry. "For whatever reason, they didn't want me. I also had a chance to sign with the Giants or the Braves. I did not sign with the New York Giants, because they wanted to send me to Class-A ball and pay me Class-C money, and the Braves were going to send me to Class-C ball and pay me Class-A money. The difference was $150 a month. That is why I signed with the Milwaukee Braves." In June of 1952, the Braves signed Henry for $350 a month and sent him to the Eau Claire Bears, their Class-C club of the Northern League, located in Eau Claire, Wisconsin. He reported to the team on June 11. This marked the first time that Aaron shared the ball field with white players. A month later, Henry played in the Northern League All-Star Game and was later named the Northern League's MVP. Aaron had spent only six weeks with the Indianapolis Clowns of the

Negro Leagues, before they folded. The note in the envelope said, "Forget everything else about the player. Just watch his bat."

In 1953, Henry was sent South to the Jacksonville Braves, the Boston Braves' Class-A club of the Sally League, and he played second base. There were only five black players in the Sally League at that time. That same year, during Spring Training, the Boston Braves moved to Milwaukee, Wisconsin, and became the Milwaukee Braves. Henry met his first wife, Barbara Lucas, in Jacksonville. They would have five children together. Aaron led the Sally League in hitting and was voted MVP. After the season ended in 1953, Henry traveled to Puerto Rico to play for the Caguas team in the Winter Leagues. Aaron mostly threw underhanded until he played Winter Ball in Puerto Rice. There he learned to throw over-handed. Puerto Rico is where he became an outfielder. In Puerto Rico, every time a player hit a home run they received a carton of Chesterfield cigarettes. Yes, Henry smoked back then, and he was not proud of it.

In 1954, left-fielder Bobby Thomson broke his ankle in Spring Training sliding into second base. Henry was given the #5 to wear and was promoted to the Milwaukee Braves as their starting left-fielder. Henry only spent one season in the Minor Leagues. On April 13, 1954, the great Henry Aaron went 0 for 5 in his first game at Crosley Field in Cincinnati, as a Milwaukee Brave. He would later record his first hit, a double in Milwaukee, against Vic Rashi of the St. Louis Cardinals. On April 23rd, Henry hit his first home run at Sportsman Park in St. Louis off the same pitcher. Aaron roomed with Jim Pendleton at first, and then later with Bill Bruton. On September 5, 1954, Aaron broke his ankle sliding into third base. Interestingly, Bobby Thomson came in to run for Aaron. Henry finished the year with 13 home runs and a .280 batting average. In 1955, Henry would switch to the #44. He hit 27 home runs, batted .314, scored 105 runs and drove in 106 runs. He was also selected to play in his first All-Star Game, held that year in Milwaukee.

"In my first All-Star Game, played in Milwaukee, I was sitting next to Stan Musial," said Aaron. "Stan got up to hit and turned to us and said, 'Well boys, they don't pay us to pinch hit so I might as well hit a home run.' "Musial hit a home run that won the game for us. I know people talk about Ruth calling his shot but that's the gospel truth," said Aaron. Henry Aaron and Stan Musial would become best of friends. During the 1960s, they traveled to Vietnam and roomed together, while visiting our troops. It was the first time Henry Aaron had ever had a white roommate.

Aaron won his first batting title in 1956, while hitting .328. Henry once said, "Playing in the big leagues wasn't nearly as hard as getting there." Aaron's bat weighed 10 oz. less than Babe Ruth's. "I always held my bat with my left hand right on the knob," said Henry. "I used to always get a blister right here, pointing to his palm. This happened because I did a lot of hitting with my wrist." Henry never hit more than 47 home runs in a single season, but he did hit double-digit home runs for 23 seasons.

In 1957, Henry hit 44 home runs; drove in 132 RBI's, scored 118 runs, and was voted the National League MVP. During the 1957 World Series against the hated New York Yankees, Henry batted .393, and hit three home runs, including a three-run shot in Game Four to win the Milwaukee Braves' first World Series. The Braves' franchise had not won a World Series since 1914, when they played in Boston.

Henry had his first three-homer game at Seals Stadium in San Francisco on June 21, 1959. That same year he won his second batting title hitting .355. This 25-year old had 223 hits but the Braves lost the pennant to the Dodgers in a playoff game. His salary increased to $17,000 a year.

The following are some interesting facts about Henry

Aaron and his life and career. "Home Run Derby" was filmed in Los Angeles, California, at Wrigley Field in 1959. The show aired in 1960. Aaron won six times and won the most money from the Home Run Derby, $13,500. There was also some hardship. Henry had experienced divorce from his first wife, Barbara, and lost a son as an infant. She had given premature birth to twin boys named Lary and Gary. Unfortunately, Gary did not survive the birth. In 1962, Henry's daughter Dorinda, was born on his birthday, and he and his brother Tommie Aaron became roommates with the Milwaukee Braves. Three times that year, they both hit a home run in the same game. Hank Aaron's first *Sports Illustrated* cover occurred on August 16, 1969. He was 35 and in his 16th season of Major League baseball. Henry was still 160 home runs short of "the Babe's" record of 714. It just seemed like he had slipped up on baseball and Ruth. On May 17, 1970, Hank recorded his 3,000th hit off Cincinnati Reds' pitcher, Wayne Simpson. He became the eighth player in Major League history to get to 3,000 hits. He hit 47 home runs in 1971 and it began to dawn on folks that he indeed had a chance. On February 29, 1972, Hank Aaron became the richest player in Major League history when he signed a three-year, $600,000 contract to remain with the Atlanta Braves. At the time, Hank had hit 639 career home runs, 75 behind the great Babe Ruth. As the 1973 season unfolded, Henry married his second wife, Billye in Jamaica, and appeared on "The Flip Wilson Show" in October of that year. He would also be seen on "Hollywood Squares" and was a guest on Dean Martin, Merv Griffin, Mike Douglas and Dinah Shore shows. But, Aaron was also treading on sacred ground as Ruth was considered a baseball god, and what does he get? Hate mail! The chase for Ruth's home-run record had exposed the hatred that surrounded the game at that time. "It should have been the greatest period of my life, and it was the worst," said Henry.

After finishing the 1973 season with 40 home runs, his career total now rested on 713, one away from tying Babe Ruth. Henry Aaron, Davey Johnson and Darrell Evans had made history by becoming the first three players on the same team to each hit 40 or more home runs in the same season. After the games, he would sometimes sleep in the locker room or he would slip out a back entrance. He could not celebrate with his teammates. In anticipation of breaking Babe Ruth's record, television manufacturer, Magnavox, signed him in January of 1974, to a five-year $1 million contract.

The Braves were scheduled to open the 1974 season at Riverfront Stadium in Cincinnati. Braves' Manager Eddie Mathews wanted to keep Henry out of the lineup. Mathews told the Baseball Commissioner that he wanted Henry to break the record at home, but I believe Mathews feared for the safety of Aaron's life. The U.S. Postal Service has estimated that Henry had received 930,000 pieces of mail during the year, or 3,000 letters a day. Some of the mail received was supportive, but a lot of the mail had been hate mail, including death threats. The FBI got involved. "I just wanted to live until next season," was Aaron's response after getting death threats as he approached Babe Ruth's career home run record. Dinah Shore was second on the postal service list with 60,000 pieces of mail. A security team was now traveling with Aaron, and his daughter was receiving police protection. Henry, now 40 years old, did not travel with the team and often avoided attention by registering at hotels under the alias George Ruth. But Baseball Commissioner, Bowie Kuhn ruled that every team should play their best players and would not allow Henry to sit out. "Once I got to the ballpark nothing could distract me from the game," said Henry. On April 4th, a sellout crowd of 52,154 showed up. They were not disappointed. Aaron complied and hit home run #714 in his first at-bat off Reds' pitcher Jack Billingham. Henry sat out the second game and went hitless in the third. The Braves now returned to Atlanta for three games with the Los Angeles Dodgers.

On Monday night, April 8, 1974, NBC decided to air the Braves' and Dodgers baseball game played in Atlanta. Curt Gowdy was on the call for NBC. But it was the radio calls that have stood the test of time. There were 53,775 fans in attendance including celebrities like Georgia Governor Jimmy Carter, Redd Fox and Sammy Davis, Jr. Henry's dad, Herbert, threw out the first pitch. Monte Irvin, an official in Baseball Commissioner Bowie Kuhn's office, was sent to represent Kuhn. The Atlanta fans booed Irvin when they found out the Commissioner was not present. Aaron felt slighted and never forgot. The ratings went through the roof and recorded a 22.3 rating. It took until Game Seven of the 2001 World Series to top that rating.

"He's sitting on 714." Most baseball fans believe it's one of the top five calls of all-time. These two guys are forever joined in baseball lore by less than forty words, spoken into a microphone one early evening on April 8, 1974, by Braves' broadcaster Milo Hamilton, 47 years ago. It was the first game of the new season. The Atlanta Braves were at home against the Los Angeles Dodgers. Umpire "Satch" Davidson was behind home plate. Against Dodger left-handed pitcher, Al Downing, who also wore #44, Aaron drew a walk and scored a run in the second inning. With misty rain falling, Henry came to bat in the bottom of the fourth inning with no outs and Darrell Evans on first. The Braves were behind 3-1. Dusty Baker was on deck that day as Henry approached the plate. "Hank would always stop and tell me what he was looking for from the pitcher," said Baker. "But this day he said, 'I'm going to end this thing right here.'" With a 1-0 count, Downing threw a slider. Aaron unloaded and drove the ball 400 feet into leftfield over the head of a leaping Bill Buckner and into the Braves' bullpen. The blast was caught by Braves' relief pitcher, Tom House. Here's how the Atlanta radio call by Milo Hamilton sounded, as Henry Aaron settled into the batter's box. "He's sitting on 714! Here's the pitch by Downing, swinging, there's a drive into left centerfield, that ball is gonna beee...OUTTA HERE! IT'S GONE! IT'S 715! There's a new home-run champion of all time and it's HENRY AARON!"

If you were listening to the Dodgers' radio broadcast, you heard Vince Scully say these words after an 11-minute ovation. "What a marvelous moment for baseball. What a marvelous moment for the country and the world. A black man is getting a standing ovation in the Deep South for breaking the record of an all-time baseball idol."

As Aaron rounded the bases, Dodgers' first baseman, Steve Garvey shook his hand. As he passed second base he became aware of two young men running beside him and patting him on the back. How could security have allowed this to happen? This was "can't miss" TV. As Henry crossed home plate, he was besieged by teammates and his parents, Herbert and Estella. "I never knew my mother could hug so hard," said Henry. After a moment or two, it started to rain and a microphone was brought out. Aaron thought to himself, what if this game gets rained out? He would have to go though this all over again, but the rain finally stopped. Henry said at the end of his short speech, "I just thank God it's all over with." The Braves won that night 7-4, and Henry now had a new nickname, "Home Run King." The press was livid with Mathews as he refused to let anyone in the locker room after the game, except players and their families. The champagne flowed as the team celebrated with Henry. Afterwards, there was a party at Henry's house where he retired to a room, got down on his knees and cried.

In 1974, the year he broke Babe Ruth's career home-run record, Henry Aaron was the last of the Negro Leaguers playing in the Major Leagues. Willie Mays had retired in 1973. Sammy Davis, Jr., offered Hank $25,000 for his 715th home run ball. Aaron said "No thanks" and kept it in a safety deposit box. Shortly after, 230 billboards in the City of Atlanta saluting Hank Aaron were on display. In mid-June, the Braves played the Mets at Shea Stadium and Aaron was presented the New York City's Gold Medal, its highest honor, by Mayor Abraham D. Beame, outside of City Hall. Aaron also toured Harlem in a motorcade and spoke to over 5,000 people at Marcus Garvey Park.

Braves' Manager Eddie Mathews was fired shortly after the 1974 All-Star Game and Aaron expected to be offered the job. Hall-of-Famers Eddie Mathews and Hank Aaron have some history together as teammates. During their 13 years playing together they hit a combined total of 863 home runs, the most ever by two teammates. And last but not least, I can't help but find it interesting that Al Downing never struck out Henry Aaron in the four years they competed against each other.

The list of Hall-of-Famers from Mobile, Alabama, was impressive. They included Hank Aaron, Satchel Paige, Willie McCovey, Billy Williams and Ozzie Smith. Also from Mobile were Cleon Jones, Tommy Agee and Amos Otis. But it was Willie Mays whom Aaron competed against, his entire career. Both were raised in Alabama, only 225 miles apart. In the 1950s, only eight percent of Major League baseball, primarily in the National League, was made up of African-Americans, yet they dominated most of the awards, winning eight of ten MVP Awards. Roy Campanella won three times, Ernie Banks won twice, and Willie Mays, Don Newcombe and Henry Aaron won one each. Every decade or so, there comes along a player whom other players will get up off the bench to watch to see what happens. With Hank Aaron there was a quiet excellence. He had a lack of flair that his predecessors like Ruth, DiMaggio, and Mantle had. Yet, he drove in more runs than Lou Gehrig and scored more runs than Willie Mays. Aaron always considered 1959 to be his finest year with a bat. Henry recorded 400 total bases. Some players who never reached 400 total bases in a single season included Ted Williams, Mickey Mantle, Ernie Banks and Willie Mays. "Total bases combined the ability to get on base with the power to move base runners around," said Henry. Aaron once said with a smile, "I was faster than Mays. He just wore his cap up on his forehead so it would fly off when he ran. He thought it made him look fast." When Willie heard about Henry's death, Mays said, "He was a very humble and quiet man and just simply a good guy. I have so many fond memories of Hank and will miss him very much."

Henry hit a total of 733 home runs as an Atlanta Brave, with the last one coming in his final at-bat off Rawley Eastwick of the Reds, on October 2, 1974. Aaron became the designated hitter for the Milwaukee Brewers a month later. Aaron was traded to the Brewers of the American League for outfielder Dave May and pitcher Roger Alexander. He signed a two-year contract at $240,000 a season. During those two years, he added 22 homeruns to his total, with his 755th and last home run coming on July 20, 1976, against Dick Drago of the California Angels. Aaron played his last baseball game on October 3, 1976, against the Detroit Tigers. The Brewers retired Henry's #44. While living in Milwaukee, Henry became a Vince Lombardi and Green Bay Packers' fan. Lombardi allowed him and Bud Selig to stand on the sidelines near the Packers' bench during the game. Hank Aaron would later become a die-hard Cleveland Browns fan. "I loved watching Jim Brown and Ozzie Newsome," said Henry. "I would fly to Cleveland on Sunday, dressed for

10-degree weather and sit in the Dog Pound with the real fans. One day, the owner Art Modell saw me and invited me to sit with him in his suite."

In an interview in 1965, Aaron said he had hoped to be a black manager one day in the Major Leagues. Henry never rested. He spoke out against the lack of African-Americans in management positions in the front offices of Major League baseball. He disliked the idea of Pete Rose being placed in the Hall of Fame and suggested that anyone involved in the Houston Astros sign-stealing scheme be run out of the game.

Baseball has recently lost a lot of its history in the past year. We saw the deaths of 110 Major League players in 2020, by far the greatest collections of Hall-of-Famers to die in one year. It wasn't even close. It was the most in 40 years. Eight sitting Hall-of-Famers passed, with five of them in a 42-day period. As of this writing, we have lost three more baseball Hall-of-Famers this year. Their names are Tommy Lasorda, Don Sutton and Henry Aaron.

Stories are powerful. If told often enough, the stories live on forever.

There are so many wonderful thoughts by former teammates and opponents. What follows are some of my favorites. Muhammad Ali once said about Hank Aaron, "The only man I idolized more than myself."

"Trying to throw a fastball by Hank Aaron is like trying to sneak a sunrise past a rooster," said Phillies' pitcher, Curt Simmons.

"We called him 'Supe,' short for Superman," said teammate, Darrell Evans.

Teammate Davey Johnson once asked Aaron, "What pitch are you looking for?" "Breaking ball." said Hank. "Why is that," asked Johnson. "Because they can't throw a fastball by me," said Aaron. "That's for sure," laughed Davey.

"The one thing people should know about Henry is how

good an all-around player he was," said Tom Seaver.

Mickey Mantle once said, "As far as I'm concerned Henry Aaron is the best baseball player of my era."

Jackie Robinson once wrote that he had broken the color barrier and Hank Aaron had broken the number barrier. Aaron still had the letter.

"Chipper" Jones may have said it best. "He had an aura about him," said Braves' Hall-of-Fame third baseman "Chipper" Jones. "He was in constant peace, while he probably had every right to be militant and angry and leery of everyone he came in contact with. He never was. He always had this gentle smile, always had this peace about him. Wherever he went, it was like watching God walk by."

The Atlanta Braves retired Aaron's #44 in April of 1977 and unveiled a statue of him swinging for the fences at Atlanta-Fulton County Stadium in 1982. They later moved the statue to Turner Field, in 1997, and changed the stadium address to 755 Hank Aaron Drive. A new statue now stands at Truist Park, erected in 2017.

"My biggest home run was not the one that broke Babe Ruth's record, it was the home run I hit off Billy Muffet in 1957, to clinch the National League pennant for the Braves," said Aaron. This hit occurred on September 23, 1957, at County Stadium in Milwaukee, Wisconsin, in front of 40,926 hometown fans. "Vinegar Ben" Mizel started the game for the Cardinals. "I ended up the MVP that year, and we won the World Series," exclaimed Aaron.

Aaron once said in jest, "It took me 17 years to get 3,000 hits. I did that in one afternoon on the golf course." Henry hit home runs off some of the very best pitchers of his day. He got Nolan Ryan twice. He hit seven home runs off of Sandy Koufax, eight off of Bob Gibson, eight off of Juan Marichal and a whopping 17 dingers off of Don Drysdale. Aaron hated stepping in the batter's box against the "Dominican

Dandy." "Juan Marichal could throw all day within a two-inch space, in, out, up or down. I'd never seen anyone as good as that," said Aaron.

Henry played 23 seasons (1954-1976). Aaron remains first in the Major Leagues in total bases (6,856), runs batted in (2,297), and extra bases hits (1,477). He is second in home runs (755), at-bats (12,364), behind only Pete Rose and third in hits (3,771), behind Rose and Cobb, and fourth in runs scored (2,174). Henry hit between 40 and 47 home runs eight times during his career. He won the National League's single-season home run and RBI titles four times each, led in runs scored, three times, and slugging percentage four times. In 1969, Henry hit 44 homeruns and only struck out 47 times. Henry hit .300 or better 14 times. Aaron also won three Gold Gloves and was faster than you think. He was as quick on the base paths as he was in the outfield. In 1963, he finished second in stolen bases behind Maury Wills. Henry Aaron became the second youngest player to reach 1,000 hits, after Ty Cobb. Henry made the All-Star team every year he played except his first and last seasons. Aaron averaged 37 home runs per 162 games played over his 23-year career. Remarkably, if you were to subtract Aaron's 755 home runs from his total hits, he would still have 3,016 hits; 2,294 of those being singles. He also hit 624 doubles, 98 triples and never struck out 100 times in a season, but he did ground into a double play 328 times.

Henry Aaron was voted into the Baseball Hall of Fame Museum in 1982. He was inducted alongside Frank Robinson, "Happy" Chandler and Travis Jackson. Hank Aaron was left off the Hall-of-Fame ballots of nine different voters in his first year of eligibly for Cooperstown. Still, he received 97.8% of the votes to earn enshrinement. Only Ty Cobb had received a higher percentage of votes with 98.2 percent. "I always felt that if you gave me four chances I could always hit a ball out of the ballpark," said Aaron.

In his later years Hank was asked what memorabilia he kept from his career. "I don't have anything. I've given it all to the Hall of Fame," said Hank. "I don't even have a ring." Henry Aaron appeared on the cover of Time and Newsweek. After his baseball career was over, Henry made amends with the Atlanta Braves and returned as a Vice President and Director of Player Development, an office that he held for 13 years. At that time he was baseball's only black executive. He later became a Senior Vice President in 1989 and worked on behalf of the Hank Aaron Chasing-the-Dream Foundation, a project which helped gifted children develop their talents. Other businesses that Henry invested in included a fast-food chicken restaurant, several doughnut shops and car dealerships. In 1998, Tom Morehead, Ed Fitzpatrick and Henry Aaron joined together to become the only African-Americans in the U.S. to own and operate a car dealership. Hank Aaron autographed a baseball for every customer who purchased a new car.

In 1999, the 25th anniversary of Aaron's breaking Babe Ruth's home run record; the "Hank Aaron Award" was created by Major League baseball to honor the best hitter in each league.

In 2001, President Bill Clinton awarded Henry with the Presidential Citizens' Medal for exemplary service to the nation. Henry Aaron also received the Presidential Medal of freedom from George W. Bush in 2002.

San Francisco Giants' Barry Bonds passed Henry Aaron's home run total in 2007 and ended his career with 762. But because of Bonds' alleged use of steroids, most fans and writers feel the Aaron is still the true home run champion.

Ralph Garr was Henry's teammate from 1968 to 1974. "He didn't make too many mistakes," said Garr. "I never saw him pop up to the catcher." I had the privilege to sit between Phil

Garner's dad and Ralph Garr at an Astros' game in Houston. Garr was a scout at that time and we talked about playing with Henry. "Hank would study the opposing pitchers by taking his cap off in the dugout and looking at the pitcher though the little hole in the top of his cap," said Garr. "That way, he could focus on where the pitcher held his hands, his motion, his stride, and the way he turned his hips. I'd had never seen anyone else do that." I never forgot that story and then Dusty Baker mentioned it the other night when speaking about Henry. Working at a Hungry Bull Steak House located in Augusta, Georgia, in 1974, I traveled to Atlanta see Henry play, after he broke the home run record. I later met Henry at a book-signing event and got him to sign a copy of his book, I Had A Hammer. I felt blessed to be in his company.

During Henry's playing days he suffered from a sciatic nerve problem, but played through the pain. In his later years, Henry Aaron could be seen using a walker after suffering a fall. This fall required him to undergo a partial hip replacement.

Shortly after 6 pm Tuesday night, February 2, 2021, the magnificent Tim Kurkjian joined Dennis & Andy's Q & A Session on SportsradioCC 1230 am and 95.1 fm. Tim can be funny and always a pleasure to speak with. He is so knowledgeable and started off by telling a story of how he was once mistaken as an employee of Applebee's, while he was waiting for his plane at the airport. Laughter would take center stage for the rest of our interview. Dennis started by saluting Tim for his excellent reporting on the passing of the great Henry Aaron. Tim responded. "The highlight of my 41 years of covering baseball came in 2018 when Hank joined Dave Fleming, Eduardo Perez and me in the booth for four innings of a Braves and Cubs game. I sat next to Hank Aaron for an hour and a half," said Tim. "He was so gentle, so kind, and so funny; he had such great stories, and he had total recall of everything. Dennis and Andy, I stopped keeping score of the game," exclaimed Kurkjian. "I no longer cared about the game. All I cared about was listening to Hank Aaron. When the game was over, I checked twitter and some guy actually wrote 'If you ever meet anyone who looks at you like Tim Kurkjian did at Henry Aaron tonight, you should marry that person.' That's how captivated I was with Hank Aaron," said Tim. "Anyone who has ever met him thought the same thing." Tim Kurkjian stayed on with us for 30 minutes. You can hear the rest of the interview on my website www.purvisbooks.com. Just click on Dennis & Andy's podcast on menu page. It may be as close to baseball heaven as I will get. Thanks Dennis and thanks Tim.

Hammerin' Hank Aaron died of natural causes in his sleep on Friday morning, January 22, 2021, at his Atlanta home. He was 86. Henry was one of the last Major League stars to play in the Old Negro Leagues. He had received the Covid-19 vaccine just two ½ weeks earlier, in an effort to insure African-Americans that the shots were safe. Henry is survived by his wife Billye, two sons Lary and Henry, Jr., two daughters Dorinda and Gaile, all of whom he had with his first wife, Barbara; and his step-daughter Ceci from Billye Aaron's first marriage. The Atlanta Braves will wear #44 patches on their sleeves in 2021. The Atlanta Falcons and Atlanta United will retire the #44; and the flags at the Georgia State Capitol building flew at half-staff until Aaron's funeral on Wednesday, January 27, 2021.

I could just never picture Henry Aaron passing away. He was going to live forever. Aaron was a larger-than-life symbol of what we should all be. Henry refused to be defined by fear. He had an extraordinary career. The #715 remains one of the most important numbers in the game. I find it interesting that Aaron is the first name on the list of all Major League players to record a hit in Major League baseball. There was not enough space on the back of his baseball card to tell it all. I wish I could have told him how great a player he was, one more time before he passed away. I think all Henry ever wanted was one more day of summer. The world will go on without Henry Aaron, but I promise it will not be as much fun. Henry Aaron held the record for home runs with 755 for 33 years. You want to know the difference in yesterday's player versus todays? Listen to this. "The most embarrassing thing to me in my 23 years of playing was walking back to the dugout after striking out," said Aaron. Henry once said, "I don't want them to forget Ruth, I just want them to remember me." He got his wish. As Dorothy said in the *Wizard of Oz*, "I will miss you most of all, 'Scarecrow.'"

ANYONE, ANYTIME, ANYWHERE

He reminded me of "The Incredible Hulk," whose most popular catch phrase was, "You wouldn't like me when I'm angry." This basketball coach was more than just a Philly icon. His goal was to make a good life possible for many who came from nothing, and he was brilliant at recruiting kids like himself. Along the way, he rescued a lot of stray boys during his career. This coaching legend created winning teams with underprivileged kids from broken homes, poor kids from drug-infested neighborhoods, kids overlooked by the college games' national powers, and young boys trapped by lack of privilege. More important than molding young basketball players, he molded young men's lives. Heck, even Ray Charles could have seen that. The man was a true believer in second chances. He was a father figure and made it possible for many kids who came from nothing, to attend college and play basketball. This coach had the ability to connect with each and every player regardless of age, race or where they came from. He owned a fiery personality that occasionally got him in trouble, but demanded that his kids show discipline on the court and pursue their studies in the classroom. This guy just had guts, despised turnovers and his teams played such great match-up zone defense, you could hardly get the ball over half court. He believed that love and family had always been stronger than fear.

The most important competition in college basketball is one that most fans never see, recruiting. If your guys are not as good as those other guys, it's going to be hard to win. Sports not only bring excitement, but also tremendous national attention to the school. Along with the attention comes money. To combat cheating in recruiting, scholarships for athletes were created by the NCAA in 1964. Now coaches could say, "Let little Johnny come play basketball for me, and we will give him an education for free."

John Chaney became the guiding light for the basketball program at Temple University. He never loaded his schedule with easy outs and would schedule anybody, never turning down a chance to play against the best teams in the country. His mantra became, "Anyone, Anytime, Anywhere."

John Chaney was born poor on January 21, 1932, in a low-lying section of town known as Black Bottom, located in Jacksonville, Florida. His home often flooded from excessive rainfall. Early on, his father deserted the family. His mother was a housekeeper, and his stepfather worked as a janitor and carpenter. During WWII, his stepfather moved the family to the Philadelphia area when John was in the ninth grade. In 1951, standing 6 foot 4, Chaney became the player of the year in the Philadelphia high school system. Too poor to provide a suit of clothes for John to wear to the awards ceremony, his stepfather let him wear his oversized suit with the sleeves hanging down past his wrists and pants dragging the floor. Chaney wanted to play basketball at Temple, but he received no offer from Temple or any other white colleges. John Chaney became a small-college All-American at Bethune-Cookman College, located in Daytona Beach, Florida. John graduated in 1955. He later played for the Harlem Globetrotters, and for ten years he played and shined in the semipro Eastern League, located in Sunbury and Williamsport, Pennsylvania. Chaney was voted the MVP of the Eastern League.

Chaney's first coaching gig occurred in junior high school and then another later, at Simon Gratz High School in Philadelphia. John Chaney coached from 1972 to 1982 at Cheyney State College (now Cheyney University), and his team won the 1978 Division II National Championship. He was also chosen the Division II Coach of the Year, twice.

In 1982, at the age of 50, John Chaney became the head coach at Temple University. He was the first African-American head coach in Philadelphia's Big Five: Temple, Penn, Villanova, St. Joseph and La Salle. His first team went 14-15. It was to be his only losing season ever. The Temple Owls became a national power as Chaney's teams won often with few if any turnovers, a stifling match-up zone defense, and his fiery personality. John Chaney hated turnovers. He once said, "A team may out rebound us or outshoot us, but when you give that ball away, there is no greater sin."

Despite having only one consensus All-American play at Temple by the name of Mark Macon, this kid helped lead the Owls to a 32-2 record and the #1 ranking in the nation during the 1987-88 season. Chaney was voted the National Coach of the Year in 1987 and 1988, and eventually was elected to the Naismith Basketball Hall of Fame in 2001. Macon not only played in the NBA, but later became an assistant coach for Chaney at Temple.

Chaney could be combative on occasion. He was twice suspended from coaching for bad judgment. The first time was in 1994 against John Calipari's UMass team, where Temple lost by one point. Chaney felt that Calipari had intimidated the officials, and he shouted at Calipari "I'll kill you," during the postgame interview. Chaney was suspended one game. The second time came in 2005 against St. Joseph, when Chaney put a player by the name of Nehemiah Ingram in the game to intentionally bang with St. Joseph player, John Bryant. Bryant eventually ended up with a broken arm. Chaney was suspended for five games. Calipari and Chaney eventually reconciled their differences.

Chaney always seemed combative and cranky, come game time. With his loud, booming, raspy voice and his fiery temper, he could be heard all over the gym. His deep, dark eyes reminded you of the Temple mascot, the Owl. With his game face, he could stare you down to nothing. He called this face his "One-Eyed Jack." Just ask some of the referees. On the more positive side, John also loved telling stories and, at times, he could be extremely funny.

To create team spirit, Chaney did not allow his kids to celebrate play on the court with high-fives and chest bumping. To instill team-first discipline, he held practice every morning at 5:30 a.m. There was method in his madness. This also left the rest of the day for his kids to attend classes. His practices at dawn became legendary.

John Chaney only had one losing season in 34 years. Chaney finished his coaching career with 741 wins, while losing only 312. His record at Cheyney State was 225-59, and his record at Temple was 516-253. Along the way, while spending 24 years at Temple, John's teams played in 17 NCAA tournaments and won six Atlantic 10 Tournament Championships. Temple did make it to the Elite Eight on five different occasions, but never to the Final Four. The outspoken, John Chaney announced his retirement in March of 2006. Up to the end of his career, Chaney still felt that the academic testing requirements of the NCAA for athletic eligibility were culturally biased.

John Chaney died on a Friday, January 29, 2021. He was 89 years old. He is survived by his wife of 67 years, Jeanne Dixon Chaney, three children and several grandchildren.

It's true, John Chaney taught basketball, but more importantly, he also taught life lessons. He would do just about anything to convince a kid he could be a winner, and not just a winner in basketball, but a winner in life. If John Chaney is remembered for only one thing, I think it will be that he helped kids turn their round ball skills into college degrees.

ONCE IN A BLUE MOON

The hardest question in the world of sports is what does it take to become a champion? Being a champion does not come with a manual. There are no recipes or instructions. The one thing for sure that is needed is hard work. The older you get, the more you realize how difficult it is to get to that spot. You have to learn to embrace the heartache. This is your chance to show that you deserve a place at a champions' table. This is why you put up with the pain, the nonsense and heartache. This fellow ate "no" for breakfast. Many athletes find themselves surrounded by others who tell them, they can't do this, they can't do that, it's not your time or it's not your turn. Still, he became a boxer. He took his shirt off more times than Olympic swimmer, Michael Phelps.

Missing several of his front teeth, this fellow spoke like he had four or five pieces of Bazooka Gum in his mouth, and he was so strong he could crush a golf ball in his hand. There are very few sports where you can see your opponent taste his own blood; boxing is one of those sports. The man was a beast. His opponents became walking bruises. With a straight, stiff jab he could light you up like a Christmas tree. This guy rarely gave ground in the ring, while sending his opponents to "never-never land," and he could hit you so hard your dog would be retarded.

What he didn't realize in the beginning was that boxing is not a strength sport, it's a skill sport. You have to be taught how to box. Hand speed and balance are far more important than muscles. But he didn't just learn to box, he stalked his prey. This guy was as serious as a tax audit.

Have you ever felt like you had a monster chasing you? That was Leon Spinks. As an amateur, Spinks' win-loss record stood at 178-7, with 133 of those wins coming by knockout. Professionally, Leon Spinks had his hand raised in victory 26 times, 14 of those by knockout. But there was one win that shocked the boxing world. It was a rags to riches story if there ever was one. For some of us, it's about catching a foul ball, for others it's about winning the lottery. Whether it was a "shot in the dark" or a "month of Sundays," the "long shot" came in for Leon Spinks. "Once in a Blue Moon" occurred in Las Vegas, Nevada, on February 15, 1978. Leon Spinks holds the distinction as the only boxer to take a title from Ali in the ring. It was one of the few times that Ali left the ring with a bruised and puffy face.

Leon Spinks was born on July 11, 1953, In St. Louis, Missouri. Leon was the oldest of eight children raised by their single mother, Kay. As a child he was anemic and was bullied while growing up extremely poor, in the Pruitt-Igoe housing projects of St. Louis. His father would come around once in a while, just to ridicule Leon and the rest of the kids. During an interview some 40 years ago, Leon said, "My dad had gone around and told people I would never be anything. It hurt me. I've never forgotten it. I made up my mind that I was going to be somebody in this world. Whatever price I had to pay, I was going to succeed at something."

So, Leon and his younger brother Michael protected themselves from bullies by learning how to box at a nearby center known as the 12th and Park Recreation Center, owned and operated by Kenny Loehr. In 1955, Loehr, an ex-marine, started training local St. Louis boxers and continued for over 60 years. He passed away on February 5, 2015. Kenny was inducted into the Golden Gloves Hall of Fame in 1988 and the USA Boxing Hall of Fame in 2005.

Leon eventually dropped out of high school in the tenth

grade and became a welder, before joining the Marines. While in the Marines, Spinks began his amateur boxing career by becoming a member of the famed 1976 USA Olympic boxing team. Leon also lost his two front teeth in a boxing match. "I got head butted while sparring in the Marines, and they pulled them out," said Spinks. He later lost two more teeth. Spinks won the bronze medal at the inaugural 1974 World Championships, followed by the silver medal at the 1975 Pan American Games and the gold medal at the 1976 Summer Olympics. Seven members of that 1976 team won medals; one silver, one bronze and five won gold. Three of the gold medal winners included "Sugar Ray" Leonard (light welterweight), Leon Spinks (light heavyweight), and his brother Michael Spinks (middleweight). These three would also go on to win professional titles. Leon became a three-time National AAU Light Heavyweight Champion. Leon Spinks had to face Cuba's Sixto Soria in the Olympic finals. Even though Spinks was small for a heavyweight at 6-foot-1 and 197 pounds, he floored Soria with a big knockdown late in the first round and continued to throw punches in bunches in the second round, until the referee stopped the fight in the third. After the Olympics, Spinks turned professional and, with the help of his trainer, George Benton, won his first professional fight against Bob Smith in Las Vegas, with a fifth round TKO (technical knockout). Leon continued to knock out his next three opponents, all in the first round. It took Leon three rounds to put away Bruce Scott with a knockout. Then the knockout streak ended with a draw, against Scott LeDoux. Spinks won his next fight in a unanimous decision, which improved his record to 6-0-1.

Muhammad Ali had just finished and won a 15-round slugfest with big Ernie Shavers and was looking for a less taxing opponent before having to take on Ken Norton, whom he had already fought on three occasions. Norton was next in line for a title shot. Even though he had only fought seven professional fights, Leon Spinks just happened to be the right man at the right time. Even though Ali was involved, only one network, CBS, bid for the TV rights. Spinks was a 10-1 underdog. Despite Ali's rally in the final round, Spinks, now only 24, defeated the 36-year-old Muhammad Ali by split decision. Leon Spinks was now the undisputed WBC Champion. "I'm not The Greatest," said Spinks afterwards, "Just the latest." "Sugar Ray" Leonard later said, "I cried after that fight for two reasons. Ali was my idol, and I was happy for Leon. I believe there was only one person who believed he'd win and that was Leon." Leon Spinks and his gap-toothed grin appeared on the cover of the February 19, 1978 issue of *Sports Illustrated*.

One month after that fight, Spinks was stripped of his crown for refusing to defend his title against Ken Norton. Spinks wanted to fight Ali again, and Ali wanted the same thing. By September of 1978, Spinks had gone on a spending spree that included buying cars, houses, jewelry and hiring a bodyguard by the name of Laurence Tureaud, otherwise known as "Mr. T." Spinks also got into several scrapes with the law. Their second fight, seven months later, was held on September 15, 1978, at the Superdome in New Orleans, Louisiana, and lasted for 15 rounds. Before a record crowd of 72,000 fans and a television audience estimated at 90 million people, Ali put on a clinic but could not put Spinks away. Ali regained his crown in a unanimous decision. Spinks received 3.75 million for the rematch and managed to win a few more fights before setting up a title shot in 1981 with Larry Holmes. The fight was stopped in the third round and Holmes won by TKO. Later that same year, Spinks was hit over the head and robbed while in Detroit. The robbers took his clothes, jewelry and gold dental plate and left him in his hotel room unconscious. Spinks eventually slimmed down to the cruiserweight division, but failed to win the title by losing a TKO to Dwight Muhammad Qawi. Spinks fought for the last time in 1995 and ended his career with a 26-17-3 record. He was 42.

Spinks moved to Las Vegas and met and married Brenda Glur in 2011. Brenda was his third wife as he had been divorced twice. He also burned through his earnings quickly and made a living by joining the memorabilia circuit and later joined a group of ex-fighters who allowed their brains to be studied by the Cleveland Clinic Lou Ruvo Center for Brain Health. In 2012, it was found that Spinks suffered from brain damage caused by excessive blows to the head, combined with heavy drinking. In the 1990s, Spinks even tried his hand at professional wrestling and won the FMW Brass Knuckles Heavyweight Championship in 1992. He also worked as a custodian at a YMCA located in Nebraska, cleaning out locker rooms.

Ali won a tough hard-fought battle with Ken Norton but lost his October 2, 1980, fight to Larry Holmes. Ring Doctor Ferdie Pacheco begged Ali to retire. Ali finally retired after losing to Trevor Berbick in 1981. Muhammad Ali left us at age 74.

In 2011, Spinks was hospitalized twice for abdominal pains, but recovered both times. He was inducted into the Nevada Boxing Hall of Fame in 2017. Leon Spinks was diagnosed with prostate cancer in 2019. He used a wheelchair and ate through a feeding tube. Cory Spinks, one of Leon Spinks' three sons, spent some time with his dad in the hospital two days before he was removed from life support. Cory was the undisputed welterweight champion from 2003 to 2005 and the IBF middleweight champ twice between 2006 and 2010.

Leon "Neon" Spinks fought his last round in life in a Las Vegas hospital, on February 5, 2021. Spinks was living in Henderson, Nevada, and died from prostate cancer that had spread to his bladder. He was only 67, but seemed much younger. His wife, Brenda Glur Spinks, was at his side when he passed. He is also survived by another son Darrell and grandson Leon, III, who were also boxers. His son Leon Calvin was killed in a shooting in 1990, in East St. Louis, while driving home from his girlfriend's house.

Theodore Roosevelt once said, "Do what you can with what you have, where you are." All he ever wanted to do was to make his father proud.

That was Leon Spinks.

HAUNTED BY JANUARY

Author Mitch Albom once wrote, "No Life is a waste. The only time we waste is the time we spend thinking we are alone." This guy was surrounded by family, friends, coaches and players his entire life. Sports are not something most of us get to play on a professional level, but they are something we need. It makes us feel a part of something bigger and better than ourselves. Sports give us something to look forward to. Sports allow people to escape their personal life for a few hours. For him, football wasn't just a sport, it was his life.

This man was a shining light for the game of football, a preacher with a whistle. He was a guy you had on speed dial. The man walked around like he had a pocketful of sunshine. He could be intense, but not over the top. He could be emotional and cry in front of a room full of athletes. If you were a football player, you expected to win with this coach on your sidelines. This was a guy who lived the ultimate football life. The man was very organized; he didn't tie his shoes without an agenda. You could not outwork him. You couldn't out-prepare him, and you always knew exactly where you stood with him. He remembered everything. Offensively, he was unpredictable. He didn't even know what he was going to do. This man couldn't tell you what he had for breakfast yesterday, but he could tell you the exact sequence of plays his team ran before they scored the go-ahead touchdown in a game played six weeks ago.

There is a difference in being a great coach and being a great head coach. The man was a master at getting his team's attention, and there was no doubt that he cared deeply for all his players and coaches. A good coach understands that his team can never be perfect. Yes, they can do everything right during a game and still wind up on the losing end. So, when that happens, you watch the game tape, check on the health of your players and get back to work.

This fellow was a magna cum laude in coaching old school football. The man believed that when you put the ball in the air, three things could happen and two of them were bad (incomplete pass or an interception). This coach's goal was to play keep-away and run the clock. His opponents called it "Martyball." He was a winner and nobody loved football more than Marty Schottenheimer, but so few people ever get what they really want out of life. Marty wanted to coach a Super Bowl champion. He was haunted by January.

Standing on the sidelines, square-jawed and wearing his gold-rimmed glasses, he looked more comfortable than an old man wearing a baseball cap. You wouldn't recognize him in a coat and tie. He believed that you never fail in sports. If you play the game and win, you win. If you play the game and lose, you learn. Abraham Lincoln once said, "The best way to destroy your enemy is to make him your friend." That was the way Coach Marty Schottenheimer went about things in life.

Martin Edward "Marty" Schottenheimer was born on September 23, 1943, in Canonsburg, Pennsylvania, a town located about 22 miles from Pittsburgh. This part of the country was known for two things, rich minerals and football players. Born into the family of German immigrants, Marty's grandfather, Frank, worked in the local coal mines. His dad, Edward, ran a grocery store while his mom, Catherine, took care of four kids, an aunt and uncle, and two grandparents at their home. Marty went to Fort Cherry High School after moving with his family to McDonald, Pennsylvania, where he excelled in several different sports, including basketball and football. He graduated in 1961. Marty played basketball for Fort Cherry High School's 1961 state championship team. His play at linebacker and offensive center for Coach Jim Garry, earned him a scholarship to play linebacker for the Panthers football team, at the University of Pittsburgh, from 1962 to 1964. He turned down scholarship offers from Virginia, Maryland and Penn State. Marty was big for a linebacker, standing 6 feet 3 inches tall, he weighed 225 pounds. His best season at Pitt occurred in 1963 when they posted a 9-1 record with their only loss coming against the Naval Academy, quarterbacked by none other than Roger Staubach. Marty earned varsity letters in 1962, 1963 and 1964. He played in the North-South Game, the Coaches' All-American and College All-Star Games and the Senior Bowl. Marty graduated from Pitt and majored in English Literature. He also received second team All-American honors as a senior under head coach John Michelson and was drafted with the 56th pick in the seventh round of the 1965 AFL Draft, by the Buffalo Bills. He was also chosen by the Baltimore Colts of the NFL in the fourth round with the 49th pick, that same year. Marty chose the Bills, used his signing bonus to pay for his parents' home and then played four years (1965-1968) with Buffalo and participated on the Bills' 1965 AFL Championship squad. Interestingly, in his first season in the pros, he won a title as a player. Marty played very little at first, as Buffalo had a fine group of linebackers with Harry Jacobs, Mike Stratton and John Tracey. On November 6, 1966, Marty recorded his first NFL interception against Miami and ran it back 20 yards. The Buffalo Bills won the 1966 AFL East title but lost to the Kansas City Chiefs, who went on to lose 35-10 to the Green Bay Packers in the very first Super Bowl. On December 9, 1967, Marty intercepted two passes against the Boston

Patriots and grabbed a third interception on December 24th, against the Oakland Raiders. Marty wore #56 from 1965 to 1967, and then changed to #57 in 1968. He was also selected to the AFL All-Star team that same year.

In the off-season between 1966 and 1967, Marty married the love of his life, and her name was Pat. They would have two children together, a daughter, Kristen and a son, Brian. Brian would also work in the NFL as a coach, like his dad.

In a 1969 preseason game, Marty intercepted two passes in a game against the Houston Oilers. He was later traded to the Boston Patriots, before the 1969 regular season started. Marty wore #54 and stayed with the Pats until July of 1971, when he was traded again to the Pittsburgh Steelers for Mike Haggerty. Before the 1971 regular season began, Schottenheimer was again traded to the Baltimore Colts, for an undisclosed draft pick. He retired from football as a player at the end of the 1971 season and spent the next several years selling real estate. His NFL career lasted 79 games and included six interceptions returned, for a total of 133 yards and one touchdown. His longest interception return occurred in 1967 for 45 yards. Marty also recovered one fumble.

In 1974, Marty came out of retirement and signed a contract to play football with the Portland Storm of the World Football League as a player-coach. An injury in preseason to his shoulder kept him out of the lineup, but he stayed with the team as their new linebacker coach.

In 1975, you could find Marty in New York coaching linebackers for the Giants. In 1977, he became their defensive coordinator. In 1978 and 1979, Marty coached the linebackers for the Detroit Lions. In 1980, Marty moved again, this time to the Cleveland Browns and became their defensive coordinator. On October 22, 1984, in the middle of the season, Marty replaced Sam Rutigliano, as Cleveland's head coach. Cleveland's record at that time was 1-7, when owner Art Modell fired Rutigliano. Marty led the Browns to a 4-4 record, finishing the season with a 5-11 win-loss record. In 1985, Cleveland selected the University of Miami's quarterback Bernie Kosar in the NFL supplemental draft. With Schottenheimer calling the shots, Kosar under center, and a talented defense, the Browns won the 1985 AFC Central Division and became consistent contenders during the late 1980s. A huge comeback by Dan Marino and the Miami Dolphins beat the Browns 24-21, to end Cleveland's 1985 season.

A 12-4 record earned the Browns home-field advantage for the 1986 playoffs. Browns' kicker, Mark Moseley, made a field goal to beat the New York Jets, 23-20. It was Cleveland's first playoff victory in 17 years. The following week, the Denver Broncos were down 20-13 with 5:32 remaining on the clock. John Elway engineered a 98-yard drive for a touchdown and sent the game into sudden-death overtime. This effort became known in NFL lore as "The Drive." A field goal by Broncos' Rich Karlis beat the Browns that day, 23-20. The Browns continued to play well and finished the 1987 season 10-5 and won their third AFC Central title in a row. They beat the Colts 38-21 the following week and then lost again to the Denver Broncos 38-33 the next week. With 1:12 remaining in the game and the Browns with the football at Denver's eight-yard line, Kosar handed off to halfback Earnest Byner. But Byner was stripped of the football by Denver's Jeremiah Castille just before crossing the goal line. The Broncos recovered the football and ran the clock out for the win. This act became known as "The Fumble." The 1988 season was tainted by injuries, yet the Browns still finished their season with a 10-6 record and made the playoffs as a wild-card team. The Browns lost that day, 24-23 to the Houston Oilers. The Cleveland Browns did not reach the Super Bowl, while falling one win short, three different times. Schottenheimer left the Browns after the 1988 season ended. His regular season record was 44-27 and a 2-4 in the playoffs. The Browns had made four playoff appearances, won three AFC Division titles and made two trips to the AFC Championship game, losing twice to the Denver Broncos.

On January 24, 1989, Marty Schottenheimer was hired as the head coach of the Kansas City Chiefs. The 1990 season would be the Chiefs' coming out party. Winning three of their first four games they finished their season with an 11-5 win-loss record, the team's best record since 1969, and they clinched a spot in the playoffs. The Chiefs also made the playoffs in 1991, and hosted the Los Angeles Raiders in the very first post-season game to be played in Arrowhead Stadium history. It was their first home playoff game in 20 years. The Chiefs won that day 10-6, only to lose the next week to the Buffalo Bills. Kansas City finished the 1992 season 10-6, but lost the following week to the San Diego Chargers. On April 20, 1993, The Chiefs traded for Joe Montana and spent the off-season installing offensive coordinator, Paul Hackett, "West Coast Offense." Montana had led the 49ers to four Super Bowls. In June, Kansas City signed running back Marcus Allen. Montana and Allen led the Chiefs to an 11-5 record and clinched their first AFC West title since 1971. The Chiefs and "Montana Magic" proceeded to beat the Pittsburgh Steelers followed by the favored Houston Oilers, but took a loss against the Buffalo Bills in the AFC Championship Game after Montana was knocked out of the game. The Chiefs played well in 1994, but managed a 9-7 record. Miami's Dan Marino bested Montana 27-17 to end the Chiefs' season. It also ended Joe Montana's career, as he announced his retirement on April 18, 1995.

Montana was replaced by Steve Bono, who guided the Chiefs to a league-best 13-3 record and undefeated 8-0 season at home. Kansas City led the NFL in rushing offense (138.9 ypg), scoring defense (15.1 ppg), and turnover ratio (+12). Bono also received a Pro Bowl berth with his performance. But it was not enough as the Chiefs fell to the Colts 10-7 at Arrowhead, during an awfully cold day. In 1996, Kansas City missed the playoffs for the first time since 1989. They retooled their lineup in 1997 and went 13-3, and won their second AFC title in three years. Kansas City lost to the eventual Super Bowl Champion Denver Broncos, 14-10. Marty Schottenheimer resigned at the end of the 1998 season, after the Chiefs fell to a 7-9 record. Marty spent a total of 10 seasons in Kansas City and posted a 101-58-1 regular season record. His teams won three division titles, had seven playoff appearances and one trip to the AFC Championship game in 1993.

From 1999 to 2000, Marty worked as a football analyst for ESPN. In 2001, Marty headed up the Washington Redskins for a season. Washington finished the year 8-8, and Marty was let go. The San Diego Chargers hired Marty in 2002 to replace Mike Riley as head coach. After posting a 12-4 record and winning the AFC West division, he was named NFL Coach of the Year by the Associated Press in 2004. Marty made bad teams good and good teams even better, very quickly. Marty Schottenheimer led the team to two playoff appearances and a 47-33 overall record, while in San Diego. Unfortunately, he lost to the New York Jets in 2005 and the New England Patriots in 2007, bringing his playoff record to 5-13. Rather than return for the final year on his contract, Marty chose to decline a one-year extension. Marty was fired on February 12, 2007. He was replaced by Norv Turner. Marty would spend one more year coaching football with the Virginia Destroyers of the United Football League (UFL), in 2011. On October 21, 2011, the Destroyers beat the two-time defending UFL champion Las Vegas Locomotives 17-

3, earning Schottenheimer his first championship as a head coach. He was also the general manager for the team and won the Leagues' Coach of the Year Award for his efforts.

Marty Schottemheimer spent 30 years in coaching. His last game occurred on January 14, 2007. He is the only NFL coach with 200 or more wins in the regular season, but not elected into the Pro Football Hall of Fame. At the time of his death, he was the seventh winningest coach in NFL history. The other six coaches to win 200 or more games at that time are as follows: Don Shula, George Halas, Bill Belichick, Tom Landry, "Curly" Lambeau, and Andy Reid. Marty's teams won 10 or more games a season 11 times. His NFL regular-season record stands at 200-126-1. In fact, he had a better winning percentage than head coaches Chuck Noll, Tom Landry and Marv Levy, all members of the Pro Football Hall of Fame. His NFL postseason record was a dismal 5-13, leaving him with an overall record of 205-139-1. The only blemish in his coaching career is that he never won the next to the last game, let alone the last game in a season.

The book entitled Martyball was written by Jeff Flanagan, in 2012. Martyball was all about the running game, a passing game that limited turnovers and a strong defense. Some said Schottenheimer played not to lose. During his 21 seasons as a head coach, his teams participated in 13 playoffs, but no Super Bowls.

Marty always joked that he lived in Kansas City, but his real home was Arrowhead Stadium. In 2010, Marty was inducted into the Kansas City Chiefs' Hall of Fame, where he joined former head Coach, Hank Stram. After walking away from the game he loved, Marty moved his family to Lake Norman in North Carolina to spend more time with them and to chase those little white golf balls. Marty Schottenheimer died Monday night, February 8, 2021, in Charlotte, North Carolina. Marty was 77. He had been diagnosed in 2014 with Alzheimer's disease. This disease progressed slowly and Marty underwent treatment to slow the progression. By December of 2018, Marty was still able to travel and did make brief pre-recorded speeches supporting the Kansas City Chiefs' head coach, Andy Reid. Marty was placed in hospice care on January 30, 2021. He is survived by his wife of 53 years, Pat, children Brian and Kristin, four grandchildren, and too many friends to count. Brian, 47, was a backup quarterback for the Florida Gators in the mid 1990s. Brian was fired as the Seattle Seahawks offensive coordinator last month, but then hired by the new Jacksonville Jaguars' head coach Urban Meyer as their passing game coordinator and quarterback coach for 2021.

When asked why he was such a successful coach, it was said by his players that Marty Schottemheimer cared more about the men who played for him than the athlete.

PAPER HEAD

He was an extraordinary player and his talent was undeniable. When you watched him play you never noticed pressure, just pure joy. This man never backed away from trouble. When he came face to face with fear and confrontation, he'd take a step forward. Drafting this guy was like finding a lottery ticket on the ground. He had a way of empowering people around him with his play. This guy walked with long deliberate steps that told you that he knew where he was headed. The man was a game changer. He just seemed ten feet taller than everyone else. You couldn't tell if he was grieving or gloating. He was not scared of anyone at all. On the field, the man was like a shark, same dead eyes.

It was a joy to play football on the defensive side of the football in the 1960s. When you compete, when you battle, and push yourself against the greatest athletes in the world the way he did, that doesn't just inspire other football players to raise the bar, it inspires everyone from every walk of life. It's the journey that inspires everyone, not just the destination. Besides, the defensive rules were different then. Ray Nitschke once said, "If you are not willing to hit people, you don't belong on the field." This guy could snap a ball carrier in half like a bag for dry pasta. In the beginning, Irv Cross sustained several concussions during his first year in the NFL. One of the concussions he received in Pittsburgh sent him to the hospital. As a result, his teammates nicknamed him "Paper Head." Cross would fly into a tackle. Hall-of-Fame running back Jim Brown once said, "No one in the league tackles harder than Irv Cross." Maybe they should have nicknamed him "Code Red." Irv Cross played with so much passion and emotion, because others made fun of him when he was younger.

Irvin Acie Cross was born July 27, 1939, in Hammond, Indiana, to Acie and Ellee Cross. His dad was a steelworker and his mom was a homemaker while having and raising 15 children. Born into a struggling family, one of those kids was Irv Cross. Irv was number eight. His childhood was full of ups and downs, and some left lasting marks. "I'm going to be a football player when I grow up," said Irv.

In 2018, Irv told The *Chicago Tribune* that his father was a heavy drinker and often beat his mother. "It tears me up. It was frightening," said Irv. "You could tell it was coming. We tried stopping him a few times. We'd jump on his back. It's absolutely raw for me." Unfortunately, Ellee Cross died during childbirth when Irv was 10 years old. He always wondered whether the beatings by his father had caused his mother's health problems.

Irv attended, played football, basketball, ran track, and graduated from Hammond High School in 1957. As a senior, Irv was named The Times Male Athlete of the Year. He was later inducted into the Hammond Sports Hall of Fame. Irv received a scholarship to play football during Ara Parseghian's first recruiting class at Northwestern University. Irv became a big hitter, who became a big star, in the Big 10. He lettered all three years from 1958-1960 and was selected team captain for the Wildcats. Irv played wide receiver, defensive back and defensive end and was chosen Honorable Mention All-Big Ten Conference, in 1960. As a junior, Cross caught a 78-yard touchdown pass as the Wildcats beat Notre Dame 30-24. In fact, Northwestern beat Notre Dame under Parseghian's guidance, three times between 1958 and 1961. As a result, Parseghian left Northwestern to become the head coach at Notre Dame in 1963. The old saying goes "If you can't beat 'em, join 'em." Cross was also named Northwestern University's Male Athlete of the Year in track and field, in 1960. In 1961, Irv Cross received a Bachelor of Science degree from Northwestern University School of Education and Social Policy. Also in his graduating class was a future broadcasting fellow by the name of Brent Musburger.

Irv Cross was the 98th pick by the Philadelphia Eagles in the seventh round of the 1961 NFL Draft. He was one of the first African-American starters for the Eagles' franchise. Eight games into his rookie year (1961), Cross went from a third string player to the starting right cornerback position. Tom Brookshier, the former starting right cornerback, suffered a broken leg that ended his career. As mentioned above, Cross endured several concussions his rookie year. The worst concussion occurred, while blocking on a punt return for fellow teammate Timmy Brown, against the Pittsburgh Steelers. Irv spent three nights in the hospital and the doctor warned that if he were to return to action too soon, the next concussion could be life threatening. To protect himself, Irv Cross had a helmet made with extra cushion. "I just tried to keep my head out of the way while making tackles," he told *The Philadelphia Inquirer*. "But that's just the way it was. Most of the time, they gave you some smelling salts and you went back in. We didn't know."

Cross intercepted a career-high five passes during his second season. Irv was selected to the NFL Pro-Bowl in 1964 and 1965. Cross was later traded at the end of the 1965 season to the Los Angeles Rams for Aaron Martin and Willie Brown. In 1969, Cross returned to the Eagles as a player/coach. While playing football, Irv also became the first black man to report the sports on KYW-TV in Philadelphia. He also did drive-time sports for WNTP. Irv Cross wore the #27 during his entire NFL career. Cross retired as a player before the 1970 season began, to become a coach for Philadelphia.

His career stats will read: played nine years in the league with the Philadelphia Eagles and Los Angeles Rams; played in 125 games, had 22 interceptions, 14 fumble recoveries, eight forced fumbles and two defensive touchdowns. Cross also averaged 27.9 yards on kickoff returns and punt returns. Cross would later be inducted into the Indiana Football Hall of Fame.

There were a lot of firsts in Irv Cross's life. In 1971, Irv Cross was offered a front office job by the Dallas Cowboys, but instead chose to become the first African-American man to work on a national television sports show. Cross was hired as an analyst and commentator for CBS Sports. In 1975, Cross joined another club with only one member. He joined Brent Musburger and Phyllis George as the co-host on *The NFL Today*. (Phyllis George died in May of last year at the age of 70). He remained a part of this ground breaking show until 1989. In 1990, Musburger was fired over a contract dispute and Cross was also let go. Greg Gumbel replaced Cross, along with Terry Bradshaw. Cross returned to CBS and worked NFL games, NBA basketball, track and field, and gymnastic events. He spent a total of 23 years at CBS and stayed with them until 1994.

From 1996 until 1998, Cross served as the Athletic Director at Idaho State University. He also served as the Athletic Director at Macalester College in Saint Paul, Minnesota, from 1999 to 2005.

There is no doubt that Irv Cross was a pioneer. I would bet that most of you reading this story never knew Irv Cross, the two-time Pro Bowl cornerback for the Philadelphia Eagles and Los Angeles Rams. You knew him as the 15-year co-host of *The NFL Today*. As an analyst, the impact he had on people who never really knew him was immediate and breathtaking. He didn't just capture you with his broadcast of what was going on during the game; he made you feel it. Cross earned the Pete Rozelle Radio-Television Award in 2009, an award given out by the Pro Football Hall of Fame for recognition of contributions to radio and television coverage. Guess what? Irv was the first black man to also receive this award.

In December of 1992, Monday Night Football came to the Astrodome, as the Houston Oilers took on the New Orleans Saints. Irv Cross was on the field that night, and I had a sideline pass. It was there that I got to meet the man I enjoyed watching play football for the Philadelphia Eagles. Growing up in North Carolina during the 1960s, we always had the Giants, Redskins or Eagles on TV on Sundays. He was kind and quiet, a perfect gentleman.

Irv Cross left us on a Sunday, February 28, 2021. He was 81 and resting in a hospice located in North Oaks, Minnesota, near his home in Roseville. Cross was diagnosed with dementia in 2018, brought on by CTE. Cross had arranged to have his brain donated to the Boston University CTE Center after his death. Irv also suffered and died from heart disease known as (ischemic cardiomyopathy). He is survived by two daughters: Susan and Lisa from his first marriage, and two other children: Sandra and Matthew with his second wife Elizabeth. He also had one grandson named Aiden. His first marriage ended in divorce.

On the day we meet our maker, he will not ask you what your win-loss record was, but he will know what kind of person you were. Irv Cross may have died in 2021, but I'm sure his spirit will endure.

MARVELOUS

He fulfilled a promise to his mother to be the best. The oldest of six, he was a loner with no father. There is no doubt that he became one of the greatest middleweight champions of all time. When you stepped into the ring with this man, it could go one of two ways, bad or really bad. This guy rarely had a bad day and he always reminded himself that lions are not supposed to be tamed. The man was relentless, vicious and determined to remain standing as the victor at the end of the fight. This guy reminded me of a truck going down hill, gathering speed and then running over you. The man was a master at mixing up his punches. He could be extremely intimidating, had a chin made of concrete, and he was as healthy as a horseshoe. He was very athletic and could make you miss. This fellow was quiet and different; the kind of guy you could know for ten years and still be pretty sure you had never really met him before. In all his fights, no one ever saw him buckle from a hit. He may have gotten cut, but he never buckled.

In the beginning, his future was so bright the man had to wear shades. This guy could draw a crowd in an empty lot. Interestingly, he signed all his amateur photos Marvin Hagler "Future middleweight champion of the world." Fighting out of a southpaw stance, with a mustache, while his bald head glistened in the light, nobody was more ferocious during the 1980s than "Marvelous" Marvin Hagler. You see, left-handers grow up in a world not designed for them. If you sit next to one while eating you will more than likely bump elbows. Yet, lefties are always in demand in the boxing ring or on a pitcher's mound. The only test for a southpaw: is he breathing? If he is, management will give him a shot to be successful.

When writing about boxing during the 1970s and 1980s, fight experts cite Thomas "Hit Man" Hearns, "Sugar Ray" Leonard, "Hands of Stone" Roberto Duran and "Marvelous" Marvin Hagler among the era's best fighters.

Marvin Nathaniel Hagler was born on May 23, 1954, in Newark, New Jersey, to Robert Sims and Ida Mae Hagler. Marvin grew up in tenement housing located in the Central Ward of Newark. His mom and dad were never married, so Marvin took his mother's surname. His dad, Robert, left the family when Marvin was young. At the age of ten, Hagler was introduced to the sport of boxing by a social worker in Newark. He got interested in learning how to box. Marvin dropped out of school at the age of 15 and dug ditches to help support his mother financially.

In 1969, Hagler's family moved to Brockton, Massachusetts, to live with relatives, two years after the Newark riots occurred in 1967, from July 12 -17. During those riots, 26 people were killed and there was extensive property damage, including the tenement house where Hagler's family lived.

He was tired of being bullied and roughed up on the streets. He walked into a gym in Brockton owned by two brothers, Pat and "Goody" Petronelli. They became his trainers and managers for the rest of his career. At that time, you needed to be 16 to enter into an amateur boxing tournament, so Hagler lied about his age when he told the brothers he had been born in 1952, and not 1954. Marvin Hagler lost by decision the National Golden Gloves title in the Light Middleweight Division in March of 1973, to Dale Grant. Later that year, Hagler won the National Amateur Middleweight (165-pound) title in May of 1973, when he defeated a U.S. Marine known as Terry Dobbs. Hagler would finish his amateur career with a 55-1 win-lose record.

By 1973, Hagler was 19, and had filled out to 5 feet 9 inches tall and weighed 159 pounds. He also sported a reach of 75 inches. Early in his career, Hagler struggled to find quality middleweights to fight. On May 18, 1973, he knocked out Terry Ryan in his first professional fight. Hagler won his first 17 fights before suffering a draw at the hands of "Sugar Ray" Seales, on November 26, 1974. Hagler remained unbeaten in his first 26 professional fights until he met and lost to Bobby "Boogaloo" Watts on January 13, 1976. His record now stood at 25-1-1.

On March 9, 1976, Hagler lost his second fight two months later to Willie "The Worm" Monroe, who was trained by none other than Joe Frazier. Hagler received a rematch on February 15, 1977, where he knocked out Monroe in the 12th round and later beat Monroe a second time on August 23, 1979, in two rounds. In 1979, Hagler was robbed at Caesar's Palace when he received his first draw in a title fight with Vito Antuofermo. After fifteen rounds most everyone at ringside felt Hagler had won. In fact, Marvin claims that referee Mills Lane had told him after the fight, that he had won. Of course Lane denied making that comment. Antuofermo retained his title. After that fight, Hagler never trusted the judges who worked in Las Vegas. He won the next 16 fights in a row. Marvin even met Watts again for a rematch on April 19, 1980, and won by TKO.

Antuofermo eventually lost his title to Alan Minter, a British boxer, so Hagler received a second shot at the title. These two met on September 27, 1980, in London, England. Hagler destroyed Minter as the referee stopped the fight in the third round as Marvin had opened four cuts in Minter's face. The local fans retaliated as bottles and cans were thrown into the ring. Hagler was escorted to his locker-room by the police and, after 50 professional fights, Marvelous Marvin Hagler was the new World Middleweight Champion.

Hagler never thought the boxing world gave him his proper due. Unlike "Sugar Ray" Leonard, Hagler did not fight in the Olympics and he always made less money than Ray for a fight. Marvin claims he received his nickname from a journalist from Lowell, Massachusetts, who saw him fight as an amateur. In 1982, he was so upset that the ring announcer refused to introduce him before a fight by his nickname as "Marvelous" Marvin Hagler, he went to court and had his name legally changed. It was here that his real birth date became known publicly, as he had to state his date of birth in order to make the change legal.

On November 10, 1983, Hagler would test his skills against Roberto Duran. The Hands of Stone (Duran) became the first challenger to last the distance with Hagler in a world-championship bout. Hagler won a unanimous 15-round decision.

April 15, 1985, a date that lives in boxing lore, Hagler and Tommy "Hit Man" Hearns got it on. This event that was first billed as "The Fight" was soon changed to "The War." Three rounds of violence would describe the fight. Hagler was cut with either an elbow or head butt in the second round, which required the fight doctor to examine in the third round, when the cut would not stop bleeding. The doctor allowed the fight to continue. Hagler did cut easily when he received a blow to old scar tissue. At this point, Hagler weighed in with everything he had, drilling Hearns with an overhand right behind his ear. Hearns fell and then got up at the count of eight, but then collapsed into referee Richard Steele's arms. The fight was then stopped. It had lasted only eight minutes and one second. This fight was named "Fight of the Year" by *The Ring*.

Camp spies have been a part of the past in the world of boxing, forever. Newspaper man J. D. Long was hired and spied for Sugar Ray Leonard in Hagler's camp, located in

Palm Springs, California. During the pre-fight negotiations, Sugar Ray's camp wanted a larger ring of 22 feet; fighters would wear ten-ounce gloves instead of eight-ounce and a 12-round fight instead of 15. Hagler's camp approved the changes.

At the championship level, there is very little difference in who the faster fighter is or who hits the hardest. It sometimes comes down to the smallest difference that separates the winners from the losers. That was the case in this fight. Ray was made aware of two other things. First, J. D. Long wrote in his notes that he noticed that Hagler started each round of a fight by getting to the center of the ring first and waiting there, as if he were daring his opponent to tread in his territory. Sugar Ray decided to make it a point to beat Hagler to that spot before each round started. Sugar Ray was successful and beat Hagler to the center of the 22-foot squared ring before every round started. Sugar Ray was therefore effective in getting inside of Marvin's head.

The second thing Ray was made aware of was that another of Hagler's tricks was to switch from southpaw to the orthodox style of fighting between rounds. He even made the change a few times during a round. Sugar Ray's trainer, Angelo Dundee, was convinced that Marvin was not a natural southpaw and had Ray prepare for the change. As predicted, Hagler opened fight in orthodox stance, but changed to the southpaw stance to begin the third round.

On April 6, 1987, It was billed the "Superfight." This fight was being held in Las Vegas, Nevada, at Caesar's Palace, a site where Hagler had been robbed of winning before. A total of 67 sportswriters were polled before the fight, and 60 chose Hagler as the winner, 52 by knockout. The public agreed, as Ray was 4-1 underdog at the betting window. Marvin was 29 and Ray was 27 when they met. The referee was Richard Steele, a well-known personality. Steele warned

Leonard almost every round for holding, yet Ray continued. The ninth round was the most exciting, as Hagler hurt Ray with a left cross. Leonard managed to escape the corner, and ran the last couple of rounds. Leonard threw 629 punches and landed 306, while Hagler threw 792 punches and landed 291. The three judges ringside were Lou Filippo, who scored the fight 115-113 for Hagler, Jo Jo Guerra who scored the fight 118-110 for Sugar Ray, and Dave Moretti who scored the fight 115-113 for Sugar Ray. Leonard was crowned the winner by split decision.

Even though he had received $19m for his part in the fight, Hagler was outraged and felt cheated. Marvin first requested a rematch, but Leonard said he was going to retire. By 1987, Marvelous Marvin Hagler was rich and famous and set for life. He had earned nearly $40m in purses during his career. Hagler officially retired in June of 1988, claiming he was tired of waiting for Leonard to change his mind. After retirement, Hagler moved to Milan, Italy, to make spaghetti westerns. He appeared in action films entitled "Indio" and "Indio 2." In 1990, Ray finally offered a rematch to Hagler for a $15m payout, but Marvin declined.

From 1973 to 1987, Marvelous Marvin Hagler fought professionally 67 times during those 15 years, out of Brockton, Massachusetts. His career win-loss record stands at 62-3-2, with 52 of his wins coming by knockout. Hagler still holds the record for the highest knockout percentage of all middleweight champions, at 78 percent. He won 15 middleweight title fights and was the undisputed middleweight champion from 1980 until 1987, with 12 title defenses. Marvin was named Fighter of the Decade (1980s) by *Boxing Illustrated*. In 1983 and 1985, he was twice named Fighter of the Year by *The Ring magazine*. In 1993, Hagler joined the International Boxing Hall of Fame and the World Boxing Hall of Fame.

Marvin Hagler, one of the greatest middleweight boxers in history, retreated to his corner for the last time on March 13, 2021. Marvin had four children with his first wife, Bertha, which ended in divorce. His wife Kay announced his death on Facebook. He was but 66 and living in Bartlett, New Hampshire. Interestingly, after researching both Hagler and Leonard for this story, I feel that Sugar Ray and Marvelous Marvin had a lot in common. Without boxing, they could have been great friends.

Hagler had a funny side that very few got to see. He once said in an interview, "If they cut my bald head open, they will find one big boxing glove. That's all I am. I live it." There was never any doubt, that as a boxer, the man was simply Marvelous.

ALLERGIC TO GRAVITY

Bill Walton once said, "It's not how high you jump, but rather where and when." He was a complete player. The man was a roll-out-of-bed, give-you-thirty-points-a-game kind of guy. Known as a high-flying machine, he never seemed off balance and flew through the air with the greatest of ease. When this guy took off, it was like he was never coming down. He created his game while soaring through the air. A creator of shots, this fellow was one of the most spectacular shooters the game has ever known. He was hang-time before there was hang-time. He helped turn the horizontal game of basketball into a vertical one. Instant success, good as gold, the man was one of the first players I had ever seen who used "the glass." He helped change the basketball jargon used by courtside announcers. This man inspired phrases like, playing above the rim, triple double, spin-move, double-pumping, hesitation dribbling, hanging jump-shot, and the no-look pass, to describe his moves. He became known for his running one-handed bank shots over players much taller than he was. Some say he made the game look so easy. You'd rather watch him play than most others even if he never scored a basket. Everyone knew that when he had the ball in his hands, something good was about to happen. He was the godfather of "Wow." He was the player who you would put a photo of his bank-shot on your "screensaver."

While growing up on the playgrounds of Washington D. C., he played during a time when the objective was to never leave the court. Who's got next, was a question he asked often. He was the first player to really play the game of basketball, while in the air. In the 1950s, one-handed set-shots, layups and hook-shots were the norm. It was a time when the basketball nets were short and their uniform pants even shorter. Jaw-dropping, highlight basketball all started with this guy. Elgin Baylor was the smoothest basketball player of them all. He floated with the grace of a ballet dancer down-court, with the least amount of effort. Elgin may have been allergic to gravity. Baylor's only tick came from an occasional jerk of his head to the side, caused by a neck twitch which occurred only when he played basketball.

Regardless of what you thought about Oscar Robertson, "Dr. J," Julius Erving, Michael Jordan, Ervin "Magic" Johnson or Kobe Bryant; they were all mere shadows of Elgin Baylor. The line started with Baylor. "When I first got to the L.A. Lakers in 1960, I studied everything Elgin did," said Jerry West. "I was in awe of him and he was one of the most dignified people I had ever met." In fact, it was Elgin Baylor who came up with the name "Zeke from Cabin Creek" for Jerry West.

So, Elgin Baylor has left us, but for now, let's look at the bright side. When we get close to anybody or anything we will eventually lose it, in one way or another. But it's the getting close that provides the joy that is worth it all in the end. I hope you are old enough to remember Elgin Baylor. He now has a locker in that big clubhouse in Heaven.

Elgin Gay Baylor was born in Washington D.C. on September 16, 1934, to John Wesley and Uzziel Baylor. He was named Elgin after the brand of watch his father wore. His friends later nicknamed him "Rabbit." Elgin had two older brothers who also played basketball, named Sal and Kermit.

In the early 1900s, the game of basketball was off-limits to African-Americans at most of the white-dominated universities and local city basketball courts. African-

American colleges and universities began playing basketball around 1909 or 1910. Hampton Institute was the first Negro college with its own basketball gymnasium large enough to hold a basketball game with fans. Lincoln University and Union University were two others.

It all began for the Harlem Globetrotters in 1927. Professional basketball became unique in American sports because, first it was a home-grown sport, and second, it became America's leading export in the world of sports. Owner-coach Abe Saperstein had dreamed that eventually the Globetrotters would travel around the world playing basketball in places where the game had never been played before. By 1953, the world-famous Globetrotters had played the game of basketball in 60 or more countries.

The table had now been set for kids like Elgin Baylor. Integration was one of the most significant aspects of the growth of professional basketball. Outstanding individuals like Wilt Chamberlain, Oscar Robertson and Bill Russell helped pave the way for other young people of African-American heritage to become involved in the game of basketball. So, Elgin Baylor and his brothers found a way to play at night, by tunneling under the fences of the local courts in Washington D.C.   Elgin won his first trophy in 1948, at the age of 14, when he was voted the MVP of the Capitol Hill summer league. Elgin played some ball at Southwest Boys' Club and Brown Junior High, before attending high school. Baylor initially attended Phelps Vocational High School in 1951 and 1952, but dropped out due to poor grades. He had a job working at a furniture store, but realized that his life was basketball. Baylor did set the D. C. area scoring record, by dropping 44 points against Cardoza High School. In 1954, at his mother's request, he quit his job and entered the newly-opened all-black school known as Spingarm High School. By that time, Elgin had grown to six feet five inches tall and weighed 225 pounds. He also developed a nervous head-twitch that sometimes fooled his opponent, on his direction. While at Spingarm, he set the Washington D.C. high school record by scoring 63 points in one game and was selected a three-time All-City player. Future Hall-of-Fame basketball player, Dave Bing, also played baseball and basketball at Spingarm High School.

In 1958-59, Wilt Chamberlain joined the Globetrotters. Their team record that year was 179-0. It was one of the most financially successful seasons up to that point, with box-office records broken consistently.

Because of poor grades, no one offered Elgin Baylor a scholarship to play basketball in college. With the help of a friend, he was able to attend the College of Idaho. While there, he earned a scholarship playing basketball and football, and later transferred to Seattle University. In 1956, the Minneapolis Lakers drafted Elgin Baylor in the 14th round of the NBA Draft, but Baylor chose to stay at Seattle University. While with the Seattle Chieftains (now known as the Redhawks), coached by John Castellani, Baylor led his team to the 1958 NCAA Finals, against the University of Kentucky. Seattle had to beat the University of San Francisco Dons to get to the finals. Elgin, wearing #22, scored 35 points to end the Dons' 20-game win streak. Baylor led Seattle in five single-elimination games during the tournament and scored a total of 135 points, averaging 27 points per game. Seattle led the Wildcats 39-36 at halftime, but Baylor picked up his fourth foul with 16 minutes left in the game. Kentucky came roaring back. Seattle was beaten by Adolph Rupp and his Kentucky Wildcats, 84-72. Elgin Baylor received the Most Outstanding Player Award. The name Elgin Baylor was now on the radar for professional basketball teams.

Baylor was the biggest six-foot-five-inch player I've ever seen," said my friend and former referee, Dotson Lewis. Dotson had worked several of Elgin's games while he played in Seattle. In 1958, as a junior, Elgin Baylor was drafted this time with the #1 pick by the Minneapolis Lakers. Bob Short, the Lakers' owner, was desperately trying to keep his club in Minneapolis. Baylor also got married that summer, with Wilt as his best man. It was Baylor's bride Ruby, who got Elgin to accept Shorts' offer. She did not want him to become a Harlem Globetrotter. Baylor left Seattle and joined the Lakers. He signed a $20,000 contract, which seemed like all the money in the world for a young kid from D.C. Two years later, the Minneapolis Lakers became the first NBA team to move to the West Coast, and they were renamed the Los Angeles Lakers. Baylor played at a time when there was very limited TV coverage of professional basketball, and it's true that Baylor had never seen an NBA game before he actually played in one. In his first season with the Lakers, Baylor was chosen the 1958 NBA Rookie of The Year. Elgin finished second in league scoring (24.9), third in rebounding (15.0) and eighth in assists (4.3). He also scored 55 points in a single game, the third-highest for the franchise at that time. Baylor led the team from last place to the finals in his first year, but lost to the Boston Celtics in the first-ever four-game sweep. The rival between the Lakers and Celtics had begun.

Even as an NBA player, Baylor faced blatant racism. In 1959, Baylor refused to play in a game in Charleston, West Virginia, because black players were told that they could not stay at the hotel where the team was staying. When begged by his teammate "Hot Rod" Hundley to play, Baylor responded, "I'm a human being. I'm not an animal put in a cage and let out for the show. They won't treat me like an animal." The game was played while Baylor sat on the bench in his street clothes.

Known as a right-handed player, Baylor excelled at the left-handed hook shot. Baylor set a league record by scoring 64 points against the Boston Celtics, in November of 1959. The

Lakers moved to Los Angeles in 1960, the same year Jerry West joined the team. On November 15, 1960, Baylor became the first NBA player to eclipse the 70-point barrier by scoring 71 points against the New York Knicks. His record stood for two years before Wilt Chamberlain scored 100 points in a single game. Elgin's 71-point game remains tied for the league's eighth-highest total. During the 1961-62 season, Baylor missed 34 games while serving active military duty at Fort Lewis in Washington state. Remarkably, without any practice, he played only on weekends and still managed to score over 1,800 points in only 48 games. During the NBA Finals, Baylor set a scoring record that still stands today. Elgin scored 61 points in Game Six against the Boston Celtics.

"Magic" Johnson once explained. "Baylor did some things that Dr. J, Michael Jordan, Kobe and I couldn't do, and I tried to do it. I just couldn't hang that long in the air."

Elgin suffered lingering knee problems his entire career. The first two African-Americans elected to the All-NBA First-Team were Elgin Baylor and Bill Russell, in 1958-59. Baylor spent a total of 14 seasons in the NBA, and he did his part in leading the Minneapolis and Los Angeles Lakers to eight NBA Finals. He played in 846 games. Elgin was an 11-time All-Star with 10 First-Team All-NBA appearances. Baylor's career totals are as follows: he scored 23,149 points, pulled down 11,463 rebounds and dished out 3,650 assists. Baylor averaged 27.4 points, 13.5 rebounds and 4.3 assists per game, as a professional. Elgin is still the All-time leader in rebounds for the Lakers, and also is fourth in points scored and minutes played.

Jerry West once said, "Baylor never got his just due. He cared for me like a father would a son." Baylor was often called out for being one of the greatest players in the game to have never won an NBA Championship. He retired from knee and tendon injuries in 1971, nine games into the season. After his retirement, the Lakers went on to win an NBA Championship over the New York Knicks. The Lakers bestowed a championship ring to Elgin Baylor for his contributions to the team.

Baylor became an assistant coach in 1974 and a head coach in 1976, for the New Orleans Jazz. His win-loss record stands at 86-135, and he was fired in 1979. Elgin later worked as Vice President of Basketball Operations for the Los Angeles Clippers, in 1986, and won Executive of the Year honors in 2006. Baylor stayed on for 22 years with the Clippers. He resigned in October of 2008, at the age of 74.

Elgin Baylor was enshrined into the Naismith Memorial Basketball Hall of Fame, in 1977. He was joined by Charles Cooper, Lauren Gale, William Johnson and Coach Frank McGuire. Baylor's #22 was retired for all-time by the Los Angeles Lakers, on November 3, 1983, and a statue was placed outside of the STAPLES Center in his honor, on April 6, 2018. Baylor's likeness in bronze stood 16 feet 9 inches high and weighed nearly 2,300 pounds. His statue joined other Lakers' icons, Jerry West, "Magic" Johnson, Kareem Abdul-Jabbar, Shaq O'Neal and announcer "Chick" Hearn. "I didn't want anyone to see me crying," said Baylor. "But it was a big emotional moment. You can't do anything without your teammates, no one in basketball can, and I've always appreciated the guys I played with. There are just so many people you want to thank, so many people you need to thank. It was great." Baylor was named to NBA's 35th Anniversary All-Time Team in 1981, and was also named to NBA's 50th Anniversary All-Time Team, in 1996.

I arrived in Orlando, Florida, on Friday, February 7, 1992, as a guest of Miller Brewing Company for the NBA All-Star Game Weekend. Not only did we have tickets for the game on Sunday, we were invited to the pregame party for players and coaches held in the courtyard of the hotel on Saturday afternoon. It was there that I ran into Elgin Baylor. When I first spotted him in the crowd, I took his picture and then made my way over to him. After shaking his hand and saying hello, I also met NBA Commissioner David Stern, who was standing close by and talking to sportswriter Bob Ryan, of the Boston Globe. It was quite an event and I was privileged to be a part of it all.

On November 19, 2009, Seattle University renamed their basketball court in honor of Elgin. The Elgin Baylor Court can be found inside of Seattle's Key Arena. In June of 2017, The College of Idaho inducted Baylor into their Sports Hall of Fame.

Elgin Baylor's legendary life came to an end on March 22, 2021. He was 86 years old and living in Los Angeles, California, when he passed away reportedly from natural causes. His marriage to his first wife, Ruby Saunders, ended in divorce. Elgin is survived by his current wife Elaine, a daughter Krystal and two children from his first marriage, Alan and Alison.

Baylor never allowed the defense to dictate what he could or could not do with the basketball. He was always able to get his own shot. Elgin Baylor was referred to as the "Sugar Ray" Robinson of his sport. He was regarded by fellow players and fans alike as being pound-for-pound, the greatest living basketball player. Athletes like Baylor, Wilt Chamberlain and Oscar Robertson helped today's NBA superstars now to play for eight-figure salaries. There is no doubt that Baylor was the most beloved by his teammates. Elgin was team captain, a box office attraction, and the fans' favorite. He was in every way "Mr. Basketball."

Uphill Climb to Greatness

Winston Churchill once said, "The farther backward you can look, the farther foreword you can see." For this fellow, football wasn't a sport, it was his life. It turns out that the best coaches are the ones who listen and care about their players. He could read people quickly, a human lie detector. But the job of being a coach can eat you alive. He could remake a team in his image and transform them into a formidable group. When you're winning each and every week, time cannot go fast enough to get you to the next game. This guy wasn't just a coach; he was the Wizard of Oz. He owned a restless soul and never really liked the attention. I guess you could say it was stage fright. But, there is no doubt that he used the game of football to better people's lives. He wanted his kids to love the game like he did. He was like a father, the kind of guy you always told the truth to, so he could lie for you later if needed. There's no telling how far behind the game of football would be without this man. As a coach, he always felt that good players and good teams taught him more than he would ever have the opportunity to teach them. That was the case here. Sometimes our lives are defined by the losses and not the wins. Vince Lombardi once said about the game of football, "Has this become a game of madmen and I'm I one of them?" He thought like Lombardi that you needed to create turmoil to gain the players' attention. As a coach he began to realize that the clock was ticking and it would expire at some point. You must win to survive.

Some people who need help would call up and ask their coach, can you help me? With Coach Howard

Schnellenberger, he would call you with that deep baritone voice and ask you if you needed help. Coach would do anything for his players. He was family. In life, like football, there are usually two halves and, for some of us, overtime. He always made you feel like you were his best friend. Let me tell you about Howard Schnellenberger's uphill climb to greatness.

Howard Leslie Schnellenberger was born in Saint Meinrad, Indiana, on March 16, 1934. His German-American parents, Leslie and Rosena were hard working folks who gave him all they could provide. Howard walked onto his first football field when he was seven years old, and he never left. Nothing in his life came easy. Howard learned at an early age that adversity is an opportunity for heroism. Everyone has an obstacle in front of them. It may be race, being poor, overweight or just not very smart. This guy didn't have two quarters to rub together. He was from a town so small they only had three cops. You can't even surround a house with just three cops. He graduated from Flaget High School, located in Louisville, Kentucky. While there, Howard played football, basketball and baseball, before earning a scholarship to the University of Kentucky. He would start at tight end for the Wildcats and was named a 1955 All-American by the Associated Press. He graduated from Kentucky in 1956 and joined the Toronto Argonauts of the Canadian Football League in 1957. By the end of 1958, he was out of the professional ranks, smoking a pipe, and worked as an assistant coach at Kentucky under head coach Blanton Collier, in 1959 and 1960.

In May of 1959, Howard married Beverlee Donnelly of St. Johns, Quebec. Together they had three sons. Their oldest son, Stephen, suffered as an infant with endocrine cancer, but survived to live a normal childhood. He eventually became an insurance broker until he had surgery in 2003. His heart stopped and brain damage left him semi-comatose.

He was cared for at home until his death on March 9, 2008.

In January of 1961, Howard joined the coaching ranks at the University of Alabama, under the great Paul "Bear" Bryant. He made a difference quickly by recruiting both quarterbacks, Joe Namath and Kenny Stabler, for the Crimson Tide. Under Bryant, Howard helped guide the Crimson Tide to three national championships (1961, 1964 and 1965) in five seasons. Howard left Alabama in 1966 to join George Allen's staff with the Los Angeles Rams, as the tight end coach. After four seasons with the Rams, Howard was hired away by Don Shula of the Miami Dolphins, in 1970. He took over as the Dolphins' offensive coordinator that year and helped Coach Miami to their undefeated 1972 season and a win in Super Bowl VII.

On February 14, 1973, Schnellenberger signed a three-year contract to replace John Sandusky as the head coach of the Baltimore Colts. The Colts went 4-10-0 in his first full season but did manage to upset the defending Super Bowl Champion Miami Dolphins, near the end of the 1973 season. On September 29, 1974, Howard was fired by the Colts' owner, Robert Irsay, after losing to the Eagles 30-10. Irsay wanted Bert Jones to start at quarterback for the Colts, but Schnellenberegr instead chose Marty Domres. A heated discussion broke out after the game, in the locker room where Irsay relived Howard of his job as head coach. He returned to the Dolphins' staff and remained there until he was offered the head coaching position at the University of Miami in 1979.

Schnellenberger became the head coach at Miami one year after Jim Kelly signed with the Hurricanes. Kelly, wearing #12, was a freshman quarterback in 1979 when they played Penn State. Kelly was playing against Joe Paterno, a coach who said he wasn't good enough to play quarterback for Penn State. Paterno wanted Kelly as a linebacker. Kelly once said, "You can't be a great quarterback in snow and 30 mph winds." Miami won that day, 26-10. Howard changed the way recruiting was done in Florida, by only going after local Florida talent. The Miami program was all but finished when Howard arrived and had considered dropping their football program completely a few years earlier. Howard also took the learning from Bryant and Shula, and installed a passing game that allowed them to have an advantage over their opponent, who was not equipped to stop a pass first offense. By his third season at Miami, Howard's teams had finished the season in the AP Poll top 25 twice, something that had not happened since 1966. He coached the University of Miami to the national championship in 1983, defeating Nebraska in the Orange Bowl. His Hurricane record stands at 41-16. He was awarded the Eddie Robinson Coach of the Year Award in 1983 and received the Golden Plate Award of the <u>American Academy of Achievement</u> in 1984. After 1984, Howard left Miami to become a part of the United States Football League. Schnellenberger was replaced by Jimmy Johnson at Miami and later chose to continue his coaching stint in Louisville, Kentucky. He took over a broken program in 1985. The Louisville Cardinals had not had a winning season since 1978. His teams went 8-24-1 in his first three seasons, before turning the program around. His next three seasons produced a 24-9-1 record, and he led Louisville to their third and fourth bowl games in the history of their program. Louisville shut down the Alabama Crimson Tide 34-7, in the 1991 Fiesta Bowl, capping a 10-1-1 season. He was also inducted into the University of Miami Sports Hall of Fame in 1993. Howard left Louisville in 1994. Oklahoma Sooner head coach, Gary Gibbs, was forced out late in the 1994 season, and Howard was hired on December 16, 1994 to replace him. He would only stay one year posting a record of 5-5-1. A disappointed Schnellenberger resigned and decided to try the financial world and became a bond salesman.

Howard resurfaced in 1998 at the age of 64, and was named the director of football at Florida Atlantic University. His job was to build the program. With 160 walk-ons and only 22 scholarship players, they played their first game on September 1, 2001, losing to Slippery Rock, 40-7. They posted a 9-3 record during their fourth season, while transitioning to Division I-A. They eventually moved to the Sun Belt Conference in 2005. Howard was named the Sun Belt Conference Coach of the Year in 2007. In 2008, Schnellenberger led his Owls to the Motor City Bowl against the Central Michigan Chippewas. Howard retired from coaching at the end of the 2011 season. On August 20, 2014, FAU announced that their stadium would be named in honor of Howard Schnellenberger. He was also inducted into the FAU Hall of Fame in 2019. Howard received the Paul "Bear" Bryant Lifetime Achievement Award in 2021. Howard Schnellenberger coached for 47 years and his win-loss record stands at 158-151-3 as a college coach, yet he was undefeated in bowl games with a 6-0 record. His NFL record was a dismal 4-13.

Howard Schnellenberger died on March 27, 2021, just 11 days after he had turned 87 years old. Howard suffered from a subdural hematoma he received during a fall last summer. Howard is survived by his wife Beverlee of 62 years, sons Timothy and Stuart and their wives; grandchildren Joey, Marcus and Teather and their spouses; and four great grandchildren, Tyler, Lacie, Harper Ann and Angel. Howard looked worn down by life, but you wouldn't know it by talking with him. His journey was defined by his dreams in the game of football. Howard was a great coach, but even a greater character. He was living in Boca Raton, Florida. He believed that football was a game of achievement and his office space at home was full of reminders of his football life. His home had been described as a museum. Rest well, my friend. You will not be forgotten.

A Life Measured In Seconds

Legendary college basketball coach, John Wooden, once said, "Do not mistake activity for achievement." Sure, this fellow had fun driving a race car, but do not think for one second that he did not want to win. He was a tough minded, no nonsense kind of guy, who was fully focused on becoming great. He always felt at home when he stepped on the race track. If his driving skills didn't give you chills, you're never going to get them. Everyone focuses on the athletic side of race car driving, when it's really the mental aspect of the race that allows iconic results to occur. I watched this guy drive his entire career, and he still put me on the edge of my seat. He always thought he could drive better. He was never satisfied. This man was all gas and no brakes, and he drove without fear. He was a "stop what you're doing and watch" kind of driver. The man was going to get pressure with his car, going to get close to you, whether you liked it or not. A fire boiled inside of him to become great. When driving, he had a great poker face. It was like looking at a statue. When coming to the finish line next to this guy, it could go two ways for you, bad or really bad.

He was born into a racing family that had ties all the way back to the 1920s. The reasons most of them drove race cars was because they loved the feeling of speed, but loved the competition even more. For him it was a life measured in seconds. More than a dozen of his kin had been a part of the American racing scene. Family is a resource like no other. It's like having a lifetime of experience at your fingertips from a group of people who will listen to you with an open and loving heart. This is a story about life more than it is about death. It's a story about how grief can not only harm the soul of a man, but can also reveal it. This is the story of Bobby Unser. He was a larger than life, colorful character, who could talk racing until the cows come home. Have you ever thought about the word "forever?" That's what it means to be in the Hall of Fame. There was never any question that Bobby Unser was a Hall-of-Fame race car driver.

Robert William "Bobby" Unser was born in the shadows of Pike's Peak on February 20, 1934, on my mother's birthday, in Colorado Springs, Colorado. Bobby was the third oldest of the four brothers. His family moved to Albuquerque, New Mexico, when he was but one year old. His dad, Jerome Henry Unser, owned a gas station and garage along Route 66. His mom, Mary Catherine, was a homemaker. As a young boy, Bobby joined his older twin brothers, Jerry Jr. and Louis, and his younger brother Al, in rebuilding an old rusted out Model-A pickup truck. Bobby began racing in 1949 in a Modified race held at Roswell Speedway. In 1950, at the age of 15, Bobby won his first championship in Southwest Modified Stock Cars. After Bobby graduated high school, he served in the United States Air Force from 1953-1955. While in the service, he also became a top competition sharpshooter.

Bobby Unser graced the race track from 1955 to 1982. He had 258 starts, started from the pole position 52 times and won 35 races. Bobby debuted in 1955 at Pike's Peak and finished 5th behind two of his brothers. In 1956, he won the race. Unser would win six straight at Pike's Peak, from 1958 to 1963. Bobby won that race a total of 13 times.

From 1963 to 1965, Bobby raced for the Andy Granatelli Team. In 1966, he moved to the team owned by Bob Willke. He made his Indianapolis 500 debut in 1963. In his first Indy 500 race, he had started dead last, had moved up to

16th place, but crashed on the third lap. The following year, he had completed only one lap before being involved in a multicar pileup that took the lives of drivers Eddie Sachs and Dave MacDonald. His first Indycar win came in 1967 at Mosport, Ontario. In 1968, at the age of 34, Bobby won his first Indianapolis 500 with a record speed of 170 mph. The second time he won at Indy was in 1975 during a rain-shortened race of only 435 miles. More than a dozen Unsers have taken part in the racing scene. His brother Al won the Indy 500 four times, Al Jr. won it twice and Bobby's son Robby matched Uncle Louis by winning nine times at Pike's Peak. Bobby finished in fourth place behind his brother Al, A.J. Foyt and Mario Andretti, with 35 wins in the Indycar Series. Bobby also won the 1968 and 1974 United States Automobile Club National Championship.

There was a downside to racing that most of them never much talked about. Unser had a fear of heights that he had to eventually overcome to win the Pike's Peak International Hill Climb. Pike's Peak is a race against the clock that included 150 turns, beside 1,000-foot drops with no guardrails for safety. Bobby also lost his uncle Joe Unser in a crash during a practice run, before the 1929 Indy 500 and his older brother Jerry Jr., was killed in a fiery crash while practicing for the 1959 Indy 500. As for Bobby, his legs had been broken so many times, he had lost count.

Bobby was the first in Unser family to win Indy 500 in 1968. He is best-known for being the first driver to win the Indy 500 in three different decades, 1968, 1975 and 1981. Only Rick Mears has won more, with four. Bobby, his younger brother Al and Al Jr. combined for 9 wins at the Indy 500. Unser was one of only ten drivers to win the "Greatest Spectacle in Racing" more than twice. Bobby Unser was inducted into both the Indianapolis Motor Speedway Hall of Fame and the International Motorsports Hall of Fame, in 1990. In

1994, he was inducted into the Motorsports Hall of Fame of America. In 1997, he was inducted into the National Sprint Car Hall of Fame. In 1999, he was awarded the Indy 500 Front Row Award for being a nine-time front row qualifier. Bobby was inducted into the Colorado Sports Hall of Fame in 2011, and he was also selected fourth in The Greatest 33 list of Indianapolis 500 drivers that same year.

After retiring from racing, Bobby spent 20 years as a television color commentator for NBC, ABC and ESPN. Between 1986 and 1992 Bobby also covered NASCAR racing, with former driver, Benny Parsons.

Someone once wrote, "There are three things you can count on in life: death, taxes and a pile-up at the Indianapolis 500." Bobby Unser took his final lap on a Sunday, May 2, 2021. He died from natural causes, while living at his home in Albuquerque, New Mexico. Unser was 87 and had paid Father Time no mind. He is survived by his current wife, Lisa; a son Bobby Jr., and a daughter Cindy from his first marriage to Barbara; a son Robby and a daughter Jeri from his second marriage to his wife Norma; four grandchildren and too many friends to count. Bobby Unser Jr., died less than two months after his father, at the age of 65, as a result of complications from hip surgery.

Bobby Unser had lived most of his life with a steering wheel in his hands, and he never apologized for winning. In fact, part of his memorabilia collection located at his ranch in Chama, New Mexico, included a twisted steering wheel from the time his car slid under a guardrail at a Phoenix race, almost decapitating him.

THE RIFLEMAN

There's an old saying in sports that goes like this: "Second place is the first loser." When a ballplayer is the very best at what he does, fans tend to think of him as invincible. He was considered one of the best on the team because he was never satisfied. This guy was a natural. As captain of his team, one of the key lessons he talked about was that failure was not one of your destinations. This fellow believed in his team, and they were going to fight together to win. He was brash and confident and didn't say we can win; he said "We are going to win." With great feet and perfect technique, he could really protect the plate. Running into this catcher looked like an 18-wheeler jackknifed on the interstate. Runners just bounced off him. The man was amazing, and you just wanted to be around him.

Yes, he played on a great team. With names like Warren Spahn, Hank Aaron, Johnny Logan, Johnny Sain and Eddie Mathews, nametags were not required in this clubhouse. But, this guy was the apple of the bunch, and the rest of his teammates were just oranges. His teammates joked that when he was bad, he was very bad, and when he was good, he was dangerous. His Manager, Charlie "Jolly Cholly" Grimm once said about his catcher, "He had everything in his favor, perfect poise, sound judgment and aggressiveness."

As for base stealing, they should have nicknamed him "Machine Gun Kelly," as he threw out 45.9% of the base runners who tried to steal a base on him. That percentage places him eighth on the all-time list. He became known for his rifle arm, catlike movement behind home plate, and his unusual flexibility.

Like my dad, Del was a looker. Standing 6 feet 1 inch tall, he sported dark red hair, skin so fair you could almost see through it, and bright blue eyes. Del understood that winning the game was based on number of runs scored, but just think of how many other ways you can win in life. Getting to know "The Rifleman" was a gift and listening to him was a pleasure. As a player, coach, manager and broadcaster, Del Crandall spent over 44 years in the game he loved and had a lot of dirt in his spikes. Crandall once said, "When you get older, the only thing you really miss is being younger."

Delmar Wesley Crandall arrived on March 5, 1930, to Richard and Nancy Crandall. This family lived in Ontario, California, and Del was the second of three children. Del and his sisters, Barbara and Betty, grew up during the depression in Fullerton, a small town just east of Los Angeles. Both his parents worked in the citrus-packaging industry. Del found his love for baseball in the sandlots of Fullerton, shagging fly balls as a pudgy nine-year-old. Del became a catcher when he was in the fifth grade. He also met "Pep" Lemon, a former Minor-League catcher who ran the local recreation department and managed a semipro team named the Fullerton Merchants. "Everything I learned was from Pep Lemon," said Crandall. "He was the most influential man in my baseball career." At the age of 16, Lemon allowed Del to practice and catch with the Merchants. Crandall became a standout catcher at Fullerton High School and for the local American Legion Team. He was already being watched by several professional teams. Brooklyn Dodger scout, Tom Downey, was relentless in his pursuit of Crandall; but Del's dad did not want him to sign with the Dodgers, Yankees or Cardinals. His reason was simple. Those teams had too many prospects in their farm system, and his chance of making the club was slim. Instead, Crandall signed a two-year contract with Boston Braves scout, Johnny Moore.

In 1948, at the age of 17, Crandall received a $4,000 salary from Boston's Triple-A affiliate, the Milwaukee Brewers. "That was more money than my parents or I had ever seen," said Crandall. He was sent to Austin, Texas, for Spring Training with the Brewers. After struggling at the plate, he was moved to the Class-C Leavenworth Braves, located in Whitesville, North Carolina. Del was forced to play pepper every day to help cut down on his swing. After three or four weeks, he started to hit. He eventually developed a fine home-run swing. Crandall was one of the last players cut during the 1949 Spring Training season. He was assigned to the Evansville Braves of Class-B Three-I League. Del hit .351 in 38 games at Evansville and was called up to the big club. Braves' owner, Lou Perini, sent a private plane to get him. Wearing #23 for the Boston Braves, he made his debut on June 17, 1949, just three months after he had turned 19. Del entered the game against the Reds as a pinch runner during a 7-2 loss. Crandall started at catcher the following day, at Crosley Field in Cincinnati. Del appeared in 146 games for Boston Braves during the 1949-1950 seasons, before being drafted in March of 1951, into military service during the Korean War. Del was named to *The Sporting News'* Rookie All-Star Team and finished the 1949 season as the runner-up to Brooklyn Dodgers' pitcher, Don Newcombe, for the Rookie of the Year Award.

In 1950, he spent some time on the bench with a broken finger, and then he was called up by the military. Stationed in Fort Ord, California, he served with the infantry and saw active duty while serving in Japan. But, before he reported for duty, Del eloped to Las Vegas and married his high school sweetheart, Frances Sorrells. They would have six children together.

His military service ended in March of 1953, just as the

Braves departed Boston for Milwaukee. "We were all surprised by the announcement that the Braves were moving," said Crandall. "Teams just didn't move on in those days." It was the first franchise shift in Major League baseball since 1903.

The new Milwaukee Braves arrived by train on April 8, 1953. Del would now wear the #1 for the Milwaukee Braves. New faces like sluggers Andy Pafko and Joe Adcock had joined the team, along with Jim Pendleton, Billy Bruton, Bob Buhl, Johnny Antonelli and Del Crandall. With them traveled Eddie Mathews, Warren Spahn and Johnny Logan. Twelve thousand fans with signs greeted the team, and 60,000 turned out the following night for a parade. The home opener was played on a Thursday, April 14th, against the St. Louis Cardinals. Solly Hemus led off and was walked to first base. A sellout crowd of 34,357 turned out. Future Hall-of-Fame pitcher, Warren Spahn, toed the rubber for the Braves. Joe Adcock registered the first Braves' hit, and Del Crandall hit a slow roller down the third base line, as Cardinals' Ray Jablonski over-threw first baseman Bilko. Adcock scored the first Milwaukee run. The Braves won that day 3-2 in 10 innings, and County Stadium was referred to by a local sports writer as an insane asylum with bases.

It has been said that most good catchers were also good hitters. By June 29, 1953, Crandall was hitting .301 and was named to his first of eight All-Star Teams. The Braves drew 1,826,397 in their first season in Milwaukee. That mark set a new National League attendance record which they broke the following year, when they became the first NL club to top the two million mark. It didn't hurt that Hank Aaron and Gene Conley joined the team in 1954. The Braves led the National League in attendance in their first six seasons in Milwaukee (1953-1958).

In 1954, 24-year-old Del Crandall was named team captain. Typically batting in the eighth spot in the order,

Del understood the value of defense. He was one of the first catchers to throw to all three bases in an attempt to stop stolen bases. Del also made the All-Star team in 1954 and 1955. His most memorable moment at the plate occurred in 1955. In the first game of a doubleheader against Philadelphia, the Braves were behind 4-1 with the bases loaded and two outs, in the ninth inning. Crandall fouled off a few pitches and then with a 3-and-2 count, hit a grand slam to win the game. It was one of his four career grand slams and five walk-off home runs. In 1956, the Braves appeared to be ready to compete, but a slow start resulted in Grimm being fired after only 46 games played. New Manager Fred Haney instilled a more disciplined approach, and the team responded by winning their next 11 games in a row. But it was not enough, and the Dodgers finished strong and in first place.

In 1957, a 10-game winning streak from August 4th through 15th moved the Braves into first place. Milwaukee led the league in home runs with 199 and scored the most runs (772), while having the best pitching staff (Warren Spahn, Lew Burdette and Bob Buhl) in the league. The Braves met the New York Yankees in the 1957 World Series. Crandall remembered being nervous playing at Yankee Stadium. He caught five of the seven games. In the eighth inning of Game 7, Del hit a towering home run to give the Braves a 5-0 lead. The 1957 Milwaukee Braves took the Yankees to the woodshed. They were now World Champions. In 1958, Crandall, in full catching gear, graced the cover of the April 21st s. He also enjoyed his best season at the plate, batting .272 with 18 home runs and 63 runs batted in. He also hit a career high in doubles, with 23.

In 1958, Crandall started all seven World Series' games in a rematch with the Yankees. His five hits in 14 at-bats helped move the Braves to a three games to one lead, but it was not enough, as the Yankees won the next three games and the 1958 World Series. In 1959, the Crandall's moved to Brookfield, Wisconsin, just west of Milwaukee. Most thought the Braves would get back to their third World Series but it was not to be. They played sub-.500 baseball in June, July and August to drop to third place.

During his last four years in Milwaukee (1960-1963), the Braves were an aging team. Del continued to play well but missed most of the 1961 season with a sore arm. Backup catcher Joe Torre took his place and established himself as their catcher for the future. Splitting time with Torre upset Crandall, and he responded by making his last All-Star team in 1962. He also won his fourth Gold Glove Award in five years. In 1963, Bobby Bragan became the Braves' fourth manager in five years. Crandall insisted that Bragan trade him. In 1964, Crandall was sent to the San Francisco Giants in a seven-player trade that brought outfielder Felipe Alou to Milwaukee. He wore #9 for the Giants. In 1965, you could find Del in Pittsburgh as their backup catcher wearing #16. He was traded again in 1966 to Cleveland, where he wore #7. His last at-bat for the Indians occurred on September 14, 1966. Del was offered a Triple-A contract by Cleveland, but chose to retire.

In 1969, Crandall decided to manage. He led the Albuquerque Dodgers to the 1970 Texas League Championship. In 1971, Del was hired to manage the Brewers' Triple-A Evansville club. He joined the big club again in 1972 and managed the club until 1975. Crandall was fired before the last game of the 1975 season. Del finished with a 271-338 win-loss record with the Brewers. He spent the 1976 and 1977 seasons with the Salinas Angels and led them to the Class-A California League title. In 1978, Del returned to the Dodgers' organization and led the Dukes of the Pacific Coast League to four championships in the next five years. In 1983, the Seattle Mariners hired Crandall to lead their team. He was relieved of his duties in the middle of the 1984 season. From 1985-1988, Crandall worked as the color commentator for the Chicago White Sox, and continued with the Milwaukee Brewers in the same capacity from 1992 until 1997. Del finally retired for good at the end of the 1997 season.

Crandall played in 1,573 games over the course of 16 seasons. He recorded 1,276 hits, while batting .254 in 5,026 at-bats. Del hit 179 homeruns and recorded 657 runs batted in. He scored 585 times and only struck out 477 times. Del won four Gold Glove Awards, made 11 All-Star teams, and tied a National League record by catching three no-hitters.

Del Crandall and his wife Frances lived in Brea, California, close to where he had grown up. They raised six kids together: Del Jr., Ron, Billy, Jeff, Tim and Nancy. Del Crandall died on May 5, 2021, at the age of 91. He was so old he actually knew the guy they named "jumping jacks" after.

Del suffered from Parkinson's disease, heart disease and had several strokes prior to his death. From August 2020 until his death, Crandall was the last living Boston Brave, following the death of Bert Theil on July 31,   2020.

American writer, William Faulkner, once said, "The past is never dead. It's not even past." Even up until his last days, Del Crandall longed for the friendships he had made in baseball. "The things you miss the most are all the friendships you made," said Del. "You miss all the good times you've had winning baseball. You miss the people and the fans who watched us play." We will miss you too, Del.

THE WALL

Ralph Waldo Emerson once said, "What lies behind us and what lies before us are tiny matters compared to what lies within us." The man I will tell you about was a straight arrow, not even an overdue library book. Yet, he would become known as a big man on the block. Standing 7' 4" tall and weighing 275 pounds, he owned Johnny Bench-type hands and was so strong he could choke a tiger with his grip. When you saw this fellow in the lobby of a hotel you immediately thought, maybe I should wait for the next elevator. When the shark in the movie *Jaws* saw this guy, he asked for a bigger boat. On the court, this guy was a kid with grown-man moves. He had an absence of ego as if he were playing basketball with house money. A mountain of a man, his teammates kidded with him that he played with his head in the rafters. "He was one of the first to make me feel small," said Shaquille O'Neal. "I didn't realize how tall he was until I played against him. My patented elbow sandwich didn't work on him. He never said anything," said Shaq.

Every warrior has a beginning. Competition pushes us all toward greatness, and he attacked the game with such passion. This fellow was a team guy, not a stats guy. The man was aggressive, all right. He even went after his food like it was trying to escape. He may have been limited offensively, but he would become one of the best defensive centers in NBA history and king of blocking shots. There are great players, good players and great guys, but every once in a while we run across a good player who is also a great guy. That was Mark Eaton. He was a good man with a tall tale. If you bumped into him at a café, he'd apologize even if it wasn't his fault. Some of us believe our path in life has already been written, that life reveals itself to us. He believed we make our own way with our own choices. One of his Jazz teammates by the name of Mike Brown nicknamed him "The Wall." There were very few who were as dominant and scary as Mark Eaton in the paint. Still, I feel blessed to have known him.

Mark Edward Eaton was given to us on January 24, 1957. He was born in Inglewood, California. His dad, Bud, was an auto mechanics instructor and stood 6 feet 9 inches tall. His mom, Delores, was 6 feet tall, so he came from tall genes. In the beginning, Mark never liked basketball and chose water polo instead. By the time he had become a senior at Westminster High School, he had grown to 6 feet 11 inches tall, but weighed only 175 pounds. Tall, gangly, not very muscular and uncoordinated, Mark had to be talked into playing on the high school basketball team. He was lucky to stay on the team as a reserve. His high school coaches had never coached a player his size. "The coaches didn't know how to teach me to play big, and I didn't know how to play big," said Eaton. After he graduated in 1975, Eaton attended the Arizona Automotive Institute in Glendale and became an automotive service technician. Returning to Orange County, Eaton took a job earning $20,000 a year.

In April of 1977, chemistry professor and assistant basketball coach at Cypress College, Tom Lubin, discovered Eaton working on cars in Anaheim, California. Lubin had made a name for himself in the game by discovering center Sven Nater years earlier. Nater did not play basketball in high school, but went on to have a long and prosperous NBA pro career. Lubin convinced Eaton he could play the game and convinced Mark to enroll at Cypress College in 1978 and try out for the basketball team. After his freshman year, Eaton was selected by the Phoenix Suns with the 107th pick in the fifth round of the 1979 NBA Draft. Instead he returned to Cypress College. In 1980, Eaton led Cypress to the California Junior College basketball title and averaged 14.3 points per game. Mark Eaton became a UCLA Bruin in the fall of 1980. He would wear #35 at UCLA. Disappointed, Mark did not play as much as expected for Bruins' Head Coach Larry Brown. The reason was Eaton was too slow to play in Brown's fast-paced offense. In 1982, during Mark's senior year he was promised more playing time by new Head Coach Larry Farmer; but that did not pan out, as the Bruins had recruited a kid named Stuart Gray who proved to be an excellent player. Eaton played only 41 minutes his senior year and averaged 1.3 points per game and 2.0 rebounds in just 11 games. Mark was not even allowed to travel with the team on their last road trips to Oregon and Oregon State. "That was the time I felt the worst," said Mark. "I had worked so hard and it wasn't like I was causing any problems."

But, as luck would have it, a fellow you all know by the name of Wilt Chamberlain noticed Mark Eaton at a summer pickup game and took it upon himself to encourage Eaton to focus on protecting the basket, getting rebounds, and getting the outlet pass started by getting the ball in the guard's hands as quickly as possible. Eaton recalled their conversation. "After Wilt watched me chase smaller guards around the court, he said, 'Look young fella, you're never going to catch that guy and more importantly, it's not really your job.' He grabbed me and took me out on the court and put me right in front of the basket and said, 'You see this basket behind you? Your job is to stand here and block shots, your job is to stop the other players from getting to the basket, collect the rebound and then throw the ball out to the guard, let them go down to the other end and score it and then your job is to kind of cruise up to half court and see what's going on.' That little five-minute conversation turned into a 12-year career for me," said Eaton. For the rest of his life, Mark Eaton would give Wilt Chamberlain the credit for turning his basketball career around that day.

Because of his lack of playing time while at UCLA, Eaton actually paid with his own money, to participate in two professional basketball tryout camps. He received two offers, one for $15,000 a year to play in Israel and the second for $25,000 to play in Monte Carlo. But luck remained in Mark's corner. The Utah Jazz had finished in last place that year and Jazz coach Frank Layden saw Eaton as a long term project on defense. Eaton was selected by the Utah Jazz with the 72nd pick in the fourth round of the 1982 NBA Draft. "You can't teach height," said Layden, who quoted the great "Red" Auerbach. Mark Eaton had struck gold. He signed a five-year contract worth $570,000, with $45,000 guaranteed during his first season. Mark chose to wear #53 as #35 had already been taken by Darrell Griffith of the Jazz.

As a rookie, Mark started 32 games by replacing the former Jazz center, Danny Schayes, who was traded in mid-season. All Eaton did was finish the season with a record number of blocked shots (275) for the Jazz, while playing only an average of 19 minutes a game. Eaton finished his first season by averaging 3.4 blocks per game and ranked third behind Atlanta's "Tree" Rollins and San Diego's Bill Walton. Eaton's presence during his rookie season helped the Jazz improve from a 30-52 win-loss record to 45-37. They won their first Midwest Division title and made their first playoff appearance. During the 1983-84 season, Mark pulled down a team-leading 595 rebounds and blocked 351 shots. His 4.28 blocks per game led the entire NBA. Yet, all anyone talked about was his failure to block the hook shot which gave Kareem Abdul-Jabbar his 31,421st point to break the NBA career scoring record held by his friend, Wilt Chamberlain.

Eaton shattered the single season blocked-shot record

during the 1984-85 season, with 456. On April 26, 1985, Mark blocked ten shots in a 96-94 loss to the Houston Rockets, becoming the first NBA player to record ten blocks in a playoff game. That record was later tied by Hakeem Olajuwon and Andrew Bynum. Eaton had averaged 5.56 blocks per game that season. He also averaged 11.3 rebounds per game was named to the NBA All-Defensive First Team and chosen the NBA Defensive Player of the Year. During the 1988-89 season, Mark was named the NBA Defensive Player of the Year for the second time during his career and was also named to the NBA All-Defensive Team for the third time. That same year, Eaton recorded 14 blocks in a single game against the San Antonio Spurs which tied him for the third most in an NBA game since the NBA began recording blocks during the 1973 season. He was also chosen to play in his one and only NBA All-Star Game in 1989. He was joined by teammates Karl Malone and John Stockton. This was the first time the Jazz had three All-Stars in the same year.

Sooner or later, his size would become a factor in his health. After missing only nine games during his first ten seasons, Mark hurt his knees and suffered back pains late in his career. His effectiveness declined. He was limited to only 64 games played during the 1992-93 season. His back pain forced him to miss the entire 1993-94 season and his contract ran out after that season. After therapy failed to help the back pain, Mark Eaton retired from professional basketball in September of 1994. Eaton was quoted in the Salt Lake City Tribune after retirement: "It has been a great ride, but life does have a way of moving on and I must move on with it. Thank You for letting me be a part of your life and community. I'll be around."

On February 12, 1995, I attended the NBA All-Star game in Phoenix, Arizona. The game was played at America West Arena and I had tickets to all the festivities. I not only got to meet John Havlicek, who sat a few seats to my right and was nice enough to sign his autograph on the back of my ticket, but I also had dinner at Dan Majerle's restaurant. Dan played guard for the Suns. It was here that I met the big guy himself, Mark Eaton. I took a picture of him, and he invited me to sit with him for a spell. I was in Heaven.

There is no doubt that Mark Eaton helped change the outcome of the Utah Jazz franchise. They became perennial 50-plus game winners and reached the NBA playoffs in each of his ten seasons with the team. Eaton played in 875 games while scoring 5,216 points, grabbed 6,939 rebounds and blocked 3,064 shots.

Karl Malone and John Stockton had nothing on Mark Eaton. Mark Eaton was a five-time member of the NBA All-Defensive Team and led the league four times in blocked shots. Eaton still holds the NBA record for most blocked shots in a single season, with 456, and the career blocked-shots per game average, with 3.5. Eaton was named to the NBA All-Star Game in 1989 and was twice voted the NBA Defensive Player of the Year, in 1985 and 1989. When Mark retired in 1994, he ranked second in the NBA in career blocked-shots behind Kareem Abdul-Jabbar. During the 1995-96 season, the Utah Jazz retired Eaton's #53. In 2010, Eaton was inducted into the Utah Sports Hall of Fame along with former Utah player, Tom Chambers. In 2014, Eaton also had his jersey number retired at Westminster High School and Cypress College.

After retirement, Mark worked for KJZZ-TV in Salt Lake City providing color commentary for the Jazz and the University of Utah basketball games. Eaton served as the president of the National Basketball Retired Players Association from 1997 to 2007. Mark was also the founder of the Mark Eaton Standing Tall for Youth organization, which provided sports and outdoor activities for at-risk children in Utah. Mark also served as an outstanding motivational speaker. Eaton became a partner in a local restaurant named Tuscany. My stepson Bill James and his wife Mary Ann enjoy dining at Tuscany. "The food is great and we enjoy the atmosphere", said Bill. During the 2013 NBA Slam Dunk Contest, Jazz player Jeremy Evans jumped over a seated Mark Eaton to dunk the basketball. In 2018, Eaton released his book entitled <u>The Four Commitments of a Winning Team</u>. His pal, John Stockton, wrote the foreword. Jazz center, Rudy Gobert, credits Eaton as his mentor, and he later joined Eaton as the only other Jazz player in franchise history to be named Defensive Player of the Year. When Gobert heard the news, he wrote, "To my great mentor and friend, Mark Eaton, one of a kind and an amazing human being. I'm grateful for your presence in my life over the years. Gonna miss our conversations. But I know you'll be watching."

In 1980, Mark met and married his wife, the former Teri Riser Hunter. They had two sons and three daughters together. They lived for a while in Jeremy Ranch in the 1980's. Eaton, an avid outdoorsman, ordered a specially-built mountain bike, built for tall cyclists, and biked on a number of the region's first mountain bike trails. On Friday, May 28, 2021, Eaton biked with a neighbor to lunch. A short time later, Mark called his wife he was going for short ride in the neighborhood. At 8:26 p.m. Eaton was found dead after an apparent bicycle crash about a block away from his home in Summit County, Utah. He was found unresponsive by a passerby and was pronounced dead at the hospital.

I have always believed that people's paths cross and it's not by accident. Mark had just returned from Chicago where he had traveled to see his good friend, Joe West, who broke Major League baseball's umpiring record on Tuesday night by working his 5,376 regular season game. Interestingly, Joe West and I were suitemates while in college. Mark Eaton was but 64 years old.

We all want to be defined as a family by our blessings, not our tragedies, yet every family has tragedy. So, sometimes we never get to say goodbye the way we want; and when we deal with a loss so sudden, our emotions can overwhelm us. He was a quiet giant in every sense of the word.

THE GUARANTEE

Bill Belichick once said, "There is always a way to win, you just have to figure it out." For coaches, there is only one thing better than being right, being right and winning. His football life was one surprise after another. This game was his religion. The success he had, no one saw coming, not even himself. One of the keys to his success was that when he needed advice he spoke with those who were smarter than him, and when they spoke, he listened. He made the game seem easy for his coaches and players. This man made pressure look comfortable. He was the coach next door; the kind of guy you would sit next to at the airport and talk football. Nicknamed "Gentleman Jim," a happy guy; he acted like he had just found some money in the street.

He was also a lucky guy, who got to do what he loved doing. There are not a lot of people in this world who can say that. The man understood that the best of us comes out when the moment is the toughest. His motto was: "Know who you are and be how you are." He could be as smooth as a jar of jelly. Most of the time, there was calmness in his voice and failure was not a part of his vocabulary, but this coach was always getting on his players. His memory was short, but his rage sometimes went on forever. He saw things in them that they didn't see in themselves; but in the end, he had a way to make guys feel comfortable, when he knew the game was on the line.

His football legacy as the Giants' head coach is somewhat clouded, but it was his classic guarantee uttered on November 22nd, the day before Thanksgiving in late November of the

2000 season, that set him apart from his counterparts. After a great start to the 2000 season, the Giants fell to 7-4. The New York media and the Giants' upper management had a field day. After a loss to the Detroit Lions, Fassel responded this way: "This is a poker game, and I'm shoving my chips to the middle of the table. I'm raising the ante, and anybody who wants in, get in. Anybody who wants out can get out. This team is going to the playoffs, OK? This team is going to the playoffs." His coaches and players thought he was having a breakdown. It was a cinch he would be fired if wrong. New York won their last five games, beat the Eagles in the first round of the playoffs and smashed the Vikings, 41-0, in the NFC Championship Game at Giants Stadium. Fassel was carried off the field on the shoulders of Michael Strahan, Keith Hamilton and Jessie Armstead. The New York Giants were on their way to Super Bowl XXXV. The guarantee had come true.

You see, this fellow wasn't cut from classic football coach cloth. In fact, he looked more like Mr. Rogers than a football coach. In a swimsuit, Coach Jim Fassel resembled Mr. America. Even the Beach Boys were envious. Sometimes in life we make the wrong choices by mistake, but it gets us to the right place. Let me tell you about an offensive guru, a football savant, Jim Fassel.

James Edward Fassel was born on August 31, 1949, in Anaheim, California. His football life began at Anaheim High School as a quarterback before attending Fullerton College. In 1969, Fassel transferred to the University of Southern California as their backup quarterback and became part of USC's undefeated Rose Bowl Championship team. Jim finished his college football career with Long Beach State. Jim Fassel was drafted as a quarterback with the 167th pick, in the 7th round of the 1972 NFL Draft by the Chicago Bears. He was soon traded to the San Diego Chargers and then the

Houston Oilers in the same season. In 1973, you could find Jim in the Canadian Football League, playing quarterback for the Toronto Argonauts. Jim played quarterback briefly for The Hawaiians of the World Football League (WFL) in 1974, before being hired as their offensive assistant coach. He left the team at the end of the 1974 season but was asked to return at the end of the 1975 season, as The Hawaiians needed a quarterback. Jim Fassel played in the final game of the World Football League, throwing the very last pass in the league's history, as the (WFL) shut down three days after the game was played on October 22, 1975. For the next 22 seasons, Coach Jim Fassel was passed around like a bag of chips. The following eight years (1976-1983), Fassel served as the quarterbacks' and receivers' coach for the University of Utah (1976), Weber State (1977-1978), and Stanford University (1979-1983). Fassel got to work with future Hall-of-Fame quarterback, John Elway, while at Stanford. In 1984, Fassel joined the New Orleans Breakers of the United States Football League (USFL), as their offensive coordinator.

Jim Fassel finally became a head football coach for the University of Utah in 1985. He was let go at the end of the 1989 season with a 25-33 win-loss record. From 1991 to 1997, Fassel served as the offensive coordinator for the New York Giants, Denver Broncos, Oakland Raiders and the Arizona Cardinals.

Three weeks after the New York Giants beat the Buffalo Bills in Super Bowl XXV on January 27, 1991; Jim Fassel was hired by Giants' head coach Bill Parcells as their quarterback coach. Parcells then retired from football due to health problems. In 1992, Jim was promoted to offensive coordinator. After stints with the Broncos, Raiders and Cardinals, (1993-1997), Jim returned to the Giants as their head coach, in 1997. He replaced Dan Reeves. Interestingly, the New York Jets hired Bill Parcells as their new head coach.

Jim Fassel instantly became the "other guy" in the City that never sleeps. The Giants became known for their strong runs late in the season. Fassel's New York Giants posted a 10-5-1 record and finished 1st in the NFC East. He was named the 1997 NFL Coach of the Year. New York then lost to the Minnesota Vikings, in the wild card game.

The Giants finished the 2000 season, 1st in the NFC East division with a 12-4 record. In February of 2001, the Baltimore Ravens beat the New York Giants soundly in Super Bowl XXXV, 34-7. The Giants returned to the playoffs one more time in 2002, but it was not to be. Jim Fassel was fired in 2003, by the Giants, and replaced by Tom Coughlin. After seven seasons with the Giants, Fassel had posted a 58-53-1 regular season win-loss record. His team went to the playoffs three times, and their postseason record stands at 2-3. Fassel then joined the Baltimore Ravens as their offensive consultant in 2004 and was promoted to the position of offensive coordinator in 2005. On October 17, 2006, Jim Fassel was fired by the Baltimore Ravens.

Jim was asked to join Westwood One as a color commentator on their radio broadcast. Fassel stayed for two seasons, calling Sunday NFL games with Harry Kalas and Sunday Night Football with Dave Sims. Jim also participated in the NFL coverage of the playoffs, joining Bill Rosinski during the 2007 NFC Championship Games and Marv Albert during the 2008 NFC championship Games.

In January of 2009, Jim Fassel became the head football coach of Las Vegas Locos of the United Football League (UFL). The Locos won the first UFL Championship Game over the Florida Tuskers. They repeated as champions in 2010. Fassel finished his coaching career in the UFL with an 18-7 win-loss record and two UFL Championships.

On September 11, 2001, the Giants were on their way home from a road loss when they learned about the bombing of the

Pentagon and the World Trade Center in New York. Since all NFL games for the following week had been cancelled, Mayor Rudy Giuliani called on Jim Fassel and his players to help with the morale at the Trade Center site. Fassel agreed and had his team provide goodwill and moral support to the folks helping with the recovery effort. They also provided help to the recovery crews of the FDNY, the NYPD and the City of New York. Under great pressure, the Giants beat the Kansas City Chiefs in an emotional game at Arrowhead Stadium the following week.

Jim's long and illustrious career in the NFL allowed him to touch some of the finest players in the game. John Elway, Shannon Sharpe, Kerry Collins and Tiki Barber benefitted the most from his leadership. Others like Jeremy Shockey, Amani Toomer, Ike Hilliard and Michael Strahan, did the same.

Jim Fassel passed away on June 7, 2021, from a heart attack. He was taken to the Las Vegas Hospital with chest pains and died during treatment. He was 71 and living in Las Vegas, Nevada. It has been said that the strongest muscle in the human body is the heart and it's the last thing that ever wears out. It will keep beating as long as it possibly can. Jim is survived by his wife Kitty, five children and 16 grandchildren. One of his sons, John, is currently the special team's coordinator for the Dallas Cowboys. Jim and Kitty divorced in 2006, but later remarried after years of counseling.

Jim Fassel once said to his team, "I am the lucky one. I got a chance to coach you." Well said, coach, well said.

MUDCAT

Reliever, Billy Wagner, once said, "It's hard to appreciate someone until you need them." My goodness, he made the game look easy. This fellow had baseball in his heart and he will be remembered for dealing from the "bump," a ten-dollar word for pitcher's mound. He could get that baseball up there in a hurry. As for his fastball, you looked out at him and said to yourself, how can this guy throw it past me? And then he throws it past you.

He owned a smile that could stop traffic, and there is no doubt the man could throw a baseball through a waterfall without getting it wet. The difference between good and great is confidence. At times, he appeared more machine-like than human. He had everything you wanted in a starting pitcher: height, strength, intelligence, and an arm made in Heaven. He also owned velocity, accuracy, a darn-near-perfect delivery and he could count money faster than a chicken can pick up corn. He was a baseball natural. The man was all gas and no brakes, and there was some deception in his arm slot. This guy became the first African-American pitcher to win a World Series game for the American League. It was a moment made for history.

It's funny; I remember calling it hardball, not baseball. I miss that. I bet he did, too. For me, baseball is 4 to 3, not 9 to 1. It's working the count, pitching to the corners, grinding it out, hitting to the opposite field and playing scrappy and smart baseball. It's about counting outs, not scoring runs! Watching Jim "Mudcat" Grant pitch was like watching a line from the Bible come to life. Every team has a driving force, and Jim "Mudcat" Grant was the heartbeat of the 1965 Minnesota Twins. Nineteen-sixty-five was a year of firsts for Jim Grant and baseball. Not only did he become the first African-American pitcher to win 20 Major League games (21-7) in a single season in the American League, but he also pitched in his second All-Star Game, while his ERA (3.30) was shrinking faster than a cotton t-shirt. Grant led the Twins to a World Series matchup against the Los Angeles Dodgers, and in the off-season, he hosted a local Minneapolis variety television show known as the *Jim Grant Show*, where he sang and danced. Jim became the first black American League pitcher to win a World Series game, as he threw two complete games. He also became only the second American League pitcher to hit a World Series home run, in Game Six. Grant forced a Game Seven with his three-run home run in the bottom of the sixth inning. Twins' second baseman, Frank Quilici, had been walked intentionally to get to Grant. Unfortunately, Sandy Koufax and the Dodgers beat the Twins 2-0 in Game Seven and won the 1965 World Series. I loved what Jim Grant once said in an interview after the World Series, "When the out-of-town scoreboard is blank and you're still playing, that's the World Series," said Grant. Mudcat finished sixth in voting for the 1965 American League MVP and was named *The Sporting News* American League Pitcher of the Year.

My cell phone rang on June 13, 2021, on a Sunday afternoon. I usually don't get calls on Sunday, but to my surprise it was my pal, Bill Lee. Yeah, that Bill Lee: "The Spaceman." Bill wanted to let me know that he had just received my newest book <u>Legends of Greatness</u>, and when he opened the book he was at the beginning of the story about Tom Seaver. "Boy, you nailed it," said Lee, "Great job." Bill sounded excited, but I detected something more. Bill was mourning the loss of his friend Jim "Mudcat" Grant, and he wanted to make sure

I had heard the news. "Mudcat was the roommate of catcher Earl Battey," said Lee. "I attended Battey's funeral. Only five white guys were there: Jim Kaat, Jim Perry, Dan Tupper, Lee Stange and I." Bill continued, "Mudcat was also there and we were friends. I loved him and he loved me. I was born in Burbank, California, and met Jim Grant in 1972. We were playing golf one day and I drove a ball 250 yards off the tee, and the ball landed at Mudcat's feet. Most would have been upset, but Mudcat blew me a kiss," said Bill. "He later told me that my drive was like a butterfly with sneakers on." We never stop to think about all the positive ways we impact others. Relationships touch our souls. These are the things that give real meaning to life. Few of us are aware of how we positively affect those we will never meet, but it is profound. I had never met Mudcat personally, but my friend Bill Lee had, and he was beside himself.

James Timothy "Mudcat" Grant was born on August 13, 1935, in Lacoochee, Florida. This lumber town was located about 40 miles north of Tampa. Jim was one of seven children born to James Sr. and Viola Grant. James Sr. worked at the mill and died when Mudcat was two. So, the responsibility for raising the family fell on Viola, who worked at a citrus canning factory and cleaned houses in her spare time. Jim played baseball, football and basketball at Moore Academy in Dade City, Florida. Jim played semi-pro baseball in the summer for the Lacoochee Nine Devils, at third base. He was placed at third because of his strong throwing arm. Mudcat received a scholarship to play baseball and football at Florida A&M University, but unfortunately had to leave the university after his sophomore year, to help raise money for his mother and his family to survive. He relocated to New Smyrna Beach, Florida, and lived with some relatives while becoming a carpenter's helper. It was here that Grant was discovered by an Indians' bird-dog by the name of Fred

Merkie. Merkie had first seen Grant play in high school, but he was too young to sign a contract at that time. When Fred heard that Grant had left Florida A&M, he tracked Mudcat down to sign him for the Cleveland Indians.

After attending the Indians' Minor League camp in Daytona, two things happened. One: Grant left Florida for the first time in his life, when he traveled to North Dakota to pitch for Cleveland's Class-C affiliate, Fargo-Moorhead of the Northern League; and second: He received his nickname, "Mudcat" from another player by the name of Leroy Bartow Irby, who took one look at him and decided that with that wide smile and dark skin, he must be from Mississippi. You see, a Mudcat is a large catfish found living in the muddy waters of Mississippi. Grant eventually made his real name known, but would forever be known as Mudcat.

In North Dakota, Jim lost the first game he pitched, but then won 12 straight and was awarded the Rookie Pitcher of the Year. His 21-5 record with an ERA of 3.40 was brilliant. Grant pitched in the Class-B Three-I League in 1955 and ended up in Reading, Pennsylvania, with the Class-A Eastern League. It was here that he had his first losing season, 12-13. In 1957, Grant was sent to the Pacific Coast League located in San Diego, California. He went 18-7 with a 2.32 ERA and 178 strikeouts. San Diego manager Ralph Kiner said, "I've never seen a young pitcher come along as fast as he has." Grant gave all the credit to the Padres' pitching coach, Vic Lombardi.

By 1958, you could find Mudcat Grant starting for the Cleveland Indians. Larry Doby had returned to the Indians from Baltimore and took Grant under his wing. Doby gave Grant an older black player to lean on. Grant started the Indians' third game of the year and won 3-2 over the Kansas City Royals, but finished the year 10-11. He struck out 111 batters, but also walked 104. His lack of control was evident.

He would now begin to spend equal time as a starter and as a reliever. The next couple of years would be up and down for Grant. The 1960 season ended early for Grant, as he got into a screaming match on September 16th with the bullpen coach, Ted Wilks, during the National Anthem. Mudcat chose to change the words to the ending in jest, and Wilks took it personally and called Grant a racial name. Grant walked straight to the clubhouse and left the park without letting manager Jimmy Dykes know what had happened. Dykes had no choice but to suspend him without pay for the rest of the season. Wilks would later apologize, but Grant refused to accept the apology. Wilks left the Indians after the season was over. Grant and Dykes finally got on the same page in 1961, as Dykes chose to use him as a starter only. Grant started 35 games and led the team with 15 wins. On November 2, 1961 Grant was ordered to report to active duty for the U.S. Army. He was still able to pitch on weekends for the Indians. Grant was discharged in July of that year, and he finished the season with a 7-10 record. The Indians did not play well in 1963, but Grant managed to achieve his highest total of strike-outs with 157, and made his first All-Star team. He also became part of Cleveland's Community Relations Team. His personality made him a favorite to speak at churches, businesses and colleges. Between 1963 and 1964, Mudcat made more than 100 appearances. You could also catch "Mudcat and the Kittens," a nightclub act he created in and around all the jazz clubs in Cleveland. He even appeared on *The Tonight Show* with Johnny Carson. Jim and his wife Lucile gave birth to James Timothy, III, also known as "Tiny." They later adopted a second son, Rusty.

On June 15, 1964, Grant was traded to the Minnesota Twins for Lee Strange and George Banks. Grant went 11-9 his first year as a starter for Twins' manager, Sam Mele. Everything came together for the Twins in 1965, as they won a record 102 games that season. Grant gave all the credit to

Johnny Sain, his pitching coach, and to his team for their ability to score more runs. By 1967, you could find Grant in Los Angeles with the Dodgers. He and Zoilo Versalles were traded for John Roseboro, Bob Miller and Ron Perranoski. Grant loved being in L.A., even though Dodgers' manager Walter Alston used Jim out of the pen, as a reliever. Grant made 37 appearances, going 6-4 with a 2.06 ERA. Grant was selected by the Montreal Expos in the 1968 expansion draft. Jim was the Expos' very first pitcher in their first-ever game, played on April 8, 1969. He made 10 starts before being traded to the St. Louis Cardinals, in 1969. After that year, Grant was sold to the Oakland A's in 1970. Jim posted a 6-2 record with 24 saves, but was sold again to the Pittsburgh Pirates in September of the same year. Jim returned to Oakland, his last year, in August of 1971. Jim pitched his final game on September 29, 1971, at the age of 36. He retired from the game he loved in 1972.

Jim tried his hand at broadcasting for the Cleveland Indians and the Oakland A's, after baseball. He served as the pitching coach of the Durham Bulls in the mid 1980s. He also worked for an Anheuser-Busch distributor and sold Nationwide Insurance. He co-wrote a book in 2005 entitled The Black Aces, which gave an account of the 12 black Major League pitchers who had won 20 or more games in a single season. Those names include: Jim Grant, Vida Blue, Al Downing, Bob Gibson, Dwight Gooden, Ferguson Jenkins, Sam Jones, Don Newcombe, Mike Norris, J. R. Richard, Dave Stewart, and Earl Wilson. Three other African-American pitchers: David Price, CC Sabathia and Dontrelle Willis have also since topped the 20-win plateau. Jim and several of these guys were honored at the White House by then President George W. Bush, during Black History Month in 2007. Jim later moved his family to L.A., where he became a community activist.

Near the end, if you asked Mudcat, he would tell you all he wanted was one more start. Grant was inducted into the Baseball Reliquary's Shrine of the Eternals, in 2012. My friend Bill Lee became a member in 2000. Grant pitched professionally in 2,442 innings of the 571 games in which he appeared during his 14-year career (1958-1971). He started in 293 of them and threw 89 complete games. His career win-loss record stands at 145-119 with a 3.63 ERA and 54 saves. He batted .178 with 65 RBI'S. Grant hit a total of seven home runs, including his 1965 World Series blast. He recorded 1,267 strikeouts. He was a part of two All-Star Games, in 1963 and 1965, and led the American League in wins in 1965, with 21.

If you asked Jim Grant what was his greatest day in baseball, he would tell you, it was the day he signed his first professional baseball contract. It happened during Spring Training in 1958. After he signed, Jim placed his copy of the contract underneath his pillow and slept on it at night. "They say that if you put something underneath your pillow, it gets ingrained until you never forget it, and I never did forget that," said Jim.

Jim Mudcat Grant threw his last pitch in life on June 11, 2021. You don't miss yourself when you die, but you do miss those you've loved and those who have died before you. He was 85 years old and living with his family in Los Angeles, California. Jim Grant was some kind of a man, and he always chose wisdom over worry and peace over panic.

ELEVATING THE GAME

College Football Hall of Fame Coach, Pat Dye, once said, "Great football teams improve when they win. They are not satisfied with their performance." The fellow I'm writing about represented everything you would believe in the game of football. This guy had something very few coaches had, he connected with the fans. Young or old, it made no difference. He was one of them. This coach was a positive guy who understood that dark skies don't always mean rain, but he always looked like his dog had just died. The man squinted a bit when, he talked and the running joke was that if he ever fully opened his eyes you could be sure there would be six more weeks of summer. Squint as he might, this guy could also spot talent from an airplane. His impact as a coach went way beyond drawing up a play, and he worked his guys hard, yet never raised his voice. As their coach he gave his team leadership, excellence and a part of his big heart. He always thought his job was twofold, to either push his kids too far or push them to excel. As a head coach, he made sure everybody brought their A-Game every Saturday.

The man spent years teaching hard lessons to those who would listen and his players' dreams got bigger because he told them it was possible. Doing what you love to do with the people you care about just may be the definition of Heaven on earth. He also made a huge impression on the way the game is played today. At the end, his players would have walked on hot coals if they were told to do so. In this world, there could only be one Terry Donahue. If there were two, they would never stop trying to one up each other. There is no doubt the Terry Donahue elevated the game of college football. His legacy will live on in each of his players.

Terrence Michael Donahue was born on June 24, 1944, in Los Angeles, California. Terry was one of five boys in the family. He attended St. Charles Borromeo Elementary School, played football and graduated in 1962 from Notre Dame High School in Sherman Oaks. Because of his size, Terry was not recruited to play football in college, but that never stopped him. He walked on at San Jose State University his freshman year and then walked on at Los Angeles Valley College for one year. Terry also spent some time in the gym learning to box. He actually beat one fellow who outweighed him by 40 pounds. His next opponent was set to be Jerry Quarry, but Terry's father stepped in and put a stop to boxing. Terry would spend his final two college years at UCLA as a Bruin. He was scared every time he put on his uniform because he feared he would not live up to what was expected of him, yet he continued to show up and play. There he would play two seasons for the Bruins at defensive tackle, even though he stood only 6 feet tall and weighed 190 pounds. His 1965 team became the first Bruins team to win the Rose Bowl. This team was nicknamed the "Gutty Little Bruins," because nobody on the defensive line weighed more than 225 pounds; that is unheard of in today's game. Donahue graduated in 1966 with a degree in history. In 1968, you could find Terry at the University of Kansas as an unpaid defensive line coach for "Pepper" Rogers. Terry was allowed to eat with the team, but managed an apartment complex for money. He was paid $7,500 the following season.

Terry would follow Rogers to UCLA in 1971, as the offensive line coach. When Rogers left, new head coach Dick Vermeil took over and kept Donahue as an assistant. Terry Donahue became the UCLA Bruins head football coach in 1976, when Vermeil departed. Donahue led his Bruins to an upset over No. 3-ranked Arizona State, on a nationally televised Thursday night game, to open the 1976 season. The Bruins finished that season with 9-2-1 record in his first year as head coach. At first, he coached a ground oriented attack that was effective. *Sports Illustrated* announced that Donahue may be one of the best young coaches in the country. Donahue's best finish came in 1982 when he led the Bruins to a 10-1-1 record. He also posted two other ten-win seasons, in 1987 and 1988. Coach Donahue later flirted with the passing game with quarterbacks like Troy Aikman, Steve Bono, Jay Schroeder and Tommy Maddox. He understood that a rivalry game is the one you circle on your calendar. The longstanding rivalries are the ones that matter the most. His games with USC's John Robinson were important. In his final season as head coach, the Bruins defeated their arch rival, USC Trojans, for the fifth consecutive year. It was Donahue's 98th conference victory in the Pac-10, surpassing Don James for the most in conference history. He finished his 20-year coaching career at UCLA with a win-loss record of 151-74-8. Terry then announced he would be leaving his coaching job after the Aloha Bowl to work for CBS as a football analyst. He later acknowledged that he felt he had left coaching too soon.

Terry became the lead college football analyst for CBS, from 1996 to 1998. On January 1, 1997, I attended the Tostitos Fiesta Bowl in Tempe, Arizona, as a guest of the Pepsi Cola Company. My trip included a dinner two nights before the game. This is where I got to meet the CBS TV announcers, Terry Donahue and Jim Nance. Also present were the two head coaches of the Penn State Nittany Lions and the University of Texas Longhorns, Joe Paterno and John Mackovic. Running back Curtis Ennis of Penn State took on the Texas quarterback, James Brown, and UT running backs, Ricky Williams and Priest Holmes. With 65,105 fans on hand, the score ended 38-15, with Penn State on top. Texas outrushed Penn State and actually led at halftime, 12-7.

Terry Donahue left CBS to join the San Francisco 49ers' front office in 1999. In 2001, Terry was handpicked by Bill Walsh to become the 49ers General Manager. He would hold that job for four years. Donahue was fired, along with the 49ers' head coach Dennis Erickson, in January of 2005. In 2006, Donahue landed at the *NFL on FOX*. Terry also served as an analyst on *College Football Now* on *NFL Network* and *Dial Global*.

Donahue still owns the most wins of any coach in UCLA football history. Donahue had been a head coach for 20 years at UCLA, and his teams had finished ranked in the top 20, on 12 occasions during his tenure. His team also finished in the top 10 five times from 1982-1988. His teams won three Rose Bowls and five Pac-10 championships, but unfortunately, they never won a national championship. Terry coached 34 first-team All-Americans, and 14 of his players were chosen in the first round of the NFL Draft.

Terry Donahue was the first to participate in the Rose Bowl as a player, assistant coach and head coach. He recorded an 8-4-1 win-loss record in bowl games and became the first coach to win a bowl game in seven consecutive seasons. Terry was also chosen as the Pac-10 Coach of the Year twice, in 1985 and 1993. In 1998, Terry was offered the opportunity to coach in the NFL, by the Dallas Cowboys. He would have been reunited with Troy Aikman, but it was not meant to be. Negotiations with Jerry Jones went south, and Chan Gaily was hired instead. He was also contacted by the Rams and Falcons for their head-coaching jobs, but chose to stay at UCLA. Terry Donahue was inducted into the Rose Bowl Hall of Fame in 1997 and the College Football Hall of Fame as a coach in 2000. In 2001, he was selected to the UCLA Athletics Hall of Fame. In 2005, Terry joined the Sun

Bowl Hall of Fame, and the press box at the Rose Bowl was dedicated as the Terry Donahue Pavilion, in 2013.

Terry Donahue died at his home at Newport Beach, California, on July 4, 2021, after a two-year battle with cancer. He was 77 years old and is survived by his wife, Andrea, whom he met on a blind date in 1968, at the University of Kansas. They married two weeks after she graduated in 1969. They had three daughters, Nicole, Michele and Jennifer, and ten grandchildren. His life did not pass unnoticed. Even though he has left us now, there is no doubt for me that he's still winning.

THE THRILL IS GONE

Manager Jim Leyland once said, "If you go to work every day worried about your job, then you don't really have one." When this boy showed up for a tryout, he was just an overgrown kid, who wanted to have fun.

Everything that happens to us in life, good or bad, becomes a part of us, but it does not define who we are. We get to decide that. Here is his story. Off the field, he was a gentleman at heart—on the field, anything went. He was no ordinary pitcher. Watching this fellow throw put a smile on your face, unless you had a bat in your hands. Many an opponent begged out of the game when this guy was on the mound. It has been said that he could throw a baseball through a carwash and not get it wet and thought nothing of knocking you down in the dugout. There was nothing normal about this fellow's right arm. His style of pitching was tenacious. The man threw lasers. They should have named a meteor after him. There he stood on the loneliest spot in the world, the pitcher's mound at the Astrodome. He wasn't out there to sell you ice cream; the man was going to strike you out. This fellow was like a baby giraffe, all arms and legs. He stood six feet eight inches tall, but on the mound he appeared to be nine feet tall. His wing span was off the charts and his side arm fastball to a right-handed batter came directly at their ribs. With huge hands, he reminded me of Eagles' wide-receiver Harold Carmichael with a glove. This guy would become one of the most dominant pitchers to ever step on any baseball diamond, and the truth is that most of his opponents were scared to death of him.

He could be flawless on the baseball diamond and just wild enough to get everyone's attention. The man was a scary guy and in complete control. As soon as he stepped on the pitcher's mound, you could hear a pin drop. He was so much better than his competition and he always kept his foot on the gas. You could fall in love with watching J. R. Richard throw a baseball. He always looked deliberate, never in a hurry. The bigger the moment, the better J. R. threw. You would rather face Mike Tyson in a squared ring during his prime than a J. R. Richard fastball. Why do we only appreciate things from the past instead of at the time? Some would say the thrill is gone, but when I close my eyes, I can see Richard even now. He's throwing hard again, clipping corners, shaving letters, and moving that guy with the big stick in his hands back from home plate. And when his fastball pops that catcher's mitt, the backstop looks up and out at him and calls him... Baby!

J. R. Richard became the medicine this Astros' team needed. No wonder his favorite pitcher was Bob Gibson. I once asked J. R. if he could change anything, what it would be. "I'd love to start all over again," he said, with a smile. There was only one Mark Twain, one Albert Einstein, one Ernest Hemmingway and one J. R. Richard. He was born to perform. Manager Jimmy Dykes once described a rookie pitcher's first big league start like this: "You are just like a mouse in a cage with nine big cats." I think it may have been the other way around with J. R. Richard.

Every legend has a beginning. His started in Vienna, Louisiana. James Rodney Richard was born into a middle-class black family on March 7, 1950, to Clayton and Lizzie Richard. His dad, Clayton, called him J. R. Athletically talented, Richard gained notoriety while playing basketball and baseball at Lincoln High School located in nearby Ruston, Louisiana. By his senior year, J. R. had topped out at 6 feet 8 inches tall and weighed 220 pounds. J. R. was simply magnificent. Richard did not lose a single game he started in high school or concede a run for the entirety of his senior season. In one game, J. R. hit four consecutive home runs, while pitching his team to a 48-0 win against their local rival, Jonesboro Jackson High School. J. R. was selected by the Houston Astros with the second overall pick of the 1969 Amateur MLB Draft. Outfielder Jeff Burroughs went to the Washington Senators with the first pick. Richard would turn down over 200 basketball scholarship offers to sign with the Houston Astros. The $100,000 signing bonus made it an easy decision.

Richard was sent to the Covington Astros, a rookie-level minor league team in the Appalachian League. He was but 19. Richard started 12 games, but won only five. He struck out 71 batters, but also walked 52, while giving up 42 earned runs. Control problems and poor mechanics resulted in a 6.59 ERA. J. R. was promoted to the Cocoa Astros of the Florida State League in 1970. Despite a 4-11 win-loss record, his ERA came down to 2.39 and he even threw a no-hitter against the Daytona Beach Dodgers. But there was something else that was discovered. Not only did his slider top out at 94 miles per hour, but his fastball reached 100 miles per hour. Richard once said in an interview, "You never learn anything about pitching until you get tired."

During the 1970-71 off season, Richard was given the #50 and promoted again to the Oklahoma City 89ers of Class-AAA. His teammates referred to him as "The Big Fellow." He would wear the #50 for the rest of his career. In 1971, Richard threw eight complete games and led the league with 202 strikeouts in 173 innings of work. He recorded 12 wins and seven losses, before being called up to the Houston Astros. His career moment occurred the day he was called up to the Major Leagues. On September 5, 1971, at the age of 21, Richard debuted for the Houston Astros in the second game of a doubleheader at Candlestick Park, against the San Francisco Giants. The Astros had won Game One 1-0, with Jack Billingham striking out 11. The Giants were a formidable bunch led by four future Hall of Fame players: centerfielder Willie Mays, first baseman Willie McCovey, and pitchers Gaylord Perry and Juan Marichal. Mays played first base that day as McCovey was injured in Game One and Dave Kingman was suffering from appendicitis. Mays became J. R. Richard's very first strikeout, swinging, in Major League baseball. It was an auspicious beginning as Richard eventually struck out Willie Mays three times and totaled 15 strikeouts for a complete game win. Those 15 strikeouts by Richard tied Brooklyn Dodger pitcher Karl Spooner's 17-year-old record for most strikeouts by a pitcher in their first start. Interestingly, Spooner had also set the record against Mays' 1954 Giants' team. The Astros won that day, 5-3. You see, there had been no television coverage or national radio broadcast about Richard. The Giants were not aware of his 100 mph fastball or 94 mph slider. After the game, Richard and Billingham celebrated their combined 26 strikeout record thrown by a team's starters in a twin bill. This record has been tied, but still stands today.

Five days later Richard went to the mound again, but this time gave up a lead-off home run to Pete Rose in the first inning. Still, J. R. pitched five innings and gave up only two hits and the one run. He struck out five, but walked six. Richard struggled in his next two starts and spent the next several years between the Minors and Majors. Because of his wildness, he did not become a regular starter until 1975.

During the off season, between 1974 and 1975, the Astros traded pitcher Claude Osteen to the Cardinals and lost their ace, Don Wilson, who died from carbon monoxide poisoning on January 5, 1975. Wilson was 29. Richard began the

1975 season as the staff's third starting pitcher behind Larry Dierker and Dave Roberts. This flame-throwing right-hander continued to throw the ball with his effectively wild delivery. He went from pitching a complete game to walking 11 in just six innings. By the All-Star break, Richard had six wins, four losses and a 4.93 ERA in 98 innings of work. J. R. ended the season by winning three of his last four starts. Interestingly, his 12-10 win-loss record was tops for the Astros' pitching staff, and he was the only starter to have a winning record. Not only did he lead the staff with 176 strikeouts, but also led the National League with walks allowed and wild pitches thrown, with 138 and 20, respectively.

Richard experienced his breakout season in 1976. First, he took Larry Dierker's place as Opening Day starter. His season started out slowly, but by the All-Star break, his record stood at 9-9 with a 2.88 ERA. On August 26th he hit his first home run of the season. By August 31st, J. R. had improved his record to 16-13 and finished the season strong, with a 20-15 win-loss record, 14 complete games, three shutouts and 214 strikeouts. At age 26, J. R. was indeed something to watch.

In 1977, Richard finished the year leading the Astros staff in wins, starts, complete games, innings pitched, walks and strikeouts. His totals read 18-12 with 214 strikeouts, which tied him with Steve Carlton for the season high mark. Richard also hit two triples, two home runs, and recorded seven RBI's. At the end of the season, J. R. underwent an emergency appendectomy. He would spend the rest of the off-season fishing and recuperating.

Richard was the Opening Day starter again in 1978. He finished the season breaking Tom Seavers' record of 290 strikeouts by a right-hander, with 303. He also hit his seventh home run making him the Astros' career leader in home runs by a pitcher. He finished the season with 18 wins and 11 losses with a 3.11 ERA. He finished fourth behind Gaylord Perry, Burt Hooton and Vida Blue, in the Cy Young race.

The 1979 season started with Richard uncorking six wild pitches, a modern-day record in a single game at that time. Still, he finished the game with 13 strikeouts and a 2-1 Astros win. J. R. Richard would strike out 313 batters that year and join Nolan Ryan and Sandy Koufax as the only modern day pitchers to strike out 300 or more batters in consecutive seasons. With an 18-13 record, he finished third behind Bruce Sutter and teammate, Joe Niekro, in the Cy Young vote. On October 11th, Richard signed a four-year contract with Houston.

In 1980, Richard was now paired with Nolan Ryan. He was named the National League Pitcher of the Month for April. On July 3rd, J. R. was 10 and 4, and passed Larry Dierker in career strikeouts with 1,487. On July 8th, he was selected to start for the National League in the All-Star Game. He would pitch just two innings before complaining of pain in his arm and back. It fell on deaf ears. A few days after the 1980 All-Star Game, J. R. suffered a stroke and nearly died. The last game he pitched occurred on July 14, 1980. Although he started that game, later he complained of not being able to see the catcher's signs. He left the game in the fourth inning and the Astros placed him on the 21-day disabled list. The media reported he was a complainer and that he was jealous of Ryan's $4.5 million contract. Nine days later he checked into the Methodist Hospital in Houston for a series of tests. An angiogram revealed an obstruction in his right arm. On July 25th, the doctors reached a conclusion that all was normal and he did not need surgery. On July 30th, he visited a chiropractor who rotated his neck to fix the blood flow to his right arm. Later that day, while warming up, he suffered a stroke. He had emergency surgery that night. He had a synthetic graft inserted into the blood vessel in his left leg. A CAT scan of his brain showed that he had actually experienced three strokes from different obstructions. He underwent rehabilitation and missed the rest of the season. His wife Carolyn told reporters, "It took death, or near-death, to get an apology. They should have believed him." Richard was eventually cut by the Astros in 1984, after trying to make a comeback. J. R. Richard started 221 games and pitched 1,606 innings in 238 games, during his 10-year career with Astros. His record stands at 107-71, with 1,493 strikeouts and a 3.15 ERA. Richard recorded 93 hits with ten home runs and 50 RBI's. He also stole two bases.

I was very fortunate to meet "The Big Fellow" on several occasions. The first time we met he was signing autographs for the public at Padre Staples Mall here in Corpus Christi, Texas. We hit it off instantly. I had him sign a baseball and a photo. But, the best visit was when he was invited to attend a Corpus Christi Double-A Hooks Baseball banquet at the Solomon Ortiz Center. I was working that night rounding up interviews for the "Dennis & Andy's Q & A Session" radio show. He remembered me and asked me to sit with him at his table while he signed autographs for his fans. We later had a picture taken together by the Hooks' photographer. That photo is included in my book entitled This Close to Greatness.

Cincinnati Reds, Dave Parker, once said about Richard, "When he...let the ball go, he looked like he was 10 feet away from you instead of 60, which caused you to lean a little bit and made you think you had to swing the bat quicker."

I think part of the secret of J. R. Richard was that he was totally unpredictable. Every Major League pitcher will tell you that the location of a pitch is more important than its movement or velocity. Movement is a matter of spin that can be used on every pitch. Velocity is mostly God-given, but it can be improved by increasing your arm strength.

The best pitchers always have the ability to make one thing look like another. They are like magicians. They make fast pitches look slow and vice versa. They make balls look like strikes and strikes look like balls. They are also never afraid of losing, because they always believed they are going to win. For that reason they became totally unpredictable.

After baseball J. R. returned to Louisiana and entered into the oil business. He suffered a financial loss of over $300,000 in a business scam which also eventually cost him his marriage and another $669,000 in a divorce settlement to his ex-wife, Carolyn. J. R. would marry and divorce again, this time losing his home and most of the rest of his savings. He did play ball again with the Orlando Juice of the Senior Professional Baseball Association in 1989, but was later released. By 1994, the Houston Chronicle reported that J. R. Richard was homeless and living under highway 59 overpass at Beechnut Road in Houston. How could this be? In 1995, Richard finally became eligible for his Major League Baseball pension. He even appeared and played in the Astros Old-Timers' Day Game with the Astros.

Richard reached out to reverend Floyd Lewis, the minister of the Now Testament Church. With the help of this church and Lewis, Richard regained his confidence, started drawing his pension, got a job working for an asphalt company, and overcame his homelessness. J. R. Richard, a God-fearing man, became a local Christian minister and worked in the Houston community helping establish baseball programs for kids. "I always knew God was on my side," said Richard.

In 2005, the movie *Resurrection: The J. R. Richard Story*, described Richard's baseball career and his life afterwards. J. R. Richard became the ninth member of The Black Aces, an organization founded by Jim "Mudcat" Grant that consisted of all African-American pitchers who had won at least 20 or more Major League games in a single season. By

2012, you could find J.R. in the Astros' Walk of Fame. In 2015, Lew Freedman wrote a book about Richard entitled <u>Still Throwing Heat: Strikeouts, the Streets, and a Second Chance</u>. Richard was also honored in 2018 by the Negro League Baseball Hall of Fame, along with Eddie Murray, Kenny Lofton, Jim "Mudcat" Grant and Dick Allen. In 2019, Richard was inducted into the Baseball Reliquary's Shrine of the Eternals.

J. R. Richard died in a Houston hospital on August 4, 2021. He was at peace. It has been reported by his family that he had not received the vaccination for Covid-19 and experienced complications from the virus. The fire that had burned so brightly inside of him finally went out. He was only 71 years old. The kid whose father told him not to quit, never stopped. His passion for the game was contagious.

Intimidating on the mound, he became a pitcher with an exclamation point and he could beat the Dodgers. I later spoke with Texas Legend Nolan Ryan about Richard. When asked what the difference was between himself and J. R., Nolan answered, "His slider. J. R. had a great slider and no one wanted to stand in the batters box with him on the mound."

I'm sad and angry, but blessed to have spent a few minutes and shared a laugh or two with J. R. Richard. I hoped he liked me as much as I like him. I was lucky enough to call him a friend. Sometimes life goes by faster than a 6-4-3 double play.

1. Got to meet Hank Aaron in 1974 before he hit home run #715.

2. Irv Cross helped broadcast a 1992 Monday Night Football game in Houston, Texas.

3. I attended the 1975 Peach Bowl between West Virginia and N. C. State. It was there that I first saw the Mountaineers' Head Football Coach, Bobby Bowden.

4. Having lunch with center Mark Eaton of the Utah Jazz, at the 1993 NBA All-Star Game in Salt Lake City.

5. Hanging out with my good friend, Astros' pitcher, J. R. Richards.

6. On April 17, 2021, Bart Shirley, former infielder of the Los Angeles Dodgers, joined me at a book signing event.

7. Met former Chicago Cubs shortstop, Don Kessinger, at a Corpus Christi Hooks game on June 20, 2021.

8. Every Friday the R.O.M.E.O. Club meets for lunch (Retired Old Men Eating Out). I'm joined by Bobby Smith, Charles Durham, Mark Dannhoff, Marty Robinson, Buddy Kirk, Ike Isaacson, Beto Contreras, Bart Shirley, and Richard Avila.

9. I got to meet skipper Bill Virdon in Houston, at an Astros' Caravan Event in 1997.

10. Lunch with Buffalo Bills' Bobby Smith and University of Texas Hall-of-Famer, Tom Campbell.

11. Interviewed new Corpus Christi Islanders'
basketball coach, Steve Lutz, before the season
started. Lutz led his very first team to the
2022 NCAA Basketball Tournament.

12. In March of 1988, I got to meet
K. C. Jones at a Seattle Supersonics
vs. San Antonio Spurs' game, played
at the old Hemisphere Arena.

13. Met Elgin Baylor at the 1992 NBA All-Star Game, in Orlando, Florida.

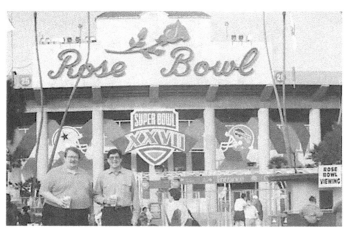

14. Attended Super Bowl XXVII in Los Angeles, with my great friend Andy Mouland.

15. Took this photo of football coach, Marty Schottenheimer, of the Kansas City Chiefs. The Chiefs were in town with Joe Montana to play the Houston Oilers.

16. Vaughn Johnson was one of the hardest hitters to ever wear the Black and Gold for the New Orleans Saints.

17. Met and interviewed Tommy Lasorda several times and even played golf with him in 1983.

18. Met and had dinner with college football analyst, Terry Donahue at the 1996 Tostitos Fiesta Bowl in Tempe, Arizona.

19. No one knew football like John Madden.

20. Joined by two of the best, halfback Butch Pressley and linebacker Shane Nelson, at a book signing event.

DADGUM

A small guy in stature; some joked that he was the size of a 50-cent glass of beer. He was suntanned; most often wore a hat, and stood with his hands on his hips while speaking. A storyteller at heart, all the Purvis side of my family looked and spoke like him. The man was everyone's friend. He could have easily been my uncle. The more you got to know him, the more respect you had for him. He was a very simple guy, a country boy from Birmingham, Alabama. As a kid, he was so ugly that his friends joked that his parents had to tie a pork chop around his neck to make the dogs play with him. Like me, this fellow grew up on the front porch. He was "down home," a Christian, with a voice as smooth as grandma's molasses. When he spoke it sounded like he had marbles in his mouth. While squinting, he used words like "dadgum," "pert-near perfect," and "sho'nuff." He put peanuts in his soft drinks, chewed on unlit cigars, was a ham for photos, and would even chew tobacco on occasion. This guy was a ray of sunshine among the darkest clouds; an artist with a whistle instead of a paint brush. He had that Blue Collar work ethic and could keep you loose or put you on edge in a heartbeat. That voice is never silenced; all I have to do is close my eyes to hear him again.

As an athlete, all we need is one coach who believes in us, and it can change your life or save it. The media referred to him as the "King of the Living Room," for his ability to persuade blue-chip players to come play for him. He could be magnetic and electrifying, while making others think like a winner and get them to believe in themselves. When a man gives you his time, he's giving you a part of his life. Bobby Bowden was funny, all right; this guy knew how to win a room. The man could recruit with the best, and some said he could even catch a fish in a kitchen sink full of dirty dishes. One of the secrets of being a really good coach is that everything remains the same until you find the right players. Then everything changes. Bowden motivated through compassion, not fear or intimidation. He was very engaging. When coach spoke, his kids listened. They didn't always understand, but they listened. Bowden's kids wouldn't blow their noses without his permission. His teams came at you at warp speed, both offensively and defensively, and he needed you to understand how hard you had to play and how long you needed to play hard.

Hall of Fame Coach, Bill Walsh, once said, "Criticism is like beef jerky. It's tough and hard to chew, but it has everything you need. Now get out of my face." In my time, your coach was trusted and respected. Everyone listened when they spoke. A coach teaches his kids about life through his stories. In this case, the tale was about the Lion and the Gazelle. They both slept at night and woke up every morning with different agendas. They both would run, but one was running to something and one was running away from something. You're either the Lion or the Gazelle he'd say, so be the Lion. There is no doubt that Bobby Bowden was the Lion.

Robert Cleckler (Bobby) Bowden was born in Birmingham, Alabama, the college football capitol of the South. The date will read November 8, 1929. He grew up in a small white three-bedroom house behind Woodlawn football stadium. His dad was a banker and his mom a homemaker. Bobby and his dad would sit on the roof of their house and watch the Woodlawn football team practice. At the age of five, his family moved to the East Lake section of Birmingham. In

January of 1943, Bobby made his way home from the YMCA after basketball practice. His knees were killing him, and his parents decided to take him to the doctor. As a 13-year-old child, Bobby was told by the doctor that he had an enlarged heart and rheumatic fever. Therefore, his parents were told he would never be able to participate in sports. He remembered lying in bed, praying to his God for good health, and listening to news about World War II on the family radio. Some think that's where his strength in faith all began for Bobby. Later in life, Bowden became excited when talking about some of the great generals from the war. "Rommel was a great tactician," said Bowden. "He knew how to think in surprises, and he could do more with less than any of the great generals. They all demonstrate discipline and that you need reserves, so if you're getting annihilated on one front, you can attack somewhere else." Some think that his analogies between football and battlefields were a vital part of his Hall-of-Fame coaching career.

Since he couldn't play ball, he played the trombone in the high school band. Eventually, the doctors allowed him to chase his dream. While standing only 5 feet 5 inches tall and weighing 120 pounds, Bobby became a star football running back while at Woodlawn High School, for Coach Kenny Morgan. Bowden was so good he was offered a scholarship to play for the University of Alabama football team, as a freshman. But sometimes love conquers all. Bobby, now a backup quarterback, became tired of sitting on the bench and not playing, and he also missed his high-school sweetheart, Ann Estock. Even though the Alabama campus was only 45 minutes away from Birmingham, Bowden was homesick for Ann, who was still attending high school. After one semester, he transferred to Howard College, now known as Samford University, located in Birmingham.

Bobby and Ann eloped and drove to Rising Fawn, Georgia,

where they were married in 1949 by the justice of the peace for $20. He was 19 and she was 16. Together they had six kids. Three of his sons, Tommy, Terry and Jeff, would all have careers coaching in college football. Tommy served as the head football coach at Clemson University and Tulane, while Bobby's son Terry was the head coach at the University of Auburn and the 1993 Coach of the Year. A third son, Jeff, served as the offensive coordinator at Florida State.

His senior year at Howard, Bowden was selected "Little All-American" at the quarterback position. Bobby graduated from Howard in 1953. From 1954-1955, Bowden served at Howard as the assistant football coach and head of the track and field team. In 1956, he left Howard and became the head football, baseball and basketball coach at South Georgia College. There, he built a winning football program. He returned to Howard and coached the football team from 1959 to 1962, posting a 31-6 win-loss record. Bowden's idol was "Bear" Bryant and he spent lots of time talking football with Alabama assistant Gene Stallings. Bowden also solicited the help of Bart Starr for five weeks to work with the Howard offense on their passing game. During the next three seasons, Howard went 24-4. Heads began to turn in his direction. In 1962, Bowden was hired by then-head coach, Bill Peterson of Florida State. Bobby stayed until 1965, and then left for the University of West Virginia, to become their assistant football coach under Jim Carlen. Carlen left in 1969 to become the Texas Tech head football coach, and Bowden replaced him. In 1974, West Virginia posted a 4-7 record. It was Bowden's first losing season as a head coach. His likeness was hung in effigy all around campus. His son, Terry, who was flanker on the football team, was upset. It didn't seem to bother Bowden at all. In 1975, West Virginia rebounded at 9-3 and beat N. C. State in the Peach Bowl. My friend, Don Guthrie and I attended that game in Atlanta,

Georgia. All we heard all night in our hotel room was "Go Mountaineers." That was Bobby Bowden's last game as the head coach for West Virginia. Bobby compiled a 42-26 record with the Mountaineers, before returning again to Florida State as their head football coach, in 1976.

The Seminole program was almost dead on the doorstep. They had won only 4 of 33 games in their three previous years. Bowden later admitted that he only took the job to help get a better job, hopefully at Alabama. By his second year, Bowden's team went 9-2. During the next 34 years, he would post only one losing season, his first (5-6). He would eventually decline head-coaching positions at LSU, Alabama, Auburn and the Atlanta Falcons of the National Football League. Every season from 1987 to 2000, the Seminoles finished with at least 10 wins and top 5 in the national polls. Florida State joined the Atlantic Coast Conference (ACC) in 1992 and won nine conference titles.

Since Clemson and Florida State were now both in the same conference, (ACC) their games played from 1999 to 2007 became known as the Bowden Bowl. Why? Because both clubs were coached by an opposing father (Bobby) and son (Tommy) duo, a first in Division I College Football. Bobby would hold the winning edge at 5-4. Bowden posted an incredible 304-97-4 win-loss record while at Florida State.

There's a wonderful story about Bobby and his son Tommy, recruiting against one another. While in high school, Jeff Francoeur played football and baseball. He was a terrific wide receiver and defensive back on the football team. Jeff led Parkview High School, located in Lilburn, Georgia, to the State 5A High School Football Championships, in 2000 and 2001. He also led his high school to the State 5A Baseball Championships, in 2001 and 2002. He was recruited for both sports near and far, by many colleges. Head football Coach, Tommy Bowden from Clemson University, was

228

after Francoeur to play for the Tigers, and he offered Jeff a scholarship to play wide receiver. Picture a scene where Tommy Bowden was visiting Jeff's family on a recruiting trip, when the phone rang in their home. As the conversation transpired Tommy Bowden realized that his dad, Bobby Bowden, the head football coach at Florida State, is the one who is calling Jeff. Tommy Bowden asked Jeff if he could have the phone and Jeff complied. Tommy then says, "Hey, Dad, it's me, I'll call you back." "It was an awkward scene," said Jeff. "But I also played baseball, and the Atlanta Braves lured me away from football, with a two-million-dollar offer to play baseball."

Tommy was later interviewed by 60 Minutes II and spoke about his dad. "On game day, he's Old Testament, an eye for an eye, tooth for a tooth. The love, grace and mercy of the New Testament, that's not covered until Monday after the game."

In 1978, my longtime sports radio partner, Dennis Quinn, spent an afternoon on the golf course with Florida State head football coach, Bobby Bowden. Everyone knew that Bowden's second love was golf. Dennis was the Sports Director for the ABC affiliate in Pensacola, Florida, known as WEAR Channel 3. Bowden had arrived at Florida State in 1976 and was out recruiting. "Pensacola was known for their abundance of great high school athletes, and Bowden wanted to get his face out there in the public and be on television," said Dennis. A local Seminole booster asked Dennis if he would play a round of golf with Bowden. Dennis was not a golfer, but he decided to drive the golf cart for the two. "He was funny, and so entertaining," said Quinn. "His players loved him, and I became a big fan."

Bobby Bowden once said, "Football is the front porch of your university." You can't begin to understand the game of college football in the Deep South, unless you go to a Florida

State Seminoles' football game. One of the great events, this game is all about surviving history. Not only will the Seminoles beat your brains out during the game, but they will scare you to death as you're leaving. Trick plays became the signature of Bowden's high-scoring, thrill-a-minute offense. His vision of playing his best athletes on defense helped pave the way to the Florida State dynasty. But all the trick plays would not have mattered if Bowden had not been able to recruit players capable of executing those plays.

There are football jobs and then there's coaching at Florida State.

Bobby Bowden was around a total of 44 years as a head football coach at Samford, West Virginia and Florida State. He won two national championships at Florida State, in 1993 and 1999. Over 150 Florida State players were drafted by NFL teams, and three have been inducted into the Pro Football Hall of Fame. Bowden once said, "I wanted my kids to think they were better people because they played for me."

Bowden coached many great college players, including two Heisman Trophy winners. In 1993, quarterback Charlie Ward won the award, and also quarterback Chris Weinke, in the year 2000. You will also recognize some of his other All-Americans: defensive back Deion Sanders, linemen Walter Jones and Ron Simmons, receiver Peter Warrick, linebacker Derrick Brooks and kicker Sebastian Janikowski. Of this group, Deion Sanders, Walter Jones and Derrick Brooks ended up in the Pro Football Hall of Fame. Bobby Bowden once said, "Your reputation is what people say about you. Your character is what God knows about you. Character is so much more important than reputation." Interestingly, Bowden was inducted into the College Football Hall of Fame in 2006, while he was still an active coach.

Along the way, Bowden also coached many future head football coaches. Of course his sons, Tommy and Terry, make the list along with Mark Richt, Chuck Amato and Skip Holtz. Add Kirby Smart, Daryl Dickey, Manny Diaz and "Jimbo" Fisher to that list, and you began to see a pattern of success.

Bowden was an engineer of life and co-authored four books. He had a huge belief in his system. If you heard him say it once, you may have heard it a hundred times. "There are five steps to coaching a football team. Number one is preparation, number two is preparation, number three is preparation, number four is preparation and number five is "Go play the game."

In his own unique way, head football Coach Bobby Bowden once told a wide receiver, "Son, you've got a good engine, but your hands aren't on the steering wheel." He was letting this kid know that yes, he could run fast, but his hands were not good enough to catch passes. Perfection and dominance may have been his best traits during his time. He believed that in order to win, you had to not lose. That means you had to play defense. Your offense had to play well enough not to get your defense in trouble. The worst part of being a coach is watching from the sidelines. Everyone wants to play. Some of us are just not built to sit and watch. Bobby Bowden lived his life with one foot in Heaven. He was known for taking cat naps occasionally and there are several photos of him napping on the plane or in a car. They always make me smile. He always credited his success in football to his faith. I always wondered why he tried so hard to fit in, when he was born to stand out.

Bowden received the Bobby Dodd Coach of the Year Award in 1980. He also collected the Walter Camp Coach of the Year Award in 1991. In 1992, Bowden received the United States Sports Academy's Amos Alonzo Stagg Coaching Award in recognition of his outstanding achievement as a coach. In 2011, in recognition of his efforts with the Fellowship of Christian Athletes, Bowden received the Children's Champion Award for Leadership Development from the Children's Hunger Fund.

Bowden recorded 40 winning seasons during his 44 years of coaching, including 33 at Florida State. While at Florida State, Bobby coached the Seminoles to 14 straight seasons with 10 or more wins, and his teams also finished their season ranked in the top five of all the major polls. While at Samford, West Virginia and Florida State, Bowden collected 377 wins, second only to Penn State's Joe Paterno. Bowden's record in bowl games (21-10-1) also stands out.

Bobby Bowden was diagnosed with Covid-19 in October of 2020, but survived. In July 2021, Bobby Bowden shared with the world that he was terminally ill with pancreatic cancer. Coach Bobby Bowden passed away quietly at his home on a Sunday morning in Tallahassee, Florida. Bowden had spent his life coaching, teaching, and preaching. The date will read August 8, 2021. He was 91. Coach was surrounded by family and loved ones. His body lay in state, and a memorial service was held in the Tucker Civic Center in Tallahassee on August 14, 2021. The man who resurrected college football in the state of Florida was buried in Trussville, Alabama. "He was an outstanding example of class and character," said Alabama Coach, Nick Saban. Bobby Bowden once said in his own funny way, about being a head coach, "We're all in the same car, but I'm driving." He was so honest and genuine. Bobby changed the way the game is played. Bowden was a father figure, the guiding light for his players. The lives he touched will be his legacy.

EXCELLENCE IN THE CREASE

The National Hockey League has got to be the Bloody Mary of sports. You can get killed playing hockey. Seeing a guy throw his gloves on the ice is like watching the gates open at the Kentucky Derby. On the ice, every shift could be life or death. Hockey is one of the few games where you take your teeth out to play. Professional hockey players pass out skull fractures for a living. I'm surprised the Stanley Cup is not full of blood. Most of our hockey heroes can't do a double Lutz, a camel or a sit-spin, but they are the guys who take you into a corner and knock you off the puck. There is an old saying that seeing a goal scored in hockey is like picking your brother out of a crowd shot at the World Series. Darn near impossible.

Standing 5 feet 11 inches tall, weighing 185 pounds, and left-handed, he was the perfect size for goaltending. One of the few goalies to be left-handed, he used his dominant left hand to hold his stick and blocker and wore his glove on his right hand. This fellow was also one strong son-of-a-gun. You couldn't beat him on the short side; he was just too quick in the crease. The shaded blue area directly in front of a hockey goal is called the crease. This area is usually designated with a red boundary line. This space is where the goalie stops most of the opposing team's attempts to score and where initially opposing players were prohibited from interfering with the goalie. The crease belonged to the goalie, and the puck had to enter the crease first before an attacking player could enter. It's the goalie's safe zone. In 1999, the NHL abolished the "no crease" rule and now allows attacking players to enter the crease without the puck, but they still cannot interfere with the goalie. This fellow with a Canadian-American upbringing won the Vezina Trophy, awarded to the goaltender of the team which allowed the fewest goals scored in the regular season, three times, but his voice sounded like two of them were stuck in his throat.

Referred to as a legend on the ice, he exuded leadership and class, while becoming one of the most dominant players ever seen at his position. If I wanted to see ice skating, I'd go see Holiday on Ice. If I wanted to see professional hockey, I watched the Chicago Blackhawks and Tony Esposito.

Esposito is not remembered so much for what he did, but the way he did it. In the late 1960s, Tony Esposito helped pioneer the now popular "butterfly style" of goaltending. This style allowed the goaltender to guard the lower half of the net by dropping to their knees on the ice, while spreading their feet apart and touching their knees together. Until then, goaltenders used the stand-up style to block attempts to score with their sticks, their blocker and their gloved hand. The butterfly style was believed to be first used by Glenn Hall of the Chicago Blackhawks, in 1961. Interestingly, Hall played his entire career without wearing a mask. On November 1, 1959, after receiving a shot to the face, Jacques Plante, goaltender for the Montreal Canadians became the first goalie to regularly wear a mask.

Anthony James "Tony O" Esposito was born on April 23, 1943, in Sault Ste. Marie, Ontario, just across the St. Mary's River from Michigan's Upper Peninsula. His older brother, Phil, was a star in his own right. Phil played 18 years in the NHL and became a Hall-of-Fame center. Tony attended college at Michigan Tech and became a three-year varsity letter winner in ice hockey. Tony was selected a three-time first-team All-American and helped the Huskies win an NCAA Championship during the 1964-65 season. Tony also became a three-time All-WCHA first-team selection (Western Collegiate Hockey Association). In 2021, Tony was named to the WCHA All-Decade Team for the 1960s. Tony turned professional in 1967, when he joined the Vancouver Canucks of the Western Hockey League. He also played with the Houston Apollos of the Central Hockey League, in 1968. At the age of 25, Tony joined the Montreal Canadians of the NHL (National Hockey League). At that time, Tony was only the third American college player to be selected by an NHL team. Wearing #35, Tony made his first appearance in an NHL game against the Oakland Seals. He played 26 minutes while relieving goalie Rogie Vachon.

Tony's first start in the NHL was on December 5, 1968, against the Boston Bruins and his brother, Phil. Phil scored twice on his younger brother, but Tony recorded 33 saves in a game that ended in a 2 to 2 tie. Tony would play in 13 regular season games that season, and then he was sent back down to the minor leagues. The Montreal Canadians beat the New York Rangers and Boston Bruins to advance to the Stanley Cup Finals. The Canadians then beat the St. Louis Blues, four games to none, and won the Stanley Cup that year. Tony Esposito had been called back up for the playoffs after goalie "Gump" Worsley had been injured, so his name was included on the winner's cup. Luckily for the Chicago Blackhawks, Tony Esposito was left unprotected by the Canadians in 1969.

In 1969, the Blackhawks claimed Tony Esposito on waivers during the intra-league draft, for the mere sum of $25,000. Timing is everything. Tony had a spectacular season with the Blackhawks, posting a 2.17 GAA (Goals Against Average) and set the modern-day record with 15 shutouts, which won him the Calder Memorial Trophy as the league's best rookie. He also won his first Vezina Trophy and was named to his First All-Star Game. It was during this record-setting season that the fans gave him his nickname "Tony O" for his ability to shutout the opponent. He proved again during the 1970 season that he was one of the league's top goaltenders, as he helped the Blackhawks finish first in the NHL's West Division. Chicago made it to the 1971 Stanley Cup Finals, but lost in seven games (4-3) to the Montreal Canadians. In 1971, Esposito posted the lowest GAA of his career (1.77) and shared the Vezina Trophy with backup Gary Smith. He was again selected to the NHL's First All-Star Team. In 1972, Tony was named to Team Canada for the Summit Series. Tony was the first goalie to win against the Soviets, while splitting time with Montréal's Ken Dryden. The Blackhawks made it back to the 1973 Stanley Cup playoffs, only to lose again in six games (4-2), to the Canadians. Tony won his third and final Vezina Trophy during the 1973-74 season. Chicago declined over the next few seasons, but not because of Tony. Esposito became a naturalized American citizen in 1981 and played for Team USA in the Canada Cup. Tony retired after the 1983-84 season.

Tony Esposito played 16 seasons (1967-1984). This six-time All-Star goalie was inducted into the NHL Hall of Fame in 1988. His #35 was also retired by the Chicago Blackhawks on November 20, 1988. Tony later became the General Manager of the Pittsburgh Penguins. He also joined his brother Phil as a scout for the Tampa Bay Lightening. In 1998, Tony was ranked #79 on "The Hockey News" list of 100 Greatest Hockey Players. His brother Phil was ranked #18. Both brothers were inducted into the Sault Ste. Marie Walk of Fame in 2007. Tony was honored by the Blackhawks on March 19, 2008, as an Ambassador of the Blackhawks' organization. The Chicago Blackhawks were one of the original six professional hockey teams. The other five included the New York Rangers, Detroit Red Wings, Toronto Maple Leafs, Boston Bruins, and Montreal Canadians.

As most players are, Tony was known for his superstitions. He would become upset by crossed hockey sticks and wanted his hockey sticks lined up in a certain way.

Whether you played left-handed, right-handed, cross-handed, or you were able to move the puck between your legs, or perform a no-look pass, Tony Esposito had your number. Tony is Chicago's career leader with 418 wins and 74 shutouts. His overall record including Montreal stands at 423-306-151 and ranks 10th in league history.

Tony Esposito left us on August 10, 2021. He was 78 and suffered from pancreatic cancer. He is survived by his wife, Marilyn, sons Mark and Jason, Mark's wife Kim, and their children, Lauren and Kamryn.

Tony Esposito, a Hall-of-Fame husband, father and grandfather, always played with lots of emotion. The fans loved him, Chicago loved him and professional hockey loved him even more.

The standing rule for watching Tony Esposito play goalie was simply, if you were one of the 18,000 fans present and shouting "Tony! Tony!" at a Chicago Blackhawks game with a camera, you would put that save on a picture and frame it.

BACKSTOP FOR THE AGES

Broadcaster, Ernie Johnson once said: "What I've got is a 'get to job' not a 'got to job.' I get to do that. When you look at your life that way, it puts a positive spin on every challenge that you have in your life." The guy I'm going to tell you about would agree with Ernie. He was a hometown kid. This man had never been picked second for anything in his life, even on the playground. He was one strong son-of-a-gun and he even walked like an athlete. This man could bench press your house. I wondered what planet he was from, because it was clearly not earth. He was a tough guy. Even the mob guys called him "Mr.", and the man would knock you sideways at home plate for a slice of pizza. If he ever said he was so hungry that he could eat a horse, then you should hide your horse.

Baseball was his life and he was good at it. As a Major League catcher, the first person he learned to motivate was himself. Being the best he could be was the only thing that really got him going. He became the heart of the Detroit Tigers' defense and led the way by showing his teammates how to play the game of baseball. Catcher is one of the most important positions in baseball, but it is still only one position out of nine starters. He insisted on being the best catcher in the game. This fellow hit baseballs to places where they don't get thrown back. The man never got cheated on a swing and crowded the plate so closely that his strike zone almost disappeared. Pitchers hated that.

Bill Freehan's best attributes were his size and toughness. Standing 6 feet 2 inches tall and weighing 205 pounds, this guy would lay you out at home plate like Sunday supper. There is difference in your record and your legacy. Your record reflects what you have done. Your legacy is what it meant. He loved baseball but hated the feeling of walking out of a ballpark at midnight when everyone else had gone home, and the only people left were cleaning the concession stands. "There's nothing as lonely as an empty ballpark at night," said Bill Freehan. Bill was truly a backstop for the ages.

William Ashley Freehan was born on a Saturday, November 29, 1941, in the city of Detroit, Michigan. Bill was the oldest of four and the eldest son of Ashley Freehan, a sales rep for a seat insulation company and Helen, his mom. Bill began his baseball career on the sandlots of the Royal Oak suburbs. He started out at shortstop until the team's catcher didn't show up one day, so he moved behind home plate. Bill became known in the neighborhood as a Little League standout. He earned enough money on a paper route to pay for his long ride to the Tigers' games. There is story of Freehan being knocked silly as a kid at home plate, by a future Detroit teammate. That other kid's name was Willie Horton. By the age of 14, Bill's dad had purchased a mobile-home business and the family was moved to St. Petersburg, Florida. Bill attended Bishop Barry High School where he played football, basketball and baseball. During the summers, Bill returned to Detroit to live with his grandparents and play sandlot baseball with friends. It was here that Bill captured the attention of Detroit Tigers' scout, Louis D'Annunzio. After graduating high school in 1959, Bill set his sites on playing baseball and football at the University of Notre Dame or Western Michigan University. But both schools wanted him to make a choice between the two sports. So, he enrolled at the University of Michigan on a baseball scholarship, where he played catcher on the baseball team for Coach Don Lund, and tight end and linebacker on the football team for Coach "Bump" Elliott. The following year he was moved to a football scholarship, because there were more of those available.

In 1961, Freehan pounded Big Ten pitching while batting .585. Every scout in the Major Leagues took notice. At the age of 19, Bill signed with his hometown Tigers for a $125,000 bonus. Still he attended school at Michigan during the off-season, until he graduated in 1966 with a 3.1 grade point average and a degree in history. "My deal with my dad was, I didn't see a dime of my bonus until I got my degree," said Bill. The Tigers sent Bill to the Class-C Northern League where he hit .343 in 30 games. He was then moved to Knoxville, Tennessee, part of the Sally League before being called up to the big club (Detroit) in late September. "I made so much money, the veteran players called me 'Brinks,' and stuff like that." said Bill. Freehan played the entire 1962 season for Denver's American Association. On February 23, 1963, Bill married Patricia O'Brien, his high school sweetheart from St. Petersburg, Florida. Bill Freehan joined the big club for good in 1963. Not only did he continue to hit well, but he only committed two errors in 73 games behind the plate. Freehan was one of the game's best defensive catchers. "The catcher has to be the captain of the field," said Bill. "I felt if I did my job behind the plate, I was contributing to the team in the best way I could."

By 1964, Bill Freehan was a household name for baseball fans. He became the first Detroit catcher to hit over .300 since Hall-of-Famer Mickey Cochrane hit .319 in 1935. Even though he had caught less than 200 games in the Major Leagues, Bill was selected to the 1964 American League All-Star Team. He also became the team's spiritual leader that year. Even the most tenured pitchers were willing to allow him to call the games. In 1965, Freehan was frequently dinged up by injuries, but still caught 129 games. He spent three weeks on the bench with back spasms and also injured his throwing hand with a foul tip off the bat of Cleveland's Max Alvis. Bill's bare hand was later struck again by a swinging bat in a game with the Twins.

In 1965, Bill won the first of his five consecutive Gold Gloves. On June 15, 1965, he set a record of making 19 putouts in a single game, while catching pitcher, Denny McLain. In 1967, Freehan experimented by moving closer to the plate, while batting. Although he was hit by pitches 20 times that season, his hitting improved. Bill hit .282 with 20 home runs and 74 RBIs. He stayed healthy and caught in 155 games. No other catcher in the Majors led his team in games played. In fact, Bill caught all 15 innings of the 1967 All-Star Game in Anaheim, California. On September 26th, at the end of the 1967 season, Bill was ejected for the first time in his career, for slamming his mask to the ground after Yankees' Horace Clark stole second base. The umpire thought he was arguing about the stolen base, but he wasn't. Freehan was upset at a strike called a ball by home-plate umpire Hank Soar. Bill always believed in competition rather than confrontation. Still, Freehan had a terrific year and was voted the 1967 Tiger of the Year by the local chapter of the Baseball Writers' Association of America. Freehan was not ejected again until 1975, nearly eight years later.

A balding, older-looking Bill Freehan caught 155 games and all seven of the World Series games, during the Detroit Tigers' 1968 Championship season. Bill set career-high marks with 25 home runs, 73 runs scored and 84 RBIs. He was also hit by pitches 24 times. In the first five games of the Series, the Cardinals tested Freehan's arm. They stole 11 bases in 16 attempts. Lou Brock stole seven of those 11 bases himself, in the first four games of that World Series. Freehan could not begin to contain Lou. During Games Six and Seven, Freehan managed to put a stop to the Cardinals' run game. It seemed appropriate that it was Freehan who caught Tim McCarver's foul popup near the first-base line for the final out of the Series. The site of Tigers' pitcher Mickey Lolich leaping into Freehan's arms will always be a Detroit sports memory.

The Tigers finished second in 1969, while Bill kept a daily diary of the season. This info was released in a book entitled <u>Behind the Mask: An Inside Baseball Diary</u>, the following year. "This was the story about a ballclub," said Freehan. "My book is about what it's like to be a catcher and go through a season." The 1970 season was not a good year for Freehan with a bat. His back continued to hurt, and his batting average slipped to .241. The team fell to fourth place, and Freehan underwent bone graft surgery on September 2, 1970, to help prolong his career. With manager Billy Martin now in charge of the Tigers, Bill had a strong season in 1971. Freehan was selected the starting catcher for the 1971 American League All-Star Team. This game was played at Tiger Stadium. Bill also hit three home runs in a single game on August 9th, against the Red Sox. Bill had a fine season in 1972, but fractured his right thumb late in season, while tagging out Boston's Carl Yastrzemski at home plate. With Tom Haller now at the catcher position for Detroit, the Tigers finished first in their division, but were defeated by the Oakland A's in the American League Championship Series. In 1973, Freehan and Martin got sideways, because Billy platooned him with Haller. Bill struggled a bit at the plate and resented Martin. Eventually, Martin was let go, late in 1973, and replaced by Ralph Houk in 1974. Houk primarily played Bill at first base that season. Bill felt he had something to prove and belted a grand slam and drove in seven runs against the Yankees, on September 8, 1974. Freehan hit .297 with 18 home runs and 60 RBIs that season. That was his way of answering the rise of catchers Carlton

Fisk and Thurman Munson.

In 1975, at the age of 34, Bill was selected by Houk as the starting catcher and caught 113 games. He was making $80,000 a year and made his 11th appearance as an All-Star. During the winter, Detroit traded for catcher Milt May, pushing Freehan to a reserve role. The writing was on the wall. On December 12, 1976, Detroit gave Freehan his unconditional release. His last at-bat occurred on October 3, 1976. He was offered a job managing in the Minor Leagues, but turned it down. "I can't feed my family on a Minor League manager's salary," said Bill. He served as president of Freehan-Bocci Company, an automobile manufacturer's agency. Bill spent one year as a color commentator for Seattle Mariners' games from 1979 to 1980, and for Tiger broadcasts on PASS Sports television, from 1984-1985. In 1989, Bill spoke with Michigan athletic director Bo Schembechler, about the baseball program. Two weeks later, Bill was hired as the Wolverines' head baseball coach. "You can't take the baseball out of the boy," said Freehan. He would hold that position until 1995. From 2002 -2005, Bill was asked to serve as a catching instructor for the Tigers.

Bill Freehan was known as one of the best catchers in the American League for almost 10 years. He caught some excellent veteran pitchers, the likes of Jim Bunning, Mickey Lolich and Denny McLain. His durability allowed him to catch more than 100 games a year for nine consecutive seasons. Bill played in 1,774 games in 15 years, won five Gold Glove Awards and he was selected to be a part of 11 All-Star Games, while playing in eight. He batted 6,073 times and recorded 1,591 hits. Bill posted a .262 lifetime batting average, with 758 RBI's, and hit a total of 200 home runs. Interestingly, his 200 home runs consisted of 100 hit at home and 100 hit on the road. His 2,502 total bases placed him behind only Yogi Berra and Bill Dickey, among American League catchers when he retired. As a catcher, Freehan laughed at pitching charts and computers in the dugout that said pitch this guy this way or that, because hitters were always adjusting and only you knew what was going on inside your pitcher's head. At retirement, Freehan held the Major League record for most chances (10,714), most putouts (9,941), and the highest fielding average for a catcher at (.993). In 1978, Freehan became one of seven members of the inaugural class of inductees to the University Of Michigan's Athletic Hall Of Honor. Bill was inducted into the Michigan Sports Hall of Fame in 1982. Bill Freehan caught more games than any other player in Tiger's team history. No less than 10 catchers from the Detroit Tigers have made an All-Star team. Mickey Cochrane and Ivan "Pudge" Rodriguez are the only two to be enshrined into the Baseball Hall of Fame. I vote for Bill Freehan. He may have been the most popular catcher in Detroit Tigers' history.

Bill Freehan passed away on August 19, 2021. He had been diagnosed with dementia in 2018 and was living at home in Walloon Lake, Michigan, with hospice care. Bill was 79. He is survived by his wife of 58 years, Patricia O'Brien Freehan and three daughters: Corey Sue, Kelley, and Cathy.

There are few environments where men of all races, colors, creeds, different backgrounds and religion can come together and put aside every one of their differences and join in a common goal to put a team together and win a game. And in doing so, each finds out something about themselves and the answer to life's most difficult question. Do I have what it takes to be the very best? Can I continue when I feel like stopping? Can I respect the differences of my teammates? Can I bounce back after defeat?

The answer from Bill Freehan was always "yes."

Thunder from the Center

To the average fan of professional football in the 1950s and 1960s, offensive linemen were faceless and irrelevant. Big, mean, and sometimes ugly, it was a time of the caveman aura. From tackle to tackle, the men in the offensive line received about as much credit as a pack horse. But it's true that if they did not act as a unit, if any one of them failed at their assignment, the offense could not function. The quarterback and running backs got all the glory, yet no one knew how important an offensive lineman was until he failed. A third down and two running play, reminded us of five bull elephants trying to get out of a phone booth. Their large cleated feet tore up divots out of the field of play that were large enough for planting trees.

The fellow you are about to get to know was a great guy who just happened to play a great game of football. Humble, strong, the man defined toughness. This guy wasn't just an offensive center, he was a football player. A man of few words, he was a lot of action. For 17 consecutive years he never missed a game, never missed a practice and there was always thunder from the center for the Minnesota Vikings, on Sundays. When he pulled on his helmet, the man would block his mother. He was so quick off the ball; the guy in front of him looked like he was on roller skates. You could not rattle this guy. He was somewhat an introvert and only comfortable when he was alone. Good looking, even keeled, he could be as serious as a blood clot. His job was to anchor the offensive line, hand out pancakes, (a term used to describe an offensive lineman knocking a defensive player flat on his back).

245

A man who ended up in Canton almost never made it off a farm in Nebraska. The Hall of Fame doesn't happen without the fans, your family, your coaches and trainers, and every teammate you ever played with. The Hall of Fame is forever. This is a team you can't be cut from or traded from. This team includes "Red" Grange, Otto Graham and Sammy Baugh. As Deacon Jones once said, "You can't even die from this team. This team is forever. It's your home for the rest of time, immortality.

Coach Bud Grant called him "One of the greatest Vikings of all time." Welcome to the Pro Football Hall of Fame, Mick Tinglehoff; welcome to immortality.

Henry Michael Tingelhoff was born on May 22, 1940, in Lexington, Nebraska, to Henry and Clara Tingelhoff. The youngest of six children, Mick grew up a farm kid with a blue-collar dad. Life was good, but not easy. Mick played center and linebacker for Lexington High School, but his parents never attended his games. The University of Nebraska was the only college to offer him a scholarship. "Dad thought football was a waste of time," said Tingelhoff. "They weren't real happy that I got a scholarship to Nebraska. They wanted me to stay on the farm." While at Nebraska, Mick played center some his sophomore year and started his junior and senior years. "We ran the ball a lot," said Mick. Tingelhoff became the Corn Huskers' co-captain his senior year. He played in the 1961 Senior Bowl, the All-American Bowl, and earned three letters during his college football career, but the only chance he had to be drafted was in the Army.

After graduation, Mick Tingelhoff entered the 1962 NFL Draft, but there were no takers. He was contacted by the Minnesota Vikings and signed as a free agent, in 1962. Mick got married to his sweetheart, Phyllis, before the Vikings' training camp. Standing 6 feet 2 inches tall and weighing 237 pounds, the Vikings feared that he may be too small or not tough enough to play offensive center. The Vikings envisioned him at the linebacker position. Boy, did they get that wrong. They moved Mick to the center position after their second preseason game, and he would spend the rest of his career as the pillar of their offensive line. He would be given the #53 to wear. His first coach in Minnesota was Norm Van Brocklin. His nickname was "Stormin' Norman." "He got mad all the time, and he was a real strict coach," said Mick. In 1967, Bud Grant took over head-coaching duties. "I don't think he ever smiled." said Mick.

From 1962 to 1978, Mick Tinglehoff played in 240 consecutive football games. He was known as a complete center, as he also handled the long-snapping duties. Mick spent his Sundays providing pass protection for Fran Tarkenton, and opening holes for running back, Chuck Foreman, who had three 1,000-yard rushing seasons. Only teammate Jim Marshall's 270 straight starts at defensive end were greater. The current NFL all-time record is held by Brett Favre, who started 297 consecutive games. Tingelhoff and former quarterback Phillip Rivers are now tied for third. Mick anchored an offensive line that claimed 10 divisional titles from 1968 to 1978. He was a member of the Vikings' club that won the 1969 NFL Championship and advanced to Super Bowls IV, VIII, IX, and XI. He is one of 11 players to have played in all four Vikings' Super Bowl appearances. The Vikings would be on the losing end of all four. Tingelhoff took on some of the best NFL middle linebackers in the game. Ray Nitschke of the Green Bay Packers, Joe Schmidt of the Detroit Lions and Dick Butkus of the Chicago Bears, are just some of the names you would recognize. "We called Dick Butkus 'Dickie Doo' to tease him. I once roomed with Dick Butkus during a Pro Bowl in L.A." said Tingelhoff.

Interestingly, Tingelhoff never missed a game. "I never got hurt because no one was hitting me. They were following the ball and I was after them and trying to block, so no one was trying to block me," said Mick. He was selected for the Pro-Bowl in six consecutive seasons and was named All-Pro five times in the 1960s. Mick retired after the 1978 season. After football, Mick worked in commercial real estate. In 2011, Mick was named the recipient of the Gerald R. Ford Legends Award. He has been inducted into the Nebraska Football Hall of Fame. Mick Tingelhoff's #53 was retired by the Vikings on November 25, 2001. He was also inducted into the Vikings' Ring of Honor on the same day. Still, he had to wait almost another decade-and-a-half to be enshrined into the Pro Football Hall of Fame on August 8, 2015. His friend, Fran Tarkenton, presented Mick for enshrinement. Tarkenton choked up when he said, "Tingelhoff waited 37 years" before adding, "But Mick's in the Hall of Fame."

During my time, I loved playing offensive center. I liked the fact that I got to touch the ball on every offensive play. Nothing happened until I snapped the ball. I also enjoyed taking the game to my opponent on run-blocking plays, and calling the blocking assignments for the rest of the offensive line. I was no Mick Tingelhoff, but I understood his love for the position.

Mick Tingelhoff left us on September 11, 2021, from complications of Parkinson's disease and dementia. He was 81 and staying in an assisted living facility in Lakeville, Minnesota. He is survived by his wife, Phyllis, sons Michael and Patrick, 12 grandchildren and two great grandchildren.

Stories of pain were rampant in the NFL. When you retire from pro football, you lose the chaos in your life. It takes some awhile to realize that they need to forgive themselves. To forgive themselves for everything they saw or did to their opponent. Just because they believed they were on the right side of things doesn't mean that everything they did on the field felt right afterwards. These were things that happened that they couldn't unsee.

Iron Man

Knute Rockne once said, "I've found that prayers work best when you have big players." This fellow just looked like a football player; the guy you would choose first on the playground. He was a big man with a mean mouth. He reminded me of a walking condominium. Standing six feet five inches tall and weighing well over 300 pounds, he was a big, imposing man; it was like parting the Red Sea, when he entered the room. He was half man, half amazing, and he just threw blockers to the side. When he hit someone during the game, you could see my television shake a little. The man was 100% trouble. Football isn't just a brutal game; it's also a beautiful one, a never-ending duel between violence and beauty. This fellow was never meant to just sit in the shade. He may have been one of the greatest defensive players of all time. The man was a lunch-bucket guy who showed up every day, gave you his best and returned tomorrow to do it all again. Friend or foe, hero or villain, his middle name should have been "danger." I thought they should have named torpedoes after him.

He played the game at and over the edge and was one of the game's most feared defenders. Yes, he was a great teammate, a throwback from the early days of professional football, but he always had to be the bad guy. This man could be a big bowl of trouble, and I'm not writing about him to put whipped cream on it. He was a lot more than just a football player. It just seemed that his bread was buttered on the other side.

Roger Brown once said, "All great quarterbacks look more

human when they are pressured." The man was a wrecking ball. He could and did change the outcome of many games. Roger Brown was one strong son-of-a-gun and he once said, "When you get on that field, you ain't got no friends." Brown didn't care if you liked him or not. If Mr. Rogers was Roger Brown's neighbor, he'd move. This guy was all over the field. He looked and played like a man made from iron. Roger warned offensive linemen who head-butted him. When push came to shove, this defensive tackle won the physical battles against his opponent. Roger Brown was a guy you could go to war with. An iron man, Brown never missed a game during his ten-year career. Having Brown at defensive tackle was like having a real lion on the Detroit defense. They say if you stand by the river long enough you will see the bodies of your enemies float by. At 84 years of age, Roger Brown has seen them all.

Roger Lee Brown was born on May 1, 1937, in Surry County, Virginia. He grew up in Nyack, New York, and attended Nyack High School, where he graduated in 1956. From 1956-1960, Brown played football for the Hawks at Maryland State College (now Maryland Eastern Shore). His dream was to play fullback, but he continued to grow and was soon moved to the defensive line. The rest is history. While there, he wore the #78 and received the nickname Roger "Nyack" Brown. During his four years with the Hawks, his teams were 24-5-1, and he led the team to the Central Intercollegiate Athletic Association (CIAA) title in 1957. He was also named an NAIA All-American in 1958 and 1959. The Hawks held their opponents to 7.3 points per game, while outscoring them 693-213.

Brown was drafted in the fourth round of the 1960 NFL Draft by the Detroit Lions. He was also chosen by the New York Titans of the AFL. He joined the Lions and signed his first contract for $8,000 a year. Sixty-one years later, the guy playing his position today makes $1,114,000. Roger became one of the first NFL players to have a playing weight that exceeded 300 pounds, but his size and speed made him one of the most dynamic players of the time. Brown received the #76 and became a part of the Detroit Lions' original Fearsome Foursome. From 1960 to 1966, he was joined by Alex Karras, Darris McCord and Sam Williams. In 1962, he was voted National Football League Pro-Lineman of the Year, and he also made the NFL All-Pro Team in 1962 and 1963. Brown was traded to the Los Angeles Rams in 1967 and played with their Fearsome Foursome until 1969. Brown wore #78 and his teammates with the Rams were also very well known: Deacon Jones, Merlin Olsen and Lamar Lundy.

During the 1962 Thanksgiving Day Game in Detroit, Roger Brown sacked Hall of Fame quarterback Bart Starr seven times, including once for a safety. This game became known in NFL lore as the "Thanksgiving Day Massacre." The Lions beat the Packers that day 26-14. Detroit actually had 11 sacks that day for 110 yards in losses, which remain a franchise record. Brown also sacked Hall of Fame quarterback Johnny Unitas for a safety, in the same season.

Roger Brown played for ten years, in 140 straight games, and never missed a game because of injury. The most money he made in one year was $30,000. Roger did admit that he experienced some injuries. "I had broken hands and broken bones while playing, but not as many as I caused. I had 12 operations," said Brown. He has been credited with 78 career-sacks, 15 fumble recoveries returned for 43 yards, three safeties and two interceptions returned for 30 yards. Brown played in the Pro Bowl for six straight years, from 1962 to 1967.

After he retired, Brown focused on the food industry. He started his own chain of eight fast-food restaurants in Chicago, and he later worked for the McDonald's Corporation, eventually owning three McDonald's in Virginia. At the age of 64, he sold those restaurants and opened the Roger Brown Restaurant & Sports bar in Portsmouth, Virginia, and the Cove Taverns located in Williamsburg and Newport News, Virginia.

In 1997, Brown was inducted into the Virginia Sports Hall of Fame. In 2008, Roger was chosen for the Lions' All-Time 75th Anniversary Team. In 2009, Brown was inducted into the College Football Hall of Fame. Brown was also inducted into the Black College Football Hall of Fame in 2015. On Sunday, October 28, 2018, Brown was inducted into the Pride of the Lions' Hall of Fame along with former teammates, Alex Karras and Herman Moore, at Ford Field during halftime of the game against the Seattle Seahawks. In 2019, he was selected at #19 on the *Detroit Free Press* ranking of the Detroit Lions' top 100 all-time players.

Many members of the Pro Football Hall of Fame lobbied for Brown over the years. Before he died in 2019, Bart Starr wrote a letter to the Pro Football Hall of Fame in support of Roger Brown. Starr wrote, "I personally believe the strength and character of an exceptional Sports Hall of Fame are directly commensurate with the quality of its members. Roger Brown brings that quality with him and he deserves to be inducted into our Hall of Fame. Joe Theismann also lobbied for Brown by writing, "Although he has not been inducted into the NFL Hall of Fame, where he should be, I'm hoping his time will come."

It's true that I never met Roger Brown, but yes, I saw him play. He was something to behold. As a big guy myself, guys like Roger gave me the confidence that I could play at that level. I followed his career from Detroit to Los Angeles and watched him play from the age of nine until I was 19. There was also another guy who played with Brown that I was interested in and his name was Roman Gabriel, quarterback for the Los Angeles Rams. You see, Roman and his wife lived off-campus while he played for the N. C. State Wolfpack, and he used to trade at my dad's convenience store called Gordon's Market. Gabriel carried several footballs in the back seat of his car and would throw passes in my dad's parking lot to all the kids in the neighborhood. How cool is that? We all loved Roman Gabriel.

Roger Brown retired from professional football at the age of 32 and spent the next 52 years waiting for a call from the Pro Football Hall of Fame. Now that he has been out of football for more than 20 years, he will have to be picked by the Hall of Fame's veterans' committee. In 2018, Brown said he hoped to make the Pro Football Hall of Fame one day. "I have always felt the main thing, I stay vertical, keep alive, it'll happen," said Brown. "And the thing that I'm waiting for now is Canton, Ohio. One of us from Detroit should be in that Hall." Like anyone else who played against him or saw him play, I hope he gets his wish.

Roger Brown left us on a Friday, September 17, 2021. Brown was 84 and surrounded by his wife Kay, friends and loved ones. No cause was given. Roger Brown's earlier thoughts proved to be correct as his Lions teammate, Alex Karras bust will now rest in Canton, Ohio. Karras was inducted posthumously in the 2020 class of Pro Football Hall of Fame by the veterans' committee. Karras died in 2012 at the age of 77.

WHERE'S MY BAT

William Gibson once said, "Time moves in one direction, memory in another." They say that baseball is the only game you can see on the radio. He would know, as his Major League career started in 1942. There was no such thing as television. Some of you may be asking yourself, "Who is this guy, and why is he in this book?" We sometimes forget that there is a lot to learn from our past. Unless you're an astute baseball historian, you may have never heard of him. This fellow was "old school" and spoke the language of baseball. He used all the colorful phrases like, around the horn, can of corn, frozen rope, seeing-eye single, big fly, ducks on the pond, hook slide, Uncle Charlie, southpaw, painting corners and crooked numbers.

The funny part is that he's always been around. This guy had socks older than I am, yet he ran like the summer wind. He has lived over 100 years and has spent over 65 years as a player, coach, manager and scout in professional baseball. The man was so old he probably remembered when the Bible first came out. No doubt he was what we called a "lifer." Heck, he may have stood for the national anthem more than any other person I know.

Eddie Robinson was a man's man, loved to laugh and claimed he was living a dream. He also had a history of coloring outside the lines. Eddie played the game the way it should be played, with reckless abandon and intensity. You could see his potential the first time you watched him play, and he never lifted a weight in his life. He loved bird hunting and could shoot the wings off a fly, so hitting a baseball was no big deal.

The first thing you miss when you leave the game is the action. The second thing is your teammates. Just think of all the players before him that Eddie Robinson had come to know: Babe Ruth, Tris Speaker, Rogers Hornsby, Hank Greenberg, Dizzy Dean, Brooks Robinson, and Hank Aaron. Eddie Robinson played with or against Ted Williams, Bob Feller, Satchel Paige, Joe DiMaggio, Jackie Robinson, Larry Doby, Robin Roberts, Warren Spahn, Yogi Berra, Whitey Ford and Mickey Mantle. He also worked for Bill Veeck, Clark Griffith, Casey Stengel, Paul Richards, Charlie Finley, Ted Turner and George Steinbrenner.

We all have an hourglass of sand. But the top is obscured so you don't know how much sand you have left. The sand represents the time we have left here on earth. The problem is none of us knows how much sand is left. Don't let your sand run out on you. So why does one person's sand run out before others? I don't think it's up to us to figure that out.

William Edward Robinson, II, was born on December 15, 1920, in Paris, Texas. He was the only child of William Sr., an automobile electrician born in Missouri, and Hazel Robinson who was born in Tennessee. Eddie's parents divorced when he was 12. Eddie could always hit any object thrown his way. At the age of 14, he purchased a Bill Doak glove for six dollars and paid it off at fifty cents a week. After high school, Eddie attended Paris Junior College. Robinson was a left-handed hitter who threw right-handed. He signed his first professional contract in 1939 with the Knoxville Smokies of the Southern Association, for a $300 bonus. Before he left town, he bought his mother a washing machine and paid off all the family debt. After Spring Training, he was assigned to the Valdosta Trojans of the Class D Georgia-Florida League. In 1941 and 1942, you could find Eddie with the Baltimore Orioles of the International League. He played a total of four years in the Minor Leagues, before being called up to the Cleveland Indians on September 9, 1942. Like a lot of his fellow teammates, Eddie enlisted in the U.S. Navy after the 1942 season had ended. After basic training, Eddie married Elayne Elder in February of 1943, and they had two children, Robbie Ann, who died before her third birthday from brain cancer, and William E. Robinson, III. The couple divorced in 1951. He spent three years in the Navy and suffered a leg injury while there that would bother him the rest of his life, but did not prohibit him from playing the game he loved at that time.

Eddie resumed his baseball career in 1946 with the Orioles; and he slugged 34 home runs and drove in 123 runs, to lead the league. He was named the International League MVP, beating out Jackie Robinson and Bobby Brown. He joined the Indians in 1947 and fouled an Allie Reynolds fastball off his ankle, in August. Eddie spent six weeks in a cast. The following year with the Indians, Eddie Robinson experienced one of his greatest moments, in 1948, as he helped lead Cleveland to a World Series victory over the Boston Braves in six games. For that Series, Robinson was the second leading hitter for the Indians, hitting .300 in 20 at-bats. That 1948 club remains the last Indians' team to have won a World Series.

Unfortunately, Eddie was traded after the 1948 season to the Washington Senators in 1949. He simply could not get along with Indians' manager Lou Boudreau, who favored veteran players to younger ones. Robinson's most productive years at the plate, and with his glove, came during the next four years. He spent two years with the Senators (1949-1950) and then two years with the Chicago White Sox (1951-1952). Robinson was selected to the American-League All-Star Team four times in 1949 and 1951-1953. Eddie was the starting first baseman in 1949 and 1952 contests. Robinson drove in the first runs for the American League in both contests. In 1951, he befriended Paul Richards, who was the manager of the White Sox at that time.

Robinson continued his playing career, but was traded like a bag of potato chips around the league. You could find him with the Philadelphia Athletics in 1953, and then he spent two years (1954-1955) with the New York Yankees, before being traded in 1956 to the Kansas City Athletics. In 1955, immediately after the World Series, Eddie married again, this time to Bette Farlow, and together they raised three sons: Marc, Drew and Paul. In 1957, he played for the Detroit Tigers, Cleveland Indians and Baltimore Orioles, all in the same year. Robinson continued to suffer from nerve pain in his leg and realized that he would not be able to continue playing. His last appearance occurred on September 15, 1957, with the Orioles.

Eddie Robinson played in 1,315 games during his 13-year career. Robinson actually played for seven of the original eight teams in the American League, the Boston Red Sox not included. He batted .268 with 172 home runs and 723 RBI'S batted in. Robinson never struck out more than 56 times a season. His 29 home runs for the Chicago White Sox, in 1951, stood as the team record for nearly 30 years. Eddie was one of only seven to hit a home run over the roof at old Comiskey Park in Chicago. The other six were: Babe Ruth, Lou Gehrig, Jimmy Foxx, Hank Greenberg, Ted Williams and Mickey Mantle. Eddie played every inning of his career at first base, with a .990 fielding percentage. In 1955, as a part-time player with the New York Yankees, Eddie belted 16 home runs while collecting only 36 hits. He also had more RBI's than hits, knocking in 42 runs. But, that's not why I decided to write about Eddie Robinson. The following fascinating story was revealed by Hall-of-Fame pitcher, Bob Feller.

On June 13, 1948, the Cleveland Indians were in town to play the New York Yankees. It was a Sunday and nearly 50,000 fans were on hand. The Indians came to New York, red hot with a 31-13 win-loss record. Awaiting them were the Yankees with a 27-21 record. But this meeting was far more important than just a regular season game. There were three additional celebrations scheduled for that day. First, it was the 25th anniversary of "The House That Ruth Built," Yankee Stadium. Second, the 1923 team was being recognized and honored for beating the New York Giants 4 games to 2, in the 1923 World Series; and third, the "Sultan of Swat," Babe Ruth's #3 was being retired. The "Babe" hit 41 home runs in 1923 and batted .393 for the year. It was also true that Ruth had hit the very first home run in Yankee Stadium. Not only had Ruth hit 714 homers during his career, but he also led the Major Leagues in home runs 12 times.

Jacob Ruppert, the Yankees' owner, had held a banquet for the 1923 club the night before, but Ruth was too sick to attend. You see, Ruth was 53 years old and dying from cancer of the throat. Ruth was noticeably thinner and traveled with a male nurse named Frank Dulaney. Ruth arrived at Yankee Stadium in a heavy wool overcoat in the middle of summer. Dulaney helped Ruth pull on his uniform for the last time in the clubhouse. Ruth then relaxed in the Indians' dugout while public address announcer, Mel Allen, announced the names of the surviving members of the 1923 team. Joe Dugan and Wally Pipp received a warm welcome from the fans. The great Lou Gehrig, manager Miller Huggins and second baseman Tony Lazzeri had already passed away. The last name announced by Allen was Babe Ruth. Dulaney removed Ruth's coat as he moved so very slowly down the dugout. Indians' first baseman, Eddie Robinson, was afraid the Ruth would fall, so he reached into the bat rack, pulled out a bat and handed it to Ruth to use for a cane. As Ruth climbed the steps to the field, the roar from the crowd was one that only Ruth could have known better than anyone else. Ruth, now standing close to his teammates, leaned on the bat with his right hand and held his cap in his left. With a terribly raspy voice from previous throat surgery, Babe began to speak. "I am proud I hit the first home run here in 1923," said Ruth. "It was marvelous to see 13 of 14 players who were my teammates, going back 25 years. I'm telling you, it makes me proud and happy to be here."

Nat Fein, a photographer for the *New York Herald-Tribune*, watched the ceremony from behind, near the third-base line. It was here that Fein took a picture of the #3 stretched across Ruth's back. That photograph named "The Babe Bows Out," won a Pulitzer Prize.

Although Ruth was supposed to manage the current Yankee club for two innings, Ruth immediately left the park after the ceremony. He was feeling too ill to stay.

Now here's the interesting part of the story. Fireballer, Bob Feller started for the Indians that day. But what Feller did not know was when the Babe left the field, he handed the bat he had used to steady himself back to Eddie Robinson. That bat had Bob Feller's name on it. Robinson, now realizing the historical significant of that bat, decides to place Feller's bat in his locker. When it became Feller's turn to bat, no one could find the bat and Feller asked out loud, "Where's my bat?" When no one could find it, Feller asked the clubhouse boy to find him another bat. Eddie Robinson stayed silent. Feller was forced to use a different bat than his own. Robinson took the bat with him when they left New York and remained quiet. According to Feller, Robinson did not tell him until 1982 that Ruth had used his bat that day and that he still had it. Feller never blamed Robinson, and the bat was never returned. The Yankees won that day, 5-3, and Ruth never returned to Yankee Stadium after that day.

Unfortunately, we can't stop time, no matter how invincible they seemed on the diamond. Ruth spent most of the next two months in the hospital and died on August 16, 1948. This bat was eventually sold.

After retiring at the end of the 1957 season, Robinson became a coach for Paul Richards, manager of the Orioles. In 1961, he followed Paul Richards to the Houston Colt 45s and worked as the team's farm director for five years. In 1966, he became assistant general manager of the Kansas City Athletics. In 1968, he reunited with Paul Richards in the front office of the Atlanta Braves. In 1972, he replaced Richards as General Manager and served in Atlanta until 1976. Yes, you guessed it. It was GM Eddie Robinson who traded Hank Aaron back to Milwaukee. In 1977, Robinson joined the Texas Rangers' front office and served as their General Manager from 1978 to 1982. Robinson was fired from the Rangers in 1982. He was instantly contacted by George Steinbrenner and offered the GM position for the Yankees. Eddie declined, because he did not want to move his family to New York. Instead, he became special assistant to Steinbrenner for the next three years, but continued to live in Fort Worth, Texas. Robinson eventually created his own one-man scouting combine and worked for several teams. At the age of 84, he finally retired in 2004 after 65 years in professional baseball. In 2011, Eddie, with the help of author C. Paul Rogers, III, wrote his autobiography entitled Lucky Me – My Sixty-Five Years in Baseball.

Eddie Robinson left us on October 4, 2021. He was 100 years old and died while living on his ranch in Bastrop, Texas. He was so old his birthday candles cost more than his cake. After the death of Chicago White Sox outfielder, Val Heim, Robinson was recognized as the oldest living baseball player. Now that Robinson has passed, the next oldest player is George Elder, who played for the St. Louis Browns. Even well into his 90s, Eddie played golf twice a week and spent time watching the Texas Rangers play baseball. Eddie was the last living Cleveland Indians' player to win a World Series' championship. He did attend Game 6 of the 2016 World Series between the Indians and Chicago Cubs, at Progressive Field in Cleveland. He celebrated his 100th birthday on December 15, 2020. Inside the white lines, Eddie Robinson faced two opponents, baseball and Father Time. Even though Father Time was pulling on the back of his jersey, he never wanted to leave the game. Author Kay Andrews once said, "Happy times and bygone days are never lost. In truth, they grow more wonderful within the heart that keeps them." You see, baseball is about stories. It's the stories that connect us to the past.

RemDawg

Willie Stargell once said, "When you start the game, they don't say 'Work Ball,' they say 'Play Ball.'" As a young boy in the 1950s, I loved the sounds of baseball that came out of mya radio. I spent countless nights listening to my transistor radio hidden under my pillow. Mel Allen, "Red" Barber, Ernie Harwell and Chuck Thompson filled my mind with baseball played by the very best, during the "Good Old Days."

The guy that I'm writing about today was a great example of the human spirit. This fellow owned a baby face, a thick New England accent, and he played baseball like a grown man. He may have been the definition of pure joy. This guy grew to understand that in life there is nothing but possibilities. There's something special about playing for your home state and, as a kid, he dreamed of playing the game of baseball for the Red Sox Nation. He became a man on a mission and, yes, his dream came true. For him, baseball was like macaroni meeting cheese for the first time. Yet, even though he played the game he loved for ten years, he made his biggest impact behind the microphone. The old saying goes like this: Sometimes you gotta do what you gotta do, while you're waiting to do what you were born to do. He became so much more than a baseball announcer. For over 43 years, he spent his time as a second baseman and a broadcaster. He could get in and out of a conversation with his on-air radio partners easily, whether it was Sean McDonough or Ned Martin. This guy put the color in color commentary. He had a great understanding of the sport of baseball, and he owned an interesting voice. As a broadcaster, he understood that he was not the show, but he was there to enhance the show. He became so well-known in the northeast; you'd have to travel to another part of the country to meet someone who had not heard his name. This fellow never got in the way of the game, but fans tuned in because they wanted to know what he thought. He knew the answer to every question. Every game he broadcast, you would think it was the biggest game of the year or the only game being played that day. Jerry was funny, exciting and you never knew what he was about to say. Listening to Jerry Remy broadcast a Red Sox game was like opening a box of Cracker Jacks. You had no idea what you were going to find inside. His popularity grew leaps and bounds in New England and, in 2007, Remy was elected the "President" of Red Sox Nation and was given the nickname "Remdawg."

Gerald Peter Remy of French Canadian descent was born in Fall River, Massachusetts, on November 8, 1952. His family later moved, and Jerry grew up in Somerset, Massachusetts. He played baseball and graduated from Somerset High School. Afterwards, he attended and graduated from Roger Williams University, located in Bristol, Rhode Island. Remy was drafted in the 19th round of the 1970 MLB Draft by the Washington Senators, but because of school, he decided not to sign at that time. In 1971, he was selected again in the 8th round, with the 129th pick of the January supplemental draft by the California Angels. Remy signed and played baseball at second base in the Angels' farm system for the next four years. His 1971 season was spent in the Rookie League with the Magic Valley Cowboys. In 1972, you could find Jerry with the Class-A Stockton Ports. Remy hit .335 in 1973 with the Class-A Quad City Angels and split his time in 1974 with the Double-A El Paso Diablos and the Triple-A Salt Lake City Angels. Remy played in 421 Minor League games, hitting .275 with 12 home runs and 152 RBI's.

Jerry Remy made his Major League debut on April 7, 1975, with the California Angels. He recorded a single off my pal, Steve Busby of the Kansas City Royals in his very first at bat, but was later picked off. Remy started 145 games at second base for the Angels that year. He hit .258 with one home run; recorded 46 RBI's and had 34 stolen bases. He also led the American League in being caught stealing 21 times. In 1976, his average rose to .263. During 1977, Jerry was selected team captain in June, becoming only the second captain in the Angels' team history. On December 8, 1977, Jerry Remy was traded to the Boston Red Sox in exchange for pitcher Don Aase and cash. Remy played in 444 games for the Angels, hitting .258 with five home runs, 118 RBI's and 110 stolen bases.

The year 1978 was a big year for Remy. Not only was he the starting second baseman for his favorite hometown team, but he was selected to play in his first and only All-Star Game. Jerry hit .278 with 44 RBI's and recorded 30 stolen bases in 148 games. Remy also hit two home runs, the last home runs of his career. Remy started at second base for the next six seasons, although he was hampered by several injuries. In 1979, he was limited to only 80 games played, and then played in 63 games in 1980. In 1981, he played in 88 games and batted .307. On September 3rd and 4th, Jerry accomplished the rare feat of collecting six hits in a single game, going 6-for-10 in a 20-inning game played over two days against the Seattle Mariners. Remy played well and more often in 1982 and 1983, but suffered a knee injury in 1984 that limited him to only 30 games. Remy made his final start at second base on May 5, 1984, and recorded his last at-bat as a pinch hitter on May 18, 1984. He was released by the Red Sox on December 10, 1985, and retired in 1986 during Spring Training. His Red Sox totals will read: 710 games played while batting .286 with two home runs, 211

RBI's, and 98 stolen bases. During his ten-year career (1975-1984), he batted .275 with seven home runs, 329 RBI's and 208 stolen bases in 1,154 games. Defensively, Jerry had a .981 fielding percentage and received recognition in 2001 as one of the top 100 second basemen of all time.

By 1988, Jerry Remy's love for baseball had helped him find success in broadcasting. He began to work for the New England Sports Network (NESN), as the regular color commentator for Red Sox broadcast. He was paired with Ned Martin and eventually Bob Kurtz from 1988 to 2000. From 2001 to 2015, Jerry joined play-by-play announcer, Don Orsillo. In 2016, Remy began working with Dave O'Brien until his death on October, 30, 2021.

In November of 2008, Jerry had surgery to remove a small cancerous area from his lung. Yes, Jerry Remy had smoked for years. While in the hospital he suffered from a bout of pneumonia and an infection. He took a short absence from his broadcasting duties. He returned to the booth four months later, to a standing ovation from the crowd. Jerry later revealed that he was also suffering from depression and would likely skip some of the Red Sox road trips and that he was receiving treatment. Remy took more time off in 2013 and did not return until 2014. He took another short leave during the 2016 season. In 2017, Remy announced that his cancer had returned. It was actually his fourth bout with the disease. In November 2018, Jerry told the public he was cancer free, but it was not to be. You don't beat cancer, you survive cancer. On June 12, 2021, Remy left Fenway Park during the third inning with shortness of breath and was admitted to the local hospital. He would later return to Fenway Park on October 5, 2021, to throw out the ceremonial first pitch before the American League Wild Card Game.

Jerry Remy's reach was far and wide. He worked hard for The Jimmy Fund that supports the Dana-Farber Cancer

Institute of New England. Not only did Jerry attend their annual telethon, but he invited cancer patients into the broadcast booth and visited with cancer patients at the hospital.

Jerry Remy wrote three books about baseball, two with author Corey Sandler and one with Nick Cafardo. <u>Watching Baseball: Discovering the Game within the Game</u> was written in 2004, <u>Jerry Remy's Red Sox Heroes: The RemDawg's All-Time Favorite Red Sox, Great Moments, and Top Teams</u> in 2009, and <u>If These Walls Could Talk: Stories from the Boston Red Sox Dugout, Locker Room, and Press Box</u> in 2019. Remy will also be remembered for writing his children's book series entitled <u>Wally the Green Monster</u>.

Jerry owned a hotdog stand named RemDawg's. It was located right outside Fenway Park. Remy also opened Jerry Remy's Sports Bar & Grill in Terminal C of the Logan International Airport. Jerry owned three other establishments over the years, but they have all been closed or sold.

Jerry and his partner Don Orsillo won four New England Emmy Awards, and Jerry was voted Massachusetts' favorite sports announcer in 2004, by *Sports Illustrated*. He was inducted into the Boston Red Sox Hall of Fame, in 2006, and elected President of Red Sox Nation, in 2007. Jerry was also inducted into the Massachusetts Broadcasters' Hall of Fame, in 2017. Remy was the first to call David Ortiz "Big Papi" on television. No doubt, Jerry would be pleased to find out that Big Papi has now been elected into the Baseball Hall of Fame Museum in Cooperstown.

Jerry Remy, a fine second baseman and even a better broadcaster, passed away on October 30, 2021. He was 68 and had suffered from lung cancer for over 13 years. Cancer finally threw Jerry Remy an unhittable curveball; his game was over. When the world of baseball found out, there were more long faces in the crowd than there are at the finish line at Belmont. Like Jim Valvano, Kay Yow and Stuart Scott, he was a living example of how to fight. He is survived by his wife, Phoebe, and three children. They had two sons, Jared and Jordan, and a daughter Jenna.

Jerry Remy once said, "Playing the Yankees in New York was like parachuting into Russia. You were just not welcome." A force in the booth, it was his voice that put millions of fans to bed each night during the baseball season. He will never really be gone.

OLD GARBAGE CAN

Vince Lombardi said, "I firmly believe that man's finest hour, his greatest fulfillment to all he holds dear is the moment when he has worked his heart out in a good cause and lies exhausted on the field victorious!" It has been said, "If you can't take it, don't play professional football. You've got to accept it; football is a game for men, not boys." My question is what kind of man?

He arrived in pro football by way of Ohio State University. A hero is not somebody who's not afraid. He's a guy who's scared to death, but does what's right anyway. This guy displayed passion in everything he did. Known as a man of faith, he combined talent with kindness and his attitude was contagious. All of his teammates liked him. With his high-pitched voice, this fellow often told strangers he was a business man, but his main business was scoring touchdowns. He was not a good loser. So, finding the end zone just came naturally to him. If you wanted someone to score a touchdown, he was your guy. He would literally propel himself into the end zone.

There is a difference in pure speed and football speed. At six feet one inch tall and weighing nearly 200 pounds, he was quick and explosive, but owned very little pure speed. He was the type of player who always ran out of the tunnel at 90 mph, with his hair on fire. This guy was a bully as a runner. The man loved running people over, especially defensive tackles. He had small hands and was described by the press as a gritty runner. It seemed like his feet and his mouth never stopped moving. Like a trash can, he was always full of himself. You couldn't dent him or knock him over. Detroit Lions' Hall-of-Fame defensive tackle, Alex Karras, nicknamed Tom Matte "Old Garbage Can" for his tough running style. "He was so solid, heavy, and low to the ground, it was like running into a trash can," said Karras. No matter how many hits he took, Tom Matte always found a way to get up.

Thomas Roland Matte was born in Pittsburgh, Pennsylvania, on June 14, 1939. Tom was the older of two sons born to his dad, Joseph Roland Matte, a professional hockey player, and his mom, Dorothy Stevens Matte, who worked as a secretary. His family later moved to Cleveland, Ohio, where he attended Shaw High School, located in a tough neighborhood known as Cleveland Heights. "I had to fight my way to school and then back home every day," said Tom. Matte eventually became an Eagle Scout. Tom played football at Shaw High School and graduated in 1957. He was then recruited by Woody Hayes, the head coach at Ohio State. Hayes was known for his run first, pass second offense. It was a perfect fit for Tom Matte. Tom wore #41 and started at running back in 1958, but was then moved to the quarterback position for the Buckeyes, from 1959 to 1960. "Quarterback is the most important position in football, but it is still only one position out of 22 starters," said Woody Hayes.

Running and passing all over the field, this kid could put on a show in college. He made passing a football look easy, and it's not. In college, it seemed Tom threw his best passes under the most difficult circumstances. Very few threw the football like he did. His teammates called him "The Arm." Even though Matte became one of the pure passing quarterbacks in the game, still he was known more for his running than his passing skills. Matte was not only the MVP of his 1960 Buckeye team, but he was also selected to the All-Big Ten Conference Team and he was chosen an All-American. He finished seventh in the voting for the Heisman

Trophy. During his college career, Tom attempted 146 passes and completed 78 for 1,176 yards and 12 touchdowns. He also threw 6 interceptions. Tom also ran the ball 258 times for 868 yards and scored three additional touchdowns.

Tom Matte was selected by the Baltimore Colts with the 7th pick in the first round of the 1961 NFL Draft. Matte continued to wear #41 with the Baltimore Colts. From 1961 to 1972, Tom rushed for 4,646 yards and scored 45 rushing touchdowns. Tom also caught 249 passes for 2,869 yards and scored an additional 12 touchdowns.

In 1965, Matte was used as an emergency quarterback, as Johnny Unitas and backup Gary Cuozzo were both injured. Matte shined against the Los Angeles Rams, with a 20-17 regular-season finale win. The following week, Matte again played well, but the Colts lost in a one-game playoff to the Green Bay Packers, 13-10 in overtime. Colts' head coach Don Shula had designed a wristband for Matte to wear with all the plays inscripted. That wristband is now on display at the Pro Football Hall of Fame in Canton, Ohio.

In the 1968 NFL Championship game against the Cleveland Browns, Tom Matte rushed for three touchdowns, as the Colts shut out the Browns, 34-0. Tom graced the cover of the January 6, 1969 *Sports Illustrated*. His best season was 1969 as he rushed for the most touchdowns. Matte rushed for 909 yards on 235 carries and scored league high 11 touchdowns. He also added 43 catches for 513 yards, for two additional touchdowns. Tom was selected All-Pro in 1968 and 1969. Tom was injured in the first game of the 1970 season against the San Diego Chargers and did not play the rest of the year, including their Super Bowl V loss to the Dallas Cowboys, 16-13. He was, however, awarded a Super Bowl ring. Tom played in all 14 games during the 1971 season, but ended up on the practice squad in 1972. Tom Matte was traded to the San Diego Chargers in 1973, but chose to retire.

In 1984, Baltimore Colts' owner Robert Irsey moved the team to Indianapolis, Indiana. Many former Colt players, including Johnny Unitas and Tom Matte, were angered. After football, Tom hosted charity golf events and spent four years broadcasting the University of Maryland football games on radio with Johnny Holiday. In 1992, Tom opened a pork rib joint at the new Baltimore Orioles' baseball park. From 1996 to 2005, Tom Matte joined Scott Garceau on radio, broadcasting the Baltimore Ravens' games.

Professional running back and part-time quarterback, Tom Matte, died from complications of leukemia on Tuesday, November 2, 2021. Tom had been treated for bleeding ulcers his entire career. He was 82 and living in Ruxton, Maryland. Tom is survived by his wife of 59 years, Judy, a daughter Katherine, a son Roland Thomas and four grandchildren.

Very few remember that on January 12, 1969, Matte became the first running back to top the 100-yard rushing mark in a Super Bowl. Tom rushed for 116 yards, on just 11 carries in Super Bowl III, against the New York Jets in a loss, 16-7. The old garbage can rumbled that day.

TERRIBLE THINGS, MAN!

In the 1950s, professional football players were seen as the new breed of the old American frontier ideal of toughness. The game was not defined by soaring touchdown passes or broken field runs, but by two guys down in the bloody pits with clinched fists and nasty thoughts. It was a muscle game they played in the 1950s, the heyday of the big running backs. Players considered it their job to hurt the opposition. Flying leg whips and sharp elbows were the norm for offensive linemen. Not to be outdone, defensive players were deadly in a pileup, elbows, knees, jabs to the ribs and x-rated comments about your mother. Intimidation was what they were after. In those days there were no MRI's, CT Scans or scopes. Treating players with pain killers was as common as birthday candles on a cake, so you took the shots, taped it up and went back in.

The game was played when ball carriers were not considered down until they were stopped and pinned to the ground. This advocated piling on and linebackers like Bill Pellington, Bill George, Joe Schmidt, and Ray Nitschke thrived. It's no accident that a large number of the players in the Pro Football Hall of Fame played a portion of their career in the 1950s and 1960s.

In 1956, his rookie season, there were only 33 players on a professional football roster, and only 13 of them played defense. The blessing was that his personality fit the times. His action on the field of play was raw, pure and real. This guy was like a trigger without a safety. His effort was contagious, all consuming, like a virus. When you are the hammer, everything else is a nail. This guy made more people hurt than food poisoning. He never knew what "slow up" meant. Standing 6 feet 1 inch tall and weighing 230 pounds, he had enough speed to pursue, and he loved to hit. He was always in a hurry to get on the field, get off the field and hit the running backs. His toughness became legendary around the league. He could be hardnosed, unforgiving and hard as an anvil. The man knew the game of football backward and forward. He always spoke his mind and could be as subtle as a smack in the mouth. This fellow may have been the single most intense player to ever wear a New York Giants' uniform. Sam Huff was scary. He was so mean-looking, you would lose your balance if you stared at him for more than 30 seconds. Huff may have been the reason Freddie Kruger moved to Elm Street. I was always glad to see Huff play on television because that meant he wasn't hiding in the back seat of my car with a knife and masking tape. Football would become more important to him than BBQ sauce was to spare ribs. Huff was the kind of fellow who would take his heart out of his chest and show it to you while it was still beating. The man would play with blood running from his nose, mad at everybody, his eyes deep-set in their sockets. He was always stirring the pot.

In the 1950s and 1960s, it was written that you would much rather play the Cleveland Browns twice than the New York Giants once. Cleveland may beat you on the scoreboard, but New York would make you ache all week. Until 1956, NFL games were not televised locally and the Giants drew less than 30,000 fans a game. That year, Frank Gifford and Sam Huff of the Giants captured the city of New York. Gifford was crowned the league's MVP and Huff became the first defensive player to become a superstar in the NFL. Before Junior Seau, Ray Lewis or Mike Singleterry, there was Sam Huff. Yes, Sam Huff was tough alright, borderline dirty. He once knocked the great Jim Brown out of a game. Do you know what this man would do to you if you were a running back? Terrible things, man! terrible things!

The NFL lost a legend on Saturday, November 13, 2021. Sam Huff made middle linebacker a permanent tradition in the game of football. Like everyone else my age, I couldn't wait for Sundays when New York Yankees' and Giants' announcer, Bob Sheppard, would introduce each player. "Ladies and gentlemen: #70 Sam Huff." Every lineman on my high school football team wanted to wear #70. Watching Sam Huff play altered my life. I wondered what Huff ate for breakfast, because I wanted some of that. I now knew what was expected of me as an athlete. Sam Huff was as sharp as a "Sugar Ray" Leonard jab. He owned a heart bigger than a rib eye steak at Toots Shore's. I'm ashamed to say that the game that Sam Huff knew and revered is gone.

Robert Lee Huff was born on October 4, 1934, in Morgantown, West Virginia. The fourth of six kids of Oral and Catherine Huff, Sam grew up in Edna Gas, West Virginia, in the No. 9 coal mining camp near Farmington, West Virginia. Huff could never recall how he came to be called Sam. On the banks of the Monongahela River, the Huff family lived in a small five-room row house painted red to cover up the color of the dust. These houses had no indoor plumbing or running water and were owned by the Consolidated Mining Company. This town no longer exists. Growing up during the Great Depression, Sam went barefooted until he started school. His father, two of his brothers and several uncles, cousins and nephews all worked in the mines. Relatives with black lung disease were common. Huff began playing football in the 7th grade. He attended the now closed Farmington High School (700 students) where he played several sports. Starting at offensive guard and defensive tackle, he helped lead the team to an undefeated season in 1951. Huff was selected All-State and named on the First Team All-Mason Dixon Conference team, in 1952. As an adult male, it was expected that you would spend more than half your life four miles underground in the coal mines.

After graduating from high school in 1952, Sam was recruited by Head Football Coach Art "Pappy" Lewis and signed by the Mountaineers of West Virginia. Sam had also been recruited and visited the University of Florida and the U.S. Military Academy at West Point. Sam married his high school sweetheart Mary Helen Fletcher. They had three children; Robert Lee "Sam" Huff, Jr., Catherine Ann, and Joseph D.

Wearing #75 for the Mountaineers, Huff started at the offensive guard position his sophomore year, and he was then moved to defensive tackle the next two years. During his four years at West Virginia, the team recorded a 31-7 win-loss record and a trip to the Sugar Bowl. During Huffs time at West Virginia, the Mountaineers beat Penn State three years in a row. That had never been done before by any other team. Sam also kicked for the football team and played catcher for the baseball team. The year 1955 was a big year for Sam. Not only was he voted All-American, but he served as the co-captain in both the East-West Shrine Game and the Senior Bowl. Sam never owned a suit of clothes until he attended the University of West Virginia.

While in college, Sam spoke about going down in the mines with his father. His dad wanted him to know what he did for a living. Sam said they had a big machine down there that the miners nicknamed "The Sam Huff Special." Eventually, there was an explosion that killed 93 miners. "Unbelievably, I knew every one of them," said Sam. Was Sam Huff running away from his family and the coal mines of West Virginia or towards the game of football? I think the answer on both accounts was yes.

Huff received letters from all the professional teams at that time except the New York Giants. So, Sam Huff was very much surprised when he was drafted with the 30th pick in the 3rd round by the New York Giants in the 1956 NFL Draft. The first person with the Giants to call Huff was owner, Wellington Mara. There were no sports agents in those days and Mara offered Huff $7,000 to sign. In 1956, there were only 12 teams in each league and they only played 12 games during the season. So, jobs in the NFL were limited. Sam accepted the offer. The Giants' training camp in 1956 was located at St. Michaels College in Winooski, Vermont. Tired, exhausted and missing home, rookies Don Chandler and Sam Huff felt like they were wasting their time. They decided to leave camp. An assistant coach talked Huff into staying, but not Chandler. So, Huff decided to accompany his friend Don to the airport in Burlington, Vermont. When they arrived, Chandler was told that his plane would be an hour late. Soon after, a station wagon pulled up in front of the airport and out stepped Vince Lombardi. Lombardi refused to hear anything about leaving and ordered them to get into his station wagon. "If that plane had been on time," said Huff. "Chandler would have been on it and maybe I would have gone with him."

The New York Giants have a storied history. They had been purchased by Timothy J. Mara in 1925 for $500. In 1954, Jim Lee Howell, a former Giants' player and assistant coach, became the head coach. Howell chose Tom Landry and Vince Lombardi as his assistants. In 1956, Sam Huff, Don Chandler, Jim Katcavage, Andy Robustelli, Dick Modzelewski, and Ed Hughes all joined the New York Giants. Don Chandler would become his roommate until Huff was later traded to Washington. The Giants also moved their home field from the Pologrounds in New York to Yankee Stadium. Sam always insisted that he shared the use of

Mickey Mantle's locker at Yankee Stadium. Frank Gifford claimed otherwise. After the move to Yankee Stadium, most of the Giants' lived in the Concourse Plaza Hotel, located on a hill above old Yankee Stadium. Huff would get a call from Giants' defensive coach, Tom Landry, who would invite him up to his apartment to watch game film. It was Landry that switched Huff to the defensive side of the ball. You see, the middle linebacker position didn't exist until Landry perfected the 4-3 defense. The 4-3 defense replaced the 5-2 defense. The 4-3 defense consisted of four down linemen, three linebackers and four defensive backs. The linemen would slant and the linebackers blitzed, therefore funneling the ball carrier into Huff.

Sam always claimed that Landry and Lombardi didn't like each other and rarely spoke three words to each other during the day. "They were two different personalities. Landry was stoic, mechanical, unsmiling and quiet. Lombardi was volatile, grinning and exuberant. You could hear Vince laughing from four blocks away," said Sam. "You couldn't hear Landry from the next chair."

On October 7, 1956, the Giants were playing the Chicago Cardinals. Ray Beck was playing linebacker for the Giants that day when he was injured. Huff, wearing #70 for the Giants, went in as his replacement. It was his first professional game. Huff was later knocked silly during his first year in the league by tough guy, Bob St. Clair. "I saw Huff standing there. Standing by a pileup is a typical rookie thing. You can hit them so hard they'll think their head was on a swivel." said St. Clair. The Giants went on to win the next five games and finish first in the Eastern Conference, with an 8-3-1 win-loss record. The New York Giants won the NFL title in 1956 by beating the Chicago Bears 47-7. Huff was named the NFL Rookie of the Year. In 1956, the payout to the NFL Champions was $4,718.77. The losers' share was $3,111.33.

Mara offered him a $500 raise for the following season.

In 1957, Huff blocked a punt against the Green Bay Packers and returned it for a touchdown. In 1958, the New York Giants had six future Hall-of-Fame players on their team. That year, the Giants' defense held one of their opponents to zero passing yards. The New York Giants beat the Cleveland Browns three times in 1958, including the playoffs and twice in 1959. Stopping Jim Brown and Bobby Mitchell was one thing Sam Huff loved about those games. In 1958, the Giants' 4-3 defense gave up only 197 points to their opponents in 12 games or 16.4 points per game; and on December 21, 1958, in front of 61,254 fans, beat the Cleveland Browns 10-0 in the Eastern Conference title game. During that game, the Giants defense and Huff held Cleveland to 86 yards of total offense and only seven first downs. Huff intercepted one pass and shut Jim Brown down to only 8-yards rushing in seven attempts. It's interesting that no one talks about that. "Let's face it," said Huff. "No linebacker in the league could stop Jim Brown man-to-man. All you could do is grab hold, hang on and wait for help." Sam Huff only made $8,000 that year, after being named All-Pro in 1957.

The 1958 NFL Championship game was the first to be televised nationwide. The Baltimore Colts led 14-3 at halftime. The New York Giants came back to take the lead 17-14, but the game ended in a tie, 17-17. It would be the first time ever that an NFL Championship game would be decided in "Sudden Death" overtime. Neither team had any idea what to do. The referees gathered the coaches together and laid out the rules. Colts quarterback Johnny Unitas led the team down the field and fullback Alan Ameche scored from the one-yard line to make the final score, 23-17. Huff had slanted toward the left side of the Colts offense, but Ameche ran off right tackle for a touchdown. "I can still see the picture of him running through that big hole at the goal line. That still haunts me," said Huff. This game became widely known as "The Greatest Game Ever Played."

During that 1958 Championship Game against the Colts, Sam played with cracked ribs. He swore he could feel the fans watching him play. Baltimore Colts offensive center "Buzz" Nutter once said, "Sam knew where every camera was. He was the only guy who should have had his jersey number written on the bottom of his cleats. He'd end up on top of every pile so everyone would have to get up from under him. He always had that #70 pointed where the camera could see it." That night the Giants may have fallen short on the scoreboard, but the legend of Sam Huff was born. The public could not get enough of this guy.

In 1959, Huff and the Giants again went to the NFL Championship Game, which ended in a 31-16 loss to the Baltimore Colts. He was later named the top NFL linebacker in professional football. His coach, Tom Landry, was hired to coach the Dallas Cowboys after the 1959 season ended.

On August 15, 1960, during an exhibition game in Toronto, Canada, against the Chicago Bears, Sam Huff became the first ever NFL player to be mic'd up for a game. Sam Huff was such a devastating tackler and so visible on the field of play that CBS Television made a documentary in 1960 entitled "The Violet World of Sam Huff." Sam Huff became the first NFL player wired for sound with a microphone, which allowed the national television audience to hear firsthand the brutal impact of bodies meeting bodies in the trenches. He wore a one-pound backpack hidden under his shoulder pads and covered it up with a sponge. He also wore a transmitter on the front. Every play was recorded along with every hit. One of the deals Sam made was that CBS would cut out all the foul language and they did. On 10/31/1960 Walter Cronkite narrated this documentary. Cronkite started the program this way. "Today you will play pro football riding on

Sam Huff's broad back." The Bears won 16-7.

Huff claimed that his most memorable play during his career came against Jim Taylor of the Packers. Huff always respected Jim Taylor. "We really went at it," said Huff. "I remember denting my helmet hitting that sucker and splitting his helmet down the middle." Before the 1962 NFL Championship game between Green Bay and New York, Huff was given his assignment. Jim Taylor, known for making enemies, was targeted by middle linebacker, Sam Huff, and the Giants' defense. It has been said that the profanity used by both teams during this game was unprecedented. "If Taylor went to buy a program, Huff was supposed to hit him. Wherever Taylor went, Huff went with him" said, Packer offensive guard Jerry Kramer. Final score: Green Bay 16, New York 7.

Soon after the Giants lost the 1963 NFL Championship Game to the Chicago Bears, 14-10, head coach Allie Sherman began to dismantle the team. Huff was furious when he learned he had been traded to the Washington Redskins, which had finished with a 3-11 win-loss record in 1963. "As long as I live," Huff wrote in his autobiography, "I will never forgive Allie Sherman for trading me." Huff was making $19,000 a year with the Giants when he was traded to Washington. His 1964 salary with the Redskins exceed $30,000 a year plus an additional $5,000 for scouting. Sam Huffs impact was immediate as the Redskins finished second in the league in defense in 1965. It took a few years, but on November 27, 1966, the Washington Redskins met the New York Giants at RFK Stadium. With only seven seconds to go and the Redskins leading 69-41, Washington called a timeout and sent the field goal team onto the field. Redskin coach Otto Graham was later criticized for running up the score, but Huff took the blame and claimed that it was he that had called for the field goal team to get out there. Charlie

Gogolak's 29-yard field goal made the final score 72-41. It remains the highest-scoring game in NFL history, and the Redskins' 72 points are still the most ever scored by a team in a regular-season game. "Justice was done," said Huff after the game.

Huff was forced to miss several games during the 1967 season due to an ankle injury. He retired at the end of that season, but later returned after one year as a player-coach in 1969 for the Redskins new head coach, Vince Lombardi. Huff retired for good after the 1970 season ended.

Practice to Sam Huff was just like a game. "If you came into my territory, I was going to deck you, and I did." he said. "When I went out on the football field, it was the greatest feeling. I played the game for me, because I loved the game, I loved to practice. I believe it's America's game," said Huff. "It's funny but true," said Frank Gifford. "When Sam ran off the field with the defense and I was running on with the offense, he would say, 'Would you guys go out there and hold them for a while this time?'"

After retirement, Huff took a position with J. P. Stevens in New York City as a textiles sales rep. In 1970, he spent the next season as a Redskins linebackers coach; and then in 1971, he took a job with Marriott in their marketing department as a go-between for the hotel company and athletic teams. Huff stayed with the Marriott Corporation from 1971 to 1998.

Sam then spent three years (1972-1975) doing color commentary for the New York Giants games before moving on to the Washington Redskin games on radio with Sonny Jurgenson and Frank Herzog. Huff spent the next 38 years (1975-2012) on air with Washington and did the color commentary for all three of their Super Bowl victories. On air, Huff continued to rage against changes in the game. Sam hated today's players celebrating after a catch. "I'll tell you what I'd do. I would take the 15-yard penalty and knock him into the stands," said Sam. "So would Chuck Bednarick, Bill George, Joe Schmidt, all the linebackers. We wouldn't put up with that crap." On August 1, 1989, with the help of *Washington Post* sports writer Leonard Shapiro, Huff released his autobiography entitled <u>Tough Stuff: The Man in the Middle</u>. Huff retired from broadcasting after the 2012 season. During his last few years in the broadcast booth, Sam's memory began to fade. He sometimes forgot player's names or had difficulty remembering the rules of football. In 2013, Huff was diagnosed with a form of dementia.

During his 13-year playing career (1956-1969), Sam started 159 games out of 168 played: 99 with the Giants and 60 with the Redskins. He was voted to the All-Pro Team twice (1958 and 1959) and the Pro-Bowl five times (1958-1961 and 1964). Huff played in six NFL Championship Games (1956, 1958, 1959, 1961, 1962 and 1963) during his eight years with the Giants, but was only a part of one NFL Championship in 1956. In 1957, Huff returned a blocked punt for his first professional touchdown against the Green Bay Packers. Huff also had 30 interceptions for 381 yards and returned two of those for touchdowns: one each against the Redskins in 1963 and one against the Cardinals in 1969. He recovered 17 fumbles and returned two for touchdowns: one against the Steelers in 1959 and one against the Eagles in 1961. On November 30, 1959, Huff became only the second NFL player to be featured on the cover of *Time* magazine. Detroit Lions quarterback, Bobby Layne had been the first, five years earlier. Sam Huff was also named the Most Valuable Player of the 1961 Pro Bowl.

Sam Huff is a member of the NFL 1950s All-Decade Team. He is also a member of the New York Giants' Ring of Honor and the Washington Redskins' Ring of Fame. He joined the College Football Hall of Fame and the Pro Football Hall of Fame in 1982. The 1982 Pro Football Hall of Fame class included Doug Adkins, Merlin Olsen and George Musso. Huff's presenter was Tom Landry. In 1991, Huff was also inducted into the University of West Virginia Sports Hall of Fame. In 1999, Huff joined the National High School Hall of Fame. On November 24, 2005, Huff's #75 was retired by the University of West Virginia.

Very few remember that in 1960, Huff campaigned in West Virginia for John F. Kennedy for President. A decade later, in 1970, Sam Huff ran for a seat in the U.S. House of Representatives, but lost in the West Virginia Democratic primary to Bob Mollohan.

In 1986, Huff started breeding thoroughbred racehorses at Sporting Life Farms located in Middleburg, Virginia. One of his fillies, known as "Bursting Forth," won the 1998 Matchmaker Handicap. Sam was also the chief executive of the West Virginia Breeders' Classics horse races in Charles Town, West Virginia.

Interestingly, Sam Huff's favorite player was an offensive center for the Cleveland Browns by the name of Frank Gatski. Frank was also a West Virginia boy, and he was eventually inducted into the Pro Football Hall of Fame in 1985.

Sam Huff left us on a Saturday, November 13, 2021. Jim Porter, President of the Pro Football Hall of Fame announced that the HOF flag in Canton, Ohio, would be flown at half-mast. Even though Sam died eight years after he learned that he had been diagnosed with dementia, it was noted that he died from natural causes at a hospital located in Winchester, Virginia. Huff was 87. He is survived by his former wife, Mary Helen Fletcher Huff, his daughter Catherine Ann, a son Joseph D. Huff, and his live-in partner for over 30 years, Carol Holden, three grandchildren and one great-grandchild. Sam and Mary divorced in the late 1980s and their second son, Robert Sam Huff, Jr., died in 2018. Sam Huff lived a tremendous football life, yet I always felt he longed for more.

The man made defense famous.

"I never let up on anybody" said Huff. "I don't think that I ever quit on a play. If you had the football, I was going to hit you, and when I hit you, I tried to hit you hard enough to hurt you. That's the way the game should be played." Even now, when I watch Washington play, my Dad is alive again. Thank the good Lord for Sam Huff.

THE QUAIL

The 1950s have often been referred to as the Golden Age of Broadcasting. Baseball being broadcast on the radio was the background music of America. In its early days, the game could be heard in every small town barbershop, on the radio. The game and its announcers inspired the listeners and brought the players to life. That's how I learned about this great game and these great players. It was a Thursday, October 13, 1960, and I was almost nine years old. My brother Cliff was only five and my dad, Gordon, had let me join the Chestnut Hills Little League baseball team. I played right field. When there was time, Dad also began to play catch with me in our front yard. His favorite player was third baseman Eddie Mathews of the Milwaukee Braves. Dad also bought me a transistor radio. Listening to that radio, I not only learned about this game called baseball, but the names of these faraway cities and players. I went to sleep every night in baseball Heaven. The game I was about to listen to would go down in history as one of the best. It was Game Seven of the 1960 World Series between the underdog Pittsburgh Pirates and the magnificent New York Yankees. I had listened to broadcaster Mel Allen and the Yankees on several occasions before and yes, like most boys my age, my hero was Mickey Mantle. Game Seven was played at Forbes Field, the spacious home of the Pittsburgh Pirates. Through Game Six, the Yankees had dominated the Series in runs scored, with 46 versus the Pirates 17, but still the Series was tied, three games apiece. Game Seven started at 1 PM in the afternoon and lasted only 2:36 minutes, as 36,683 attended and hundred of thousands more, like me, listened on the radio. Yes, my dad let me skip school. The first World Series night game was not broadcast until 1971. Game Seven was broadcast by NBC on television by Mel Allen and Bob Prince, but on the radio, I got to listen to Chuck Thompson and Jack Quinlan call the game for NBC radio. A ticket in the reserved seating section cost you a whopping $7.70. As I grew older and my love for baseball increased, I purchased a cassette copy of Game Seven of the 1960 World Series. I can't tell you how many times I have listened to Game Seven of the 1960 World Series.

What I do remember the most is that during this game I was introduced to "The Quail," the name Pirates' broadcaster Bob Prince had given to Bill Virdon, the centerfielder and leadoff hitter of the Pittsburgh Pirates. Yes, it's true that Pittsburgh's Bill Mazeroski hit the game-winning home run to beat the Yankees that day and win the World Series, but it had been Bill Virdon who had played a huge role in the outcome of that game. "We had an outstanding relationship. Bob Prince was always full of fun, always talking, always telling a story or a joke. He was fun to be around," said Virdon. "When I got here in May of 1956, Prince started calling me "The Quail" affectionately, because so many of the hits I got were flares over the infield. He referred to them as dying quails," exclaimed Virdon.

Never in my wildest dreams did I think some 37 years later (1997), in Houston, I would get to meet The Quail in person at an Astros' Caravan Event. New Astros' skipper, Larry Dierker had hired Bill Virdon as his bench coach, and Virdon was signing autographs for the public. Dierker needed somebody he could trust who knew his way around the league. Even at the age of 66, Virdon was such a fun guy to be around. Some joked that he could arrange a "meet and greet" with Santa Claus. It was some kind of day.

William Charles Virdon was born on June 9, 1931, to Charles and Bertha Virdon. His parents had originally moved from Missouri during the depression, so Charles could find work in the automobile factories. Bill's baseball life began in Hazel Park, Michigan. As a kid, Bill grew up a Detroit Tigers fan and Hank Greenberg was his favorite. His dad, Charles, was very strict, very disciplined, and Bill was taught by his father to be strong. Bill grew tall, quick and agile. He became an excellent athlete at West Plains High School and participated in track, basketball and football. Interestingly, West Plains did not have a baseball team. It was not until the summer of 1948 that Bill had a chance to play organized baseball. Bill was pressured by his friend, Gene Richmond, to travel to Clay City, Kansas, some 300 miles away, to play for an AABC (American Amateur Baseball Congress) team, where the two of them both made the team. Virdon made the team as a shortstop, but was quickly moved to centerfield because of his arm and his athleticism. After a 50-game season, Bill decided to attend a New York Yankees tryout camp in Branson, Missouri. After the tryout camp, he returned to Kansas and continued to play ball until after his senior year. When that season ended, Bill enrolled at Drury University and went back to Branson and signed a contract with Yankees' scout, Tom Greenwade, the same scout who had signed Mickey Mantle a year earlier. Virdon signed for a $1,800 bonus.

In 1950, Virdon began his professional career in Independence, Kansas, with a Class D team from the Kansas-Oklahoma-Missouri (KOM) League. His manager, Malcolm "Bunny" Mick, had been an outfielder and pushed Virdon to become better. The story on Bill Virdon was this. He was successful because he was so hard on himself. He could make all the throws, had an amazing arm and could throw on the run. This guy had such a strong arm he could throw sunshine past a rooster. At the end of his first season Bill was promoted to the Yankees' Triple-A team known as the Kansas City Blues. Bill hit .341 in 14 games. In 1951, Bill married his wife Shirley in November of that year, and they lived in Springfield, Missouri. That same year, you could find Bill with the Norfolk Tars of the Class-B Piedmont League, and then with the Binghamton Triplets of the Class-A Eastern League in 1952.

Although his hitting numbers were down, the Yankees were impressed with his fielding and invited him to the Yankees' pre-camp in Arizona, in 1953. He was later promoted again to the Kansas City Blues that same year. This Yankee team was loaded with players everyone had heard about. Elston Howard, Bob Cerv, Bill Skowron and Vic Power all played some in the outfield. Still, Bill struggled at the plate hitting just .233 and was demoted to the Birmingham Barons of the Double-A Southern Association, at the end of the 1953 season.

As luck would have it, Bill's new roommate was now future Pittsburgh Pirate, Hal Smith. Hal convinced him to stop trying to hit a home run in each at-bat. Virdon, now wearing round, wire-rimmed eyeglasses concentrated on hitting line drives, and he batted .317 in 42 games. Bill later credited his improved hitting to better vision. He would be invited to his first Spring Training with the Yankees in 1954. New York started Hank Bauer in right field, Gene Woodling in left field and Mickey Mantle in center. "I could see that I was going to have a problem breaking in with the Yankees," said Virdon. "They had the best outfield in baseball and I was stuck behind Mickey Mantle" There's a funny story of Virdon shagging fly balls in the outfield with the Yankees. "I fielded a fly ball and fired away," said Bill. "Somehow Casey Stengel got between me and the relay man, and I proceeded to hit him in the back with one of my strongest throws and knocked him down. The other outfielders were laughing and pointing at me," exclaimed Virdon. "Stengel got up, shook himself off and hollered, 'If you guys throw like that in a game, you might throw someone out.'" With a smile, Bill said, "Two weeks later, I was traded." In April of 1954, Bill Virdon was traded with two other players to the St. Louis Cardinals for All-Star Enos Slaughter. He was sent to St. Louis's Triple-A team, the Rochester Red Wings of the International League. Virdon hit 22 home runs, batted a league-leading .333 and was second in MVP voting behind Elston Howard.

Virdon only played one year of Winter Ball in the Cuban League for the Havana Lions after the 1954 season. He would finish as a Cuban- League All-Star, batting .340 and playing a terrific centerfield. After watching Virdon play, Cardinals' Manager Eddie Stanky considered moving Stan Musial from the outfield to first base to make room for Virdon in the outfield. Wally Moon was moved from center to right field and Virdon started in center. Musial was moved from right field to first base. Bill was given Enos Slaughter's #9 to wear. Virdon debuted on April 12, 1955, against the Chicago Cubs. He was 23. In 1955, the left-handed leadoff-hitting Bill Virdon batted .281 with 17 home runs and 68 RBI's and became the bright spot on a Cardinals' team that finished next to last in the National League. He was named the 1955 National League Rookie of the Year. A slow start for Bill ended in a trade in 1956. Virdon was traded to the Pittsburgh Pirates on May 17, 1956, for outfielder, Bobby Del Greco, and pitcher, Dick Littlefield. He would wear #18 for the Pirates. Pittsburgh had not had a winning team since 1948, but they were young. Bill Mazeroski was 19 and Roberto Clemente had turned 25. When Virdon was added to the Bucs' outfield with Clemente and Lee Walls, they were considered one of the best outfields in the National League.

The Pittsburgh fans flocked to Forbes Field in 1956 when the Pirates got off to a 30-21 start. In 1957, General Manager Joe L. Brown hired Danny Murtaugh as the team's manager. "He pushed me," said Virdon, "and made sure that I got all of the instruction that I should get."

In the late 1950s, baseball was not important in Pittsburgh, but what Bill did was made it important for everybody. Bill Virdon played a fine centerfield in Forbes Field for ten years (1956-1965). He never suffered a major injury and was never placed on the disabled list. His stance in the batter's box and the wave of his bat signaled impending doom to the pitcher, yet he only reached the seats 91 times during his career.

In 1956, he hit .319 during his second season in the Majors. Bill was also considered one the fastest in the game while running from home plate to first base. He was clocked at 3.5 seconds while hitting and 3.4 seconds while bunting. Only Mickey Mantle's 3.1 seconds was better.

"He's an underrated player," said Roberto Clemente. "He doesn't get the headlines because he makes everything look easy." The man practically slept and ate baseball in large quantities. Forbes Field was the biggest ballpark in baseball. The distance measured 435 feet to the centerfield wall, 457 to left-center and 419 to right-center. With a strong arm and terrific speed, Bill led the league in 1959 and 1961, in putouts and assists. In 1962, Virdon won his first and only Gold Glove Award. "I didn't have to worry about running into fences," said Bill.

The 1960 season would be unbelievable. In 1959, Smokey Burgess, Harvey Haddix, Don Hoak and Rocky Nelson became Pittsburgh Pirates. Gino Cimoli, Wilmer "Vinegar Bend" Mizell, and Hal Smith were added the following year. The 1960 Pirates led the National League in hitting and runs scored, while placing second in slugging. Still, they only hit 120 home runs as a team. It was a magical year. They played small ball and every time they needed a run, they got it. Throughout the Series, Virdon's ability to perform acrobatic catches paid off. Although the Pirates had been picked to finish in fourth place behind the Braves, Dodgers and Giants, Pittsburgh won the National League pennant and played the dreaded New York Yankees for the title. This Series would go seven games and has been labeled as one of the best World Series in history. Here's how it ended.

With the Yankees leading 7-4 in the eighth inning of Game Seven of the 1960 World Series, Pirates' Geno Cimoli batted for pitcher Elroy Face and hit a single. Virdon then followed with a routine grounder to the Yankees' shortstop, Tony Kubek. It appeared to be a double-play ball, but the infield at Forbes Field was hard and bumpy. The ball took a bad bounce and hit Kubek in the throat. Virdon made it safely to first base and Kubek was taken to the hospital. Instead of turning a double play, the Pirates now had men on first and second with no outs. The tide had turned for the Pirates. Pittsburgh rallied for five runs in the bottom of the eighth with the help of Hal Smith's three-run homer and went ahead 9-7. The Yankees tied the score 9-9 in the top of the ninth inning, only to lose the game 10-9 on Pirates' Bill Mazeroski's leadoff home run in the bottom of the ninth inning.

For the next four years, the Pirates played sub-500 baseball, yet Virdon continued to be an excellent outfielder. By 1965, he had decided to retire. He retired officially on November 22, 1965, and started his managerial career with the Pirates, but the pay in Minor League was not very good and he spent two years in the Mets organization. Bill returned to the Pirates as a coach in 1968 and was placed on the players' roster that year, due to the military service of many of his teammates. He played in six games and his only hit was a two-run home run on July 31, 1968, the last hit of his career.

He was 37.

In 1971, Bill was still serving as a coach under Pirates' Manager Danny Murtaugh, as Pittsburgh won the 1971 World Series. Murtaugh retired at the end of the 1971 season, and Bill became their manager in 1972 and 1973. Bill was hired by George Steinbrenner to manage the Yankees in 1974. While with the Yankees, Virdon won the *Sporting News'* Manager of the Year Award. Bill was fired in the middle of the 1975 season, but was hired by the Houston Astros on August 20, 1975. The Astros played well under Virdon and fell one game short of winning the 1979 National League West Division Championship. In 1980 the Astros beat the Dodgers to win the National League tie-breaker game and played the Philadelphia Phillies for the NLCS championship. The Astros would lose the Series in five games. He again won the Manager of the Year Award in 1980. Bill would spend eight years with Houston before being fired during the 1982 season. He was replaced by Bob Lillis. Virdon then managed the Montreal Expos for two years (1983-1984). In 1986, Virdon joined Jim Leyland as the Pirates' hitting coach for one season. Bill served as a Spring Training instructor for the St. Louis Cardinals in 1990 and 1991, before rejoining Leyland in Pittsburgh again in 1992. Virdon left the Pirates after the 1995 season and in 1997 became the bench coach for the Houston Astros under first-time Manager, Larry Dierker. That was the year I met Bill in person. Virdon later returned to Pittsburgh in 2001 as a bench coach and then finally retired from baseball after the 2012 season. Bill spent a total of 25 years with Pittsburgh. Bill Virdon's career managerial win-loss record for 13 seasons stands at 999-921. Here's a fun fact. Name the only manager of the New York Yankees to never manage a game at Yankee Stadium? Bill Virdon managed the team during the two years (1974-1975) that the Yankees played their home games at Shea Stadium while Yankee Stadium underwent renovation.

In 11 years (1956-1965, 1968) Bill Virdon went to the plate 5,980 times. He averaged .267 at the plate and produced 1,596 hits, while hitting 91 home runs. He scored 735 runs and batted in 502 RBI's while stealing 47 bases. Interestingly, Bill Virdon batted .404 against the great Sandy Koufax, the highest average of any batter facing the legendary Dodgers' Hall of Fame pitcher.

Bill Virdon died on November 23, 2021, at Lester E. Cox Medical Center in Springfield, Missouri. He was 90, and no cause of death was given. He is survived by his wife Shirley and three daughters. A portion of the U.S. Route 63 in West Plains, Missouri, is named "Bill Virdon Boulevard." Bill was inducted into the Missouri Sports' Hall of Fame in 1983 and named a Missouri Sports' Legend by the Missouri Sports' Hall of Fame in 2012. The Independence Baseball Hall of fame inducted him in 2013.

A baseball lifer for sure, Bill Virdon once said before rounding third and heading for home, "The best part of my career is that I have not missed a Spring Training in 62 years."

Man in the Middle

Someone once said, "Even if you fall on your face, you're still moving forward." The man reminded of Rocky Marciano; you could knock him down, but he kept getting back up. It's true that guys who make their living putting their hand on the ground are different. His ability to function in chaos was incredible. They should have called him "Juice Man," because he supplied the electricity for his team. He had more moves than chess champion, Bobby Fisher, and would not be denied. For a defensive lineman, it's not always about the sack; it's the mistakes you force the quarterback to make because of your presence. The man was huge, a space eater. He would eat anything that wouldn't eat him and consumed food, drink and fun in large quantities. Yes, he had eyes in the back of his head. He didn't draw a breath without knowing where everyone was on the field.

The bottom line is this: You knew that with this guy in your huddle you had a good chance to win. You've heard sportswriters claim that as a nose tackle, he changed the game. Did he? Or did he just play the position better than anyone else? He wanted to show us that he was better than anyone else who had played that position. This man was so strong he required two or three players to block him, opening lanes for others. Some refer to what he had as a fire inside him to be the best. I prefer to say he was hungry to be the best and he would let nothing stand in his way. On the field he was physical. His opponents called him a mauler. He didn't just want to tackle a guy, he wanted to finish him. Opposing offensive linemen called him "sir" and asked about his family, his dog, and how things were at home. It seemed that he was always in the right place at the right time, all the time. His approach was always to hit them in the mouth first. Yes, football is a team game, but personal individual sacrifice plays a big role in Hall-of-Fame candidates for Canton. This fellow could always get to his spot. He was the kind of defensive player who could change the outcome of a game, and there were not many like that. Hall-of-Fame center Jim Otto of the Raiders called Culp, "Perhaps the strongest man I ever lined up against."

Curley Culp had always been on the Hall-of-Fame highway. On Sundays, he became the man in the middle of the Kansas City defense. A reporter once said about Curley Culp, "You knew you were in terrible trouble if he was on one knee looking at you, because he always got up."

Every legend has a beginning. His started in Yuma, Arizona. Curley Culp was born on March 10, 1946. His father, William, owned a pig farm, and his mother, Octavia Whaley Culp, was a homemaker. Believe it or not, he was the youngest of 13 children including a twin sister, Shirley. Everyone thought Curley was a nickname, but it wasn't. Curley Culp did not have a middle name. His sister Lucille came up with the names Shirley and Curley, because they were twins and the names rhymed. Curley worked on the farm and for spending money, loaded watermelons onto trucks. Culp attended Yuma Union High School where he starred in football and wrestling. Culp played offensive and defensive tackle while in high school. Curley won the Arizona State high school wrestling titles in 1963 and 1964, in the heavyweight division. Culp received a wrestling scholarship from UCLA. Curley turned it down because he wanted to also play football. Fortunately, he was also recruited to play football for Frank Kush and wrestle for Arizona State University (ASU). At Arizona State, Curley posted an 84-11-1 win-loss record, captured three Western Athletic Conference championships and was the 1967 NCAA heavyweight champ. Curley also won the prestigious Gregorian Award for scoring the most falls at the Division I championships. Curley was invited to the Olympic trials, held in Lincoln, Nebraska. He made the team as the number two best heavyweight in the country behind Larry Kristoff.

Curley also excelled in football as a nose guard at ASU and was chosen All-American in 1967, while leading his team to allowing their opponents to just 79.8 yards per game. Unbelievable! There were many great football players at ASU during Curley's tenure. Charlie Taylor, Mike Haynes, Randall McDaniel and Reggie Jackson were just some of the well-known players. In fact, Reggie Jackson was a running back and Curley had the opportunity to block for Reggie his freshman year, before Jackson decided to focus only on baseball. Culp participated in the 1967 College All-Star Game. They were beaten 27-0 by a very good Green Bay Packer team. Curley did graduate from ASU in 1970 with a bachelor's degree in business and insurance.

The Denver Broncos drafted Curley Culp with the 31st pick in the second round of the 1968 NFL Draft. Because of the College All-Star Game, he got to camp a bit late. Lou Saban of Denver wanted him to play offensive guard, but that did not work out, so they traded him during training camp, to the Kansas City Chiefs. "Training camp was tough," said Culp. "Every day was a gut check." But this Kansas City team had great players and great role players. Defensive teammates Buck Buchanan, Bobby Bell, Willie Lanier and Emmitt Thomas all ended up in the Pro Football Hall of Fame. Culp would wear #61 and his first roommate was Jerry Marsalis. In a simple twist of fate, two seasons later, Culp was playing nose tackle for the Kansas City Chiefs in Super Bowl IV.

In January 11, 1970, in front of 80,562 fans at Tulane Stadium in Houston Texas, the Chiefs beat the Vikings 23-7, in Super Bowl IV. Minnesota had been favored by 13 points. Curley Culp's role as nose tackle actually got its start before the Super Bowl. Chiefs' Head Coach, Hank Stram, felt that the Vikings' center, Mick Tingelhoff, was too small and not strong enough to block Culp, one-on-one. So, Stram moved Culp to the nose tackle position right in front of Tingelhof. This defense became known as the 3-4 defense, employing three down linemen and four linebackers. This defense freed teammates, Buck Buchanan and Willie Lanier, to get into the Vikings' offensive backfield and shut down their running game. "We had two versions of the 3-4 defense," said Culp, "the Triple Stack and the Under." Depending on which defense was called, the linemen would slide to the left or the right before the ball was snapped. That day, the Chiefs held the Vikings to 67 yards rushing, with only two first downs. They also intercepted three passes and recovered two fumbles. This move not only helped shut down the Vikings' offense, but it helped propel the popularity of the 3-4 defensive scheme well into the 1970s. Culp played seven seasons (1968-1974) for the Kansas City Chiefs. He played in 82 games, recorded nine sacks and also recovered five fumbles with the Chiefs during his career with the team.

Curley Culp was traded to the Houston Oilers on October 22, 1974, for John Matuszak and a first-round draft pick. The Oilers gave Culp #78 to wear and used their pick for Robert Brazile. The defensive coordinator for Houston was none other than "Bum" Phillips. Culp was able to convince Bum to try the 3-4 defense; instead of using the traditional 4-3 defense of the day. Standing 6 feet 2 inches tall and weighing 285 pounds, Culp was so big and strong; it required two or more players just to block him. By using him over the offensive center, lanes opened up for Elvin Bethea, Greg

Bingham and Ted Washington to upset the rushing game. The Oilers won seven of their remaining nine games, after Curley started at nose tackle.

On September 28, 1975, Curley Culp picked up a fumble in the fourth quarter against the San Diego Chargers and rumbled 38 yards for a touchdown. As Curley tells the story he mentions that his teammate, Elvin Bethea, yelled in jest at him during the play, "You're going the wrong way." It would be his one and only touchdown. In 1977, he intercepted his first and only pass and returned it for 25 yards. Bum Phillips would later say, "Curley made the 3-4 defense work. He made me look smart." In 1978, Curley married Collette Bloom. They would have two sons, Chad and Christopher.

Midway through the 1980 season, injuries began to pile up and Culp was released. He was claimed by the Detroit Lions. He would wear #77. Curley Culp retired after the 1981 season. His impact on the game afforded him a place on the *Sporting News* All-Century Team for both the Kansas City Chiefs and the Houston Oilers.

After he retired from football, Culp ran a chemical and pest control company. He later owned a taxicab and limousine service. Curley also earned a master's degree in health and human performance from the University of Houston, in 1990.

Culp was regarded as the game's best nose tackle. He played in 179 games during 14 seasons and recorded 68 ½ sacks. Culp also forced 14 fumbles and recovered 10 of those. He played on six Pro-Bowl teams and was chosen the 1975 NFL Defensive Player of the Year, with 11.5 sacks. In 1975, Culp became a member of the Arizona State University Sports Hall of Fame and was also later named the Greatest Athlete in the history of Arizona, in 2006. Culp is a member of the Kansas City Chiefs' 25-Year All-Time Team and in March of 2008, he was inducted into the Chief's Hall of Fame.

On August 3, 2013, Curley Culp joined Larry Allen, Bill Parcells, Dave Robinson, Chris Carter, Warren Sapp and Jonathan Ogden, in the Pro Football Hall of Fame. It was quite a class. During his Hall-of-Fame speech, Culp said, "I have learned that football is not just a sport, but a life lesson in what it means to be a team player. I have learned how pain can build character and endurance, and believe that life itself is like playing a very long and exciting football game, where every play can determine the outcome."

Curley Culp informed the public on November 16, 2021, that he had been diagnosed with Stage IV pancreatic cancer. Curley died 11 days later on November 27, 2021. He was 75 and living in Pearland, Texas. Culp is survived by his wife, Collette, their two sons Chad and Christopher, seven grandchildren, his twin sister Shirley and a brother, William Jr.

I never had the pleasure of meeting Curley Culp in person, but I did interview his teammate, Elvin Bethea. It wasn't very long into our interview that Elvin mentioned the play of Curley Culp. "Curley had these thick, nasty forearms that were hard as rocks," said Elvin. "He'd use those forearms to hit centers on the side of the head. He'd knock them off balance and their ears would be ringing. The rules were different back then." Elvin credited Culp's play with helping him get into the Pro Football Hall of Fame in 2003.

A PUTT THAT CHANGED HISTORY

He was the Hank Aaron of golf, humble, never bitter and full of life and joy until the end. This man was so generous with his time and wisdom. He broke down the last major color barrier in American sports and gave the African-American community hope. As a caddie in Dallas, Texas, he learned to play golf cross-handed, like the great Hank Aaron learned to hit a baseball. Ted Rhodes, another black golfer and his mentor, helped change him over to a more traditional grip.

Along the way, he received so many hateful letters and death threats that he rented two homes for safety, and he always surrounded himself with friends when he went out to eat. One time during his second year on the tour, he was leading a golf tournament. He literally had to play his way through a racist crowd. "I was on about the 15th hole, and I drove my ball down the left side of the fairway. Several people jumped the fence, grabbed my ball and threw it out in the road and stayed there and called me all kind of racial-slur names," said Elder. "And then that night, as a matter of fact, they called the motel that we were staying at and threatened my wife and my life. And the next day, we had to play with armed guards walking in the fairway."

Lee Elder, a pioneer with a putter, earned his way to the Masters by making an 18-foot birdie putt on the fourth playoff hole, to beat Peter Oosterhuis at the 1974 Monsanto Open, at the Pensacola Country Club in Florida. It was a putt that changed history. Elder was whisked away quickly after the match had been completed. He was later told why. The course had received several telephone calls that Elder would be killed if he won the tournament. Interestingly, Lee had been refused entrance to the clubhouse at this same course. In fact, he had to change his shoes in the parking lot.

Lee Elder played in the Masters six times. In 1997, Tiger Woods won the Masters by a record-setting 12 strokes. Tiger was the first African-American and Asian-American to do so. Lee Elder was there. "I was the first, but I wasn't the pioneer. Charlie Sifford, Lee Elder, Teddy Rhodes, you know, those guys are the ones who paved the way in order for me to be here, and I thank them, because if it wasn't for them, I may not have had the chance to ever play golf. When I turned pro at 20, I was able to live my dream because of those guys," said Tiger. Woods later said, "I thought of Lee Elder on that final hole."

His golf swing wasn't made in Heaven, it was made in Dallas. Robert Lee Elder was born on July 14, 1934, in Dallas, Texas. Lee was the youngest of ten children. His father, Charles, was a coal-truck driver and his mother, Almeta, ran the household. Lee became an orphan when he was nine years old. His father was killed in Europe during World War II, and his mom died three months later. For the next three years, Lee spent his time being shuttled from one relative to another, until he turned 12. Lee spent his spare time working as a caddie for $1 a round, at an all-white local public golf course in Dallas. He eventually ended up living in Los Angeles, California, with an aunt. While in L.A., he continued to caddie and eventually dropped out of Manual High School after the 10th grade. Rather than running the streets, Lee supported himself financially while honing his golf skills, during the hours set aside by the golf course for caddies to play. Elder did not play a full round of 18 holes until he turned 16. In addition to caddying, Lee worked in the pro shops and locker rooms. Elder quickly learned that you can't put a golf ball in a hole with your height, or your strength, or your speed. It doesn't matter to a golf ball how fast you can run or how high you can jump. Yet, he became a golf hustler and was often seen with a noted white gambler named Alvin Thomas. Elder not only caddied for Thomas, but also became his chauffeur. Elder often walked away from the golf course with a handsome profit by playing others from his knees, on one leg or wearing a raincoat on a terribly hot day. He won hundreds of dollars from private bets against players who had no idea how good he was.

At the age of 18, Lee met and played a round of golf with former heavyweight champion boxing great, Joe Louis. Louis, an avid golfer, was playing in an exhibition match held in Cleveland, Ohio. Louis was taught the game by another Black golfer named Ted Rhodes. It was at that tournament, that Rhodes noticed the raw talent of Lee Elder. Rhodes had played in the U.S. Open in 1948, and was one of the first Black professional golfers. It was Rhodes who switched Elder from an unorthodox cross-handed grip to a conventional grip, greatly improving Elder's golf game. Rhodes would become Elder's mentor and Lee moved into Rhodes' home in St. Louis for about three years. Lee also accompanied Rhodes on trips to Havana and Kingston, Jamaica.

Elder fulfilled his Army service in 1959, by spending two years at Fort Lewis, Washington. As luck would have it, Lee's commander, Colonel John Gleaster was an avid golfer, and he placed Lee in a Special Service unit which allowed him to play golf frequently. By 1961, Elder had finished his commitment to the Army and joined the United Golfers' Association Tour (UGA), the sports equivalent of baseball's Negro Leagues. It was sometimes referred to as the "Peanut Tour" because of its small winners' purses, usually less than $500. In the early 1960s, Elder dominated this tour. During one stretch, Lee won 18 out of 22 tournaments.

In 1963, Lee met his first wife Rose Harper, an excellent

golfer, at a tournament in Washington, D.C. They married in 1966, and she gave up her golf career to become his business manager. They managed the Langston Golf Course, for several years. They later divorced, and Elder moved to South Florida.

The Professional Golf Association (PGA) lifted its color barrier in 1961, allowing non-white players to become members. By 1967, Lee Elder was living in Washington, D. C. and had raised enough money on the UGA Tour to attend the PGA qualifying school. He finished 9th out of a class of 122 and received his tour card for 1968. That first year; Lee won about $38,000 and finished 40th on the money list. The highlight of his rookie season came in a loss on the fifth hole of a sudden death playoff to the great Jack Nicklaus, at the American Golf Classic in Akron, Ohio. Not only did Lee receive national recognition, but he won $12,000 and began to market Lee Elder golf clubs and balls, and to appear in commercials.

In 1971, Elder accepted an invitation from Gary Player to play in the South African PGA Championship in Johannesburg, South Africa. It was the first integrated tournament in that country's history. Elder would also win the Nigerian Open in 1971.

In 1972, Augusta National, the private club that runs the Masters, changed its qualifying rules to extend an automatic invitation to any player who won on the PGA Tour. As mentioned above; Lee Elder scored his first PGA victory in 1974, at the Monsanto Open. That win gained him entry to the Masters played each year at the Augusta National Golf Course, in Georgia. Lee Elder with the help of his first wife, Rose, set up the Lee Elder Scholarship Fund in 1974. This fund offered money to low-income young men and women seeking financial assistance to attend college.

When I saw Lee Elder grip a golf club, my only thought was

that God meant for this man to play golf. Elder played in his first Masters event in 1975 at the age of 40. At 11:15 AM, on April 10, 1975, wearing a green shirt, dark blue pants and a white hat, Elder drew a huge crowd. When he teed off for his first shot, the huge crowd lined the fairway. He wondered how he was going to hit the ball without killing somebody. Lee drove his very first tee shot right down the middle of the fairway. After he birdied the third hole to go one under par, he saw his name on the leader board for the first time. Lee shot 74 that day, followed by a 78 on day two and missed the cut. Elder went on to play in the Masters five more times between 1977 and 1981. His best finish at Augusta National came in 1979, when he tied for 17th on the leader board. Interestingly, nine months after Lee Elder became the first Black man to play in the Masters, Eldrick Tont Woods, known as "Tiger," was born.

In 1979, Lee Elder became the first African-American to qualify for play in the Ryder Cup. Lee Elder won a total of four PGA Tour events: the Monsanto Open in 1974, the Houston Open in 1976, the Greater Milwaukee Open and the American Express Westchester Classis, both in 1978. He also finished second 10 times.

By 1984, at the age of 50, you could find Lee playing with other seniors in the Champions' PGA Tour. Elder won a total of nine tournaments on the Champions' Tour, between 1984 and 1988. He also won the Jamaica Open in 1984 and won twice more on the Japan Senior Tour.

Lee Elder shared his story of rejection because of the color of his skin, to many. During a round at a Memphis tournament a spectator ran out on the course and picked up Lee's golf ball and threw it in a hedge. This incident was witnessed by another golfer named Terry Dill, and Lee was given a free drop. He was also turned away from hotels in the South despite confirmed reservations, and was forced to change his clothes in the parking lot because he was not allowed in the clubhouse. Elder once shared a conversation he had with Jackie Robinson, who broke the color barrier in professional baseball. Jackie advised Lee not to retaliate. "It's easy to get in trouble and hard to get out of trouble," said Jackie.

In 1990, Elder spoke out against country clubs that still excluded Black golfers from membership. He promoted Summer Youth Golf Development Programs and also raised money for the United Negro College Fund. In 1995, Elder married his second wife, Sharon Anderson. Lee Elder won the Bob Jones Award in 2019. This award is the United States Golf Association's highest honor, presented for outstanding sportsmanship. Bob Jones was the co-founder of the Masters.

In 1987, Lee Elder suffered a heart attack while playing in the Machado Classic in Key Biscayne, Florida. He recovered and one year later won the tournament, shooting a 65 in the final round.

Since 1963, every Thursday morning before each Masters' event, three former professional golfers are chosen as Honorary Starters for the Masters. Up until last year only nine players had been chosen. At 86 years old, Lee Elder became the tenth. On April 8, 2021, Lee joined Jack Nicklaus (85) and Gary Player (81). Augusta National Chairman, Fred Ridley, said, "Today Lee Elder will inspire us and make history once more. Lee, you have the honors." Although Lee did bring his clubs with him, arthritis in his knees left him without enough stability to hit a shot. Still, Elder received a standing ovation. "For me and my family, I think it was one of the most emotional experiences that I have ever witnessed, I've been involved in," said Lee. A little over seven months later, Lee Elder would pass away. During his professional career, Lee Elder had a total of 16 wins. He earned $1.02 million in purses on the PGA Tour and another $1.6 million on the

Champions' Tour.

Lee Elder lived a story book career. He died on a Sunday, November 29, 2021. He was living in Escondido, California. He was 87. He is survived by his second wife, Sharon.

"The game of golf lost a hero in Lee Elder," said Jack Nicklaus when he heard the news.

HERE IT IS, HIT IT

Understanding this guy was a head scratcher from the get-go. It has been said that to conquer fear, you must become fear. You must bask in the fear of your opponent and embrace your worst fears. One of his former managers, Tony LaRussa, once said, "My first impression of him was, here is a pitcher. He had average stuff, but amazing command and tremendous confidence, and he never showed fear. What a competitor." Don't let the halo fool you, this guy loved a good fight. From the mound, he reminded you of a truck rolling down hill without brakes. He spent hours on the bump practicing his command, catching corners and changing speeds. Developing control of his right-handed sinkerball was like finding a black cat in a coal mine. "I knew I couldn't blow hitters away, but I could put the ball where I wanted, a fourth of an inch, a sixteenth of an inch, and I could make the ball move. I knew how to attack the corners of the plate," he exclaimed.

For guys like him, there's nothing like game day. His energy is what made him special. His nickname was "The Incredible Bulk," but it should have been "High Tide," because when he was on the mound, he lifted everybody on that team. He didn't catch very well or hit consistently. I'm not even sure he knew how to do a high-five, but his sinkerball was outstanding. His shoulders were as broad as the cornerstone of a bank. With blacksmith forearms, skin thicker than a catcher's mitt, the man was a gunslinger that spilled his guts with every pitch. You expected him to holler from the mound, "Here it is, hit it."

But for some athletes, paychecks are the shackles of common man. This guy loved to eat, owned a fat belly, and weighed more than he should have. His favorite floor plan for his home included one bedroom and two kitchens. He was listed at 6 feet 3 inches tall and weighed 195 pounds, yet he acknowledged several times that he weighed well over 240 pounds. His career was cut short by food, shoulder injuries, abusing alcohol and drugs, including painkillers. Taking painkillers is like buying a ticket on the Hindenburg. Eventually, you're going down. They called him washed up, tuned out, old news and Old Yeller. LaMarr Hoyt eventually spent some time in jail and was out of baseball after only eight years. A wise man once said, "Alcohol is a man's best friend with a knife."

Dewey LaMarr Hoyt Jr., was born on New Years Day, 1955, in Columbia, South Carolina. Frank A. Clark once wrote, "The most important thing a parent can teach their children is how to get along without them." Hoyt's parents struggled to make ends meet and divorced when he was only six months old. LaMarr began his life without a mother or a father of his own, as he was raised by an aunt. Hoyt was an all-around athlete and graduated from Keenan High School in Columbia, South Carolina. He later admitted that as a kid he smoked marijuana and drank beer with the guys. On June 5, 1973, he was selected by the New York Yankees in the fifth round of the 1973 MLB June Amateur Draft. On April 5, 1977, Hoyt was traded with pitcher Bob Polinsky, outfielder Oscar Gamble, and $200,000 to the Chicago White Sox for shortstop Bucky Dent. After seven years in the Minor Leagues, he was called up and debuted in relief on September 14, 1979, for the Sox. LaMarr Hoyt married Sylvia in 1980, but they later divorced after the 1985 baseball season. Hoyt was switched to the starting rotation in 1982 and tied a White Sox club record by winning his first nine starts. Hoyt joined former Sox pitchers "Lefty" Williams (1917) and Orval Grove (1943). Hoyt ended up leading the American League in wins with 19. In 1983, LaMarr won the Amercian League Cy Young Award. Hoyt posted a 24-10 win-loss record with a 3.66 ERA. He also threw 11 complete games and allowed only 31 walks in 260 2/3 innings. Hoyt pitched a complete game 2-1 victory over the Baltimore Orioles, during the 1983 American League Championship Series.

But 1984 was not kind to Hoyt. His win-loss record fell to 13-18, with a 4.47 ERA. LaMarr had gone from winning the most games to losing the most games, in a single season. LaMarr Hoyt and Todd Simmons would be traded on December 6, 1984, to the San Diego Padres for Ozzie Guillen, Tim Lollar, Bill Long and Luis Salazar. Hoyt rebounded a bit in 1985 and made the National League All-Star Team in his first season in the league. He was also named the starting pitcher and won the Major League All-Star Game Most Valuable Player Award. While pitching in pain, Hoyt finished his first season with the Padres with a 16-8 record and a 3.47 ERA. LaMarr may have had the best control of any National League pitcher at that time.

Following the 1985 season, Hoyt was arrested twice in a month on drug-possession changes. He had become dependent on drugs. LaMarr eventually checked into a rehabilitation center after the second arrest. Hoyt claimed he had a rotator cuff injury and did not want to have surgery. So, he decided to pitch through the pain with the help of painkillers. He ended his 1986 season with an 8-11 record and a 5.15 ERA. His last game occurred on October 3, 1986, against the Cincinnati Reds. Shortly after the 1986 season ended, he was arrested again for trying to smuggle painkillers across the US-Mexico border. Hoyt was sentenced to 45 days in jail on December 16, 1986, and was then suspended by

MLB Commissioner Peter Ueberroth. On June 17, 1987, the Padres gave him his unconditional release from the team. On July 1, 1987, he was given a second chance by the White Sox, but was arrested for a fourth time in December of 1987. LaMarr Hoyt's baseball career was now over.

You can never really put all of the memories away when you leave the game as a player. LaMarr knew what it was like to try and make his memories go away. You can make new memories, good ones and those new memories can change your life.

It's funny, I always found the name LaMarr Hoyt interesting. It reminded me more of a racecar driver or a scientist. LaMarr Hoyt pitched 1,311 1/3 innings during his eight active years and posted a 98-68 win-loss record. His control was magnificent. LaMarr hit 18 batters and threw only 13 wild pitches. He gave up 1,313 hits and 637 runs. His ERA stands at 3.99, and he recorded 681 strikeouts and gave up only 140 home runs. As a hitter, Hoyt was terrible with a bat. Hoyt recorded just 10 hits in 110 career at-bats and only posted one extra-base hit.

According to his son, Mathew, LaMarr Hoyt passed away from cancer on Monday, November 29, 2021, while living in Columbia, South Carolina. He was 66. Hoyt married a second time to Leslie and they had two sons, Mathew and Josh, and a daughter Alexandra. Hoyt spent his time after baseball selling sporting goods and household appliances.

LaMarr Hoyt was never happy about the way he left things in baseball.

ALL DAY TOUGH

Fear is an interesting emotion. Sometimes it brings out the worst in people, but fear can also bring out the very best. You can see that some days on the playing field: the loyalty, the care, support and generosity athletes have for their teammates. For a few athletes, fear brings out something different: the choice to be heroic, to stand their ground, to play for each other and find a way to hold onto hope and depend on each other like family. That's a hero.

Hall of Famer, Ray Lewis once said, "There are only two types of people who play this game, those who watch the play happen and those who make the play happen." This man was all day tough and his breath smelled like quarterback. He was not the sort of guy who would chase you very far. It was much worse than that. He would catch you and then proceed to dismantle your senses from your head. If you were going to get into it with him, you might as well finish him off, because he was just going to keep coming back. The things this guy did on the football field would exhaust anyone if they were normal, but he was not normal, he was super-human. He would knock you into yesterday. As a defensive end, this guy was a forest. He thought he could make every play.

The battle for him always started up front: pass, run, or draw? He owned a PhD in sacking the quarterback. The things they could do to a quarterback in the 1970s, they would put you in jail for today. This man was 100% trouble, and he always played the game of football with a "rip your heart out" mentality. The air went out of the quarterbacks he hit, faster than a nail in a bicycle tire. He was like a volcano waiting to erupt, and the man never quit on a play. This fellow was one of the best door kickers in the league, and he made offensive linemen look stupid. He could change direction like a large-mouth bass and could hit you so hard that your eyes would roll back like a slot machine. His Atlanta Falcons' teams were filled with lots of Joes that few had ever heard of. There was no brighter star in Atlanta than Claude Humphreys. He went from seeing stars to being one.

Claude Humphreys was born on June 29, 1944, in Memphis, Tennessee. His father, Dosie, was a school maintenance engineer, and his mom, Millie Hayes Humphreys, worked as a domestic. Claude played football, basketball, ran the low hurdles and threw the shot put at Lester High School in Memphis. Humphreys enrolled and played football for the Tigers of Tennessee State University. There, #75 became an All-American lineman in 1967 and in 2012, he was voted into the Black College Football Hall of Fame.

Claude visited quite a few schools before deciding where he was going to go to college. Grambling, Texas Southern, Jackson State, Moreland and Tennessee State were just a few. Claude turned down Eddie Robinson at Grambling, because the town was small and there was nothing to do off campus. He liked Tennessee State because it was close to his hometown. His head coach was John Merritt. There were other great defensive legends like Ed "Too Tall" Jones and Richard Dent, who attended Tennessee State. The Tigers only lost four games (35-3-1) during Humphreys' three years there (1965-1967). Tennessee State won the 1967 National Championship among Historically Black Colleges and Universities (HBCU). Coach Merritt would also become his agent.

Claude Humphreys played in the College All-Star Game, which was coached by Norm Van Brocklin. Claude found himself face to face with future Hall-of-Fame offensive tackle, Forrest Gregg of the Green Bay Packers. "I thought I was pretty good, but I found out that I had a lot to learn and a short time to learn it in. Forrest Gregg gave me a lesson in how to be kept away from the quarterback," said Humphreys.

Humphreys was taken with the third pick of the 1968 NFL Draft behind tackle Ron Yary by the Minnesota Vikings and behind center Bob Johnson by the Cincinnati Bengals. Standing 6 feet 4 inches tall and weighing 252 pounds, he was given the #87 to wear. Three years after being drafted by the Falcons, their head coach Norb Hecker was fired and Van Brocklin took his place. Humphreys claimed in the beginning that he actually had very little interest in playing professional football. He was just trying to get an education. Training camp with the Falcons was brutal. They trained in Johnson City, Tennessee, where it was extremely hot. They practiced three times a day.

The Falcons' defensive alignment in 1977 became known as the "Grits Blitz." This team gave up only 129 points, at that time an NFL record low for a 14-game season. The sad part, this team struggled on the offensive side of the ball, finished their season with a 7-7 win-loss record and missed the playoffs. The Atlanta Falcons only had two winning seasons between 1968, when Humphreys joined them, and 1977, his last full season with the club.

Defensive end, Claude Humphreys, played ten frustrating seasons with the Falcons. "In Atlanta, I never got used to losing," said Humphreys. "It made me play harder." When the Falcons fell to 1-3 to start the 1978 season, Humphreys had his fill of defeat. After the game, he sat in front of his locker and thought about how things were not getting any better. "I put my stuff in my locker and left, it was that simple," said Humphreys. "I wasn't mad at anybody, because there was nothing I could do as a player, but what I did.

They said they weren't going to trade me." Claude sat out the remainder of the 1978 season and was then traded to the Philadelphia Eagles for two draft picks, the following year.

Humphreys played for Dick Vermeil in Philadelphia. His defensive coordinator was Marion Campbell. In 1980, the Eagles posted a 12-4 regular season record. Humphreys recorded a team high 14 ½ sacks and helped the Eagles become NFC Champions and earn a trip to Super Bowl XV. "No one counted sacks when I played," said Claude. "At that time, a sack was just a tackle. The most fun I had was batted balls."

Humphreys did not play well against the Oakland Raiders in Super Bowl XV, and the Falcons lost 27-10. During the game, he was penalized by the referee for roughing the passer, against quarterback Jim Plunkett, and the ref threw the yellow penalty flag at him. Humphreys picked up the flag and threw it back at the official, Ben Dreith.

After retiring from the game in 1981, Claude tried his hand at acting. He made a guest appearance on *The Dukes of Hazzard* episode entitled "Repo Man," in which he played the part of a counterfeiter named Big John. He also owned a livestock ranch in Oakland, Tennessee, and was a defensive line coach with the Falcons.

Humphreys flattened quarterbacks in 171 NFL games during his 13-year career (1968-1981), and recorded 2 interceptions and 2 safeties. In his first year, Claude Humphreys recorded 11 ½ sacks and was chosen the 1968 NFL Associated Press Defensive Rookie of the Year. Claude also recovered 11 fumbles during his career and returned one for 24 yards against the Vikings in 1969, for his only touchdown. He missed the entire 1975 season with an injured knee. In 1976, Claude was selected the Falcons' MVP. Unofficially, Claude has been credited with 130 sacks with the Falcons and Eagles. He still holds the Falcons' team record for sacks, with 99 1/2.

Humphreys retired in 1981, one season before sacks were counted as an official NFL stat. He was selected to the Pro Bowl six times (1970-1974, and 1977), was chosen First-Team All-Pro five times (1971-1974, and 1977), and Second-Team All-Pro three times (1969, 1970 and 1976).

Humphreys is a member of the Georgia Hall of Fame and the Tennessee Hall of Fame. In 2008, Tennessee State retired his #75 and inducted him into the Tennessee State Hall of Fame. That same year, Lester High School retired his number and placed him into their Hall of Fame. Humphreys joined Falcons' teammate Mike Kenn as a member of the Atlanta Falcons' Ring of Honor, in 2008.

Claude Humphreys waited 28 years for his induction into the Pro Football Hall of Fame. Claude felt he had to wait so long because the Falcon teams he played on were not very good, and they never played in or won a Super Bowl. He was named a HOF final candidate in 2003, 2005, and 2006. Then he was moved to the senior candidate list, where he was named a HOF finalist in 2008 and 2013. Finally, in February of 2014, Claude Humphreys was elected to the Pro-Football Hall of Fame, on the senior ballot. Claude Humphreys was officially inducted on August 2, 2014, along with a class that included Andre Reed, Derrick Brooks, Ray Guy, Michael Strahan, Aeneas Williams, and Walter Jones. Other Pro Football Hall-of-Fame players, who played with the Falcons, include Tommy McDonald, Eric Dickerson, Chris Doleman, Deion Sanders, Brett Favre and Morton Anderson.

The toughest linemen Humphreys ever faced, besides Forrest Gregg, were Bob Brown, Ron Yary and Rayfield Wright. Claude thought the toughest player he ever had to tackle was Larry Csonka. "In a Monday night game he just ran right up my chest," said Claude. "He was a great fullback."

Claude Humphreys passed away on a Friday night,

December 3, 2021, at his home in Memphis, Tennessee. He was 77. It's only a matter of time, before they stand in that tunnel for the last time. This is where their football life ends. Players never forget their last game. They stand there and take it all in. Claude Humphreys will now forever live in Canton, Ohio. Humphreys had suffered from diabetes and had lost a kidney to cancer. He is survived by his daughters Claudia, Chandra and Candice, and a grandson. His wife, Sandra Harrell Humphreys, died in 2013.

"I was aggressive, very aggressive," said Humphreys. "I tried to play the game to the point where, when I walked off the field, there was nothing that I didn't cover. I tried to play all out. I didn't take any prisoners."

ONE FOOT IN HEAVEN

Vince Lombardi once said, "The measure of who we are is what we do with what we have. Many words were used to define this fellow: Powerful, explosive, tenacious, resilient, tough and proud. Standing 6 feet 5 inches tall and weighing 252 pounds, he was a good-looking guy who could dunk a basketball. It was like watching a Pepsi machine jump up in the air. He was a large man with a very big head and eyebrows that had a language all of their own. This fellow reminded me of an extra in a Gladiator movie. His size would have kept him off most of the rides at Disneyland. The cleats he wore were size 14D. It took him 20 minutes to unlace them after a game. A tough defensive end is as important to the team's defense as radar is to a fighter jet. He was also strong. This man didn't throw furniture, he threw entire rooms. If you saw his footprints in the sand you would call 911. He was a great edge-rusher with a quick first step. The man was a tackling machine. He could get all over a quarterback like a cheap suit. If he was delivered to you in a box, you would have put it in water before opening. How did quarterbacks ever survive guys like Bill Glass?

Bill Glass was a fine Christian man, who just happened to play a great game of football. He was a ponderer, a thinker, a fellow who thought before he answered. This guy was top shelf, he had it all, and he played the game in a lane all his own. He was a religious man and when he lined up against you, everybody was praying that he wasn't going to hurt you, including him. Glass understood that there are no bad days, just some days are better than others. After football, he counseled prison inmates that the windshields of cars are bigger than the rearview mirrors, because it's better to look forward than backward. Glass discovered that most inmates, like him, were raised without fathers; that sports gives kids a place to belong, gives them something to do beside drink or take drugs or create mischief; and most times, it's the coach who leads the way. Coaches can become family. He taught inmates that change is the essence of life; that yesterday is over; that love isn't a memory' it's so much more than that. Real love is bigger; it is a world of its own that lives in the heart, not the head. This guy saved more inmates than antibiotics. It turns out that the Good Lord had his hand on Bill Glass from the beginning and his high-school football coach, Bill Stages, and Baylor University were a big part of that. Bill Glass had always lived his life and played the game of football with one foot in Heaven.

William Sheppeard Glass was born on August 16, 1935, in Texarkana, Texas. At the age of five, Bill's father, Vernon Sr., moved the family to Corpus Christi, Texas, to join his brother-in-law in the insurance business. Bill followed in his older brother, Vernon Jr., footsteps and started playing football in Junior High. When Bill was 14, his father died from cancer. This loss would shape his future efforts in ministry, which most often focused on the importance of a father figure in the home. Bill described himself at the time, as an awkward, clumsy kid with no self confidence. It was at W. B. Ray High School in Corpus Christi, that Bill Glass would meet his father figure, and his name was Bill Stages. Coach Stages was the head football coach, and he too had lost both his parents in a car wreck, when he was an infant. Coach Stages understood what losing your parents was about and spent an hour each day after school, not only running Bill though football drills, but lifting weights with him and mentoring him as a second father figure. Bill grew six inches and gained 60 pounds while in high school and became a force on the playing field. Bill also joined a Baptist Church and became a Christian while attending Ray High School.

Coach Stage's Ray Texans won the Texas State 4-A football title in 1959. Glass had already moved on to attend college. I am not originally from Corpus Christi and moved here in 1985. Since then, I have accumulated many friends who knew and some played for the Texans and were friends with Bill Glass. Ronny Holiday, Charles Durham, Bart Shirley and Bobby Smith are just a few I can name.

In 1953, Bill Glass chose to attend and play football for the University of Baylor, a private Christian school, for that reason. Attending Baylor also brought him and his wife Mavis together. She was drawn to Bill after reading a newspaper article where a Baylor football player was teaching Sunday school classes. They were married six months after they met and spent 60 years together, before she passed in 2017. Together, they raised three children. He would letter in football from 1954-1956 and helped start up the University of Baylor Chapter of the Fellowship of Christian Athletes. In 1956, Baylor posted an 8-2 win-loss record, and Bill had his best year, recording 154 tackles in just ten games. Baylor beat the University of Tennessee 13-7, in the Sugar Bowl played on January 1, 1957. Glass turned the tide for the Baylor Bears, when he forced a fumble on a punt return by Tennessee's Johnny Majors. The Bears recovered the fumble and scored the winning touchdown. Glass received many honors. He was voted to the 1956 All-Southwest Conference First Team, at the guard position. He made the Walter Camp Football Foundation Team and was chosen an Associated Press First Team All-American. Glass was also voted the 1956 Southwest Conference MVP by the *Houston Post*. Bill participated in the East-West Shrine Game and the Senior Bowl. Glass graduated in 1957 with a Bachelor of

Arts degree.

Bill Glass was on everybody's draft list. He was taken with the 12th pick of the 1957 NFL Draft by the Detroit Lions. During this time, with NFL games being played on Sundays, most religions viewed this as a clear violation of the Fourth Commandant. Athletes were condemned for playing football on Sundays for money and fame. At first, Glass followed this line of thinking and decided to join the Saskatchewan Roughriders of the Canadian Football League. In the Canadian Football League, most games were played on Saturdays. There, he was moved to the defensive side of the ball, playing end. But one year later, Glass had a change of heart and decided to play in the NFL. He reported to the Detroit Lions in 1958 and was given #53 to wear. Glass later addressed his decision. "I just couldn't believe that God was willing for all pro sports to go without a witness just because of Sunday game days." Therefore, he enrolled at Southwestern Baptist Theological Seminary, where he spent six off-seasons taking classes, before graduating in 1963, with Bachelor of Divinity degree. In Detroit, Glass started holding Bible study and prayer meetings at the team hotel, before games. The Lions finished the 1958 season 4-7-1. Glass became a full-time starter at right defensive end, in 1959. This Lions' defensive line consisting of Alex Karras, Roger Brown, Darius McCord and Bill Glass, would become known as the original "Fearsome Foursome." In 1960, the Detroit Lions allowed the third fewest points to be scored in the NFL. "I was a defensive end, where I fought with huge linemen, so I could get to the guy with the ball and throw him to the turf," said Glass. "There were some games that were nothing more than brawls and hand-to-hand combat. I'm not talking about dirty play, but hard, physical, demanding, and yes manly, battles." The simple fact is that the other Fearsome Foursome that played for the Los Angeles Rams received more recognition, because they played in L.A. Glass spent four years in Detroit (1958-1961) before being traded to the Cleveland Browns, in 1962.

Glass was traded along with quarterback Jim Ninowski and running back Howard "Hopalong" Cassady for quarterback Milt Plum, running back Tom Watkins and linebacker Dave Lloyd. Arriving in Cleveland, Glass became more intentional. He encouraged his teammates to attend pregame devotionals where they read scripture together and then later rewrote the chapters in their own words. He had admiration for his teammate Jim Brown, and he urged his white teammates to forget color and treat everyone alike. "Even if a black athlete is treated fairly by the coaches, he still has to live in a prejudiced society," said Glass.

For the next seven years (1962-1968), Glass started for the Browns and was selected to play in four Pro Bowls (1962-1964 and 1967), at the defensive end position. Wearing #80, Bill became the highest paid defensive lineman in the NFL. Bill Glass played a key role on Cleveland's 1964 NFL Championship team and their 1965 Eastern Division Championship team. Cleveland posted a 10-3-1 record in 1964 and advanced to the NFL Championship Game against the Baltimore Colts. On December 27, 1964, Cleveland shut out Baltimore, 27-0. The Colts' Johnny Unitas, was held to only 89 yards passing, while Cleveland's Jim Brown rushed for 114 yards in the win. It was the Browns' first championship since 1955. The Browns won 11 out of 14 games in 1965 and returned to the NFL Championship Game. This time, on January 2, 1966, the Browns would lose to the Green Bay Packers 23-12.

Glass intercepted four passes and scored one touchdown during his 12-year career. When Glass retired from Cleveland after the 1968 season, he had recorded 77.5 sacks during his 94 games with the Browns. That total also included

16.5 sacks in (1965), 15.5 sacks in (1962), and 15 sacks in (1966). All are still team records. These totals for sacks may very well help Bill Glass as a possible future candidate for enshrinement into the Pro Football Hall of Fame.

Bill Glass gave 22 years of his life to football: 10 years at the amateur level in junior high, senior high and college; and 12 years at the professional level. Even though he will be remembered by football fans as a great player on the field, his greatest achievement may have come after he put away his shoulder pads. Glass also authored 12 books including his 1965 memoir <u>Get in the Game!</u> Also <u>Stand Tall and Straight</u>, <u>Don't Blame the Game</u>, <u>Look at What's Right with Sports</u>, <u>Expect to Win</u>, and <u>Free at Last</u>, are a few of the others. In 1969, he started the Bill Glass Ministries. He drew 13,000 people at his first event. He began to focus on prison ministry in 1972. Glass discovered that most prisoners, like him, did not grow up with both parents in the home. His focus was on fatherhood and changing individual prisoner's hearts. Glass was one of the first to take famous athletes from all sports into prisons with him. You will recognize the names of Roger Staubach, Tom Landry, Michael Jordan, "Mean Joe" Greene and Mike Singletary.

In 2019, his ministry reported up to that point in its history, that Bill Glass: Behind the Walls Ministries had trained 58,550 Christians to share their faith; presented the gospel to over 6 million incarcerated individuals; and recorded 1.2 million commitments to Christ. Glass claimed that he had been in more prisons than any man that had ever lived. Bill could also point to other chapel services like Baseball Chapel and Pro Athletes Outreach, which exist in no small part because of Glass.

Bill Glass received many accolades for his work on the field and off. He joined the University of Baylor Hall of Fame in 1969. He was selected to the College Football Hall of Fame in 1985. In 1987, Glass joined the Texas Sports' Hall of Fame. In 2007, he was inducted into the Cleveland Browns' Legends Program and was listed at No. 31 on Cleveland's 100 Greatest Browns' players in 2013. Glass then joined the University of Baylor's Wall of Honor in 2016.

Bill Glass left us on a Sunday, December 5, 2021. He was 86 and buried at Central Waxahachie Bible Church in Waxahachie, Texas. He is survived by his three children, Billy, Bobby and Mindy. There is no doubt that Bill Glass raised bumps and bruises on running backs on Sunday afternoons in the NFL and then created goose bumps on his congregation's arms on Sunday nights. His legacy will live on in the countless number of lives he touched.

WHAT A LIFE IT WAS!

My favorite quotation of his was "When you can see your breath, its' good football weather." It was easy to pick him out on the sidelines; jumping up and down, cursing and raising hell. This fellow never looked like anything but a football coach. He conditioned everyone around him to winning, including his wife. Yet for some, he resembled a cartoon character. The man owned flaming red hair, a big nose, and a grin as wide as a watermelon. This guy's arms had a mind all their own and were constantly flailing back and forth, and he always seemed to be screaming at the officials. The man was funny, animated, went nuts on the sideline at a time when his opponent's coaches were very much subdued and stoic, much like Tom Landry, Paul Brown, Chuck Noll and Don Shula.

It's funny; he reminded me of a blocking sled and looked kind of like a football. This man loved to eat. He'd meet the pizza delivery guy half way. On his birthday before he blew out the candles, his wish was for another cake. You could tell he was a former lineman, because what he had just eaten was all right there on the front of his shirt. It was once said that he looked more like an unmade bed than a coach and if he won a game, he wore his same lucky outfit the next game. This guy was as much a renegade as his players, but he always wanted to be known as a coach. As a football coach, he was ahead of his time. The Oakland Raiders were the first team to hold mini-camp and the first to film their practice. He always provided an itinerary for the players on Saturday: what time to report, when to get taped, time for team breakfast, etc. When it came to the part about game time, he always wrote three words, "Go to war." The NFL eventually made him remove those words. This coach only had three rules: be on time, pay attention and play like hell when I tell you to. He was one of the few coaches to allow his players to grow their hair long and sit on their helmets when not in the game. It's funny; the only thing he ever failed at was a driver's test for his license.

Quarterback Joe Montana once said, "John made everyone want to watch football, women, kids any age, it didn't matter." It's true. Madden came across so honest and genuine. You couldn't talk football in the 1970s without mentioning John Madden. Then...all of a sudden...BOOM...he's gone! John Madden; from Hall-of-Fame coach, to broadcaster, to video game czar; what a life it was!

John Earl Madden was born on April 10, 1936, in Austin, Minnesota, to Earl and Mary Madden. He was the oldest of three, with two younger sisters, Dolores and Judy. His father was an auto mechanic and moved the family to Daly City, California, a town located just south of San Francisco, when John was six. His mom was a very religious woman and the family spent much of their time in church. John lived at 213 Knowles Street and attended grammar school at Our Lady of Perpetual Help. It was here that he met his lifelong friend and teammate, John Robinson. The Robinsons lived across the street from the Maddens. They hung out together with other friends at a local pool hall, and he earned some spending money working as a caddie, at $1.50 a bag for 18 holes. Madden and Robinson first played baseball together for the Daly City Red Sox Little League team. Madden graduated from grammar school in 1950, and moved on to Jefferson High School, where he played basketball, football and baseball, before graduating in 1954. He wore #74 at Jefferson. Madden was never much of a student in high school, but loved football. He played football one season at San Mateo Junior College, before receiving a football scholarship to play at the University of Oregon, in 1955. During the season, Madden suffered a right knee injury that required an operation, so in 1956 he moved on to play at Gray's Harbor College, located in Aberdeen, Washington. John was on the move again in 1957, when he transferred to Cal Poly, in San Luis Obispo. There, he played both offensive and defensive line for the Mustangs. John also starred at the catcher's position for the Cal Poly Mustang baseball team and was offered a $75 a month Minor League contract, by the New York Yankees and Boston Red Sox. But football was his game and he had also earned All-Conference honors at offensive tackle.

In 1957, two things happened to John that would steer him for the rest of his life. First, he met his future wife, Virginia Fields, in a bar located in Pismo Beach, California. Second, on December 2, 1957, big John Madden was drafted with the 244th pick of the 21st round in the 1958 NFL Draft by the Philadelphia Eagles, as an offensive guard. He was given the #77 to wear for the Eagles. The 1958 NFL Draft consisted of a sea of future stars. This draft included players like John David Crow, Lou Michaels, Chuck Howley, Alex Karras, Jim Taylor, Bobby Mitchell and Ray Nitschke. John and Virginia got engaged before he left for the Eagles' training camp. Unfortunately, John suffered torn ligaments and tendons in his left knee during his first training camp. Surgery was required and the doctor informed him that his football career may be over. After his time spent with the Philadelphia Eagles, John returned to Cal Poly to continue his education. By 1959, Madden had earned a Bachelor of Science degree in Education and later a Master of Arts degree in Education in 1961. John and Virginia were married on December 26, 1959. The Maddens lived in Pleasanton, California, and

326

had two boys, Joseph and Michael. Joe played football at Brown University, and Mike attended Harvard University and played receiver on their football team.

In 1960, Madden joined Allen Hancock College as an assistant football coach. He would be elevated to head coach in 1962 for two seasons at Allen Hancock College, before joining San Diego State Aztecs as their defensive coordinator in 1964, for Don Coryell. John Madden worked for Coryell for three years. "Don was the most intense coach I've ever been around," said Madden. There was another assistant at San Diego that John would learn from and his name was Joe Gibbs. Coryell would later coach the San Diego Chargers and the St. Louis Cardinals.

When John first started out coaching professionally, the Oakland Raiders were a part of the American Football League (AFL). In 1967, Madden was hired by Al Davis to coach the Oakland Raiders' linebackers. John Rauch was the Raiders' head coach at that time. Madden helped the team reach Super Bowl II that season, but the Raiders lost to the Green Bay Packers, 33-14.

On February 4, 1969, at the age of 32, John Madden became the youngest NFL head coach of that time. John Rauch left to take the head-coaching position with the Buffalo Bills, and Raiders' owner Al Davis hired John Madden. No one ever came between owner Al Davis and head coach John Madden. Al never turned down one of my requests," said Madden. John coached for 10 years, and he posted a 103-32-7 win-loss record in the regular season. From 1969 to 1978, Madden's Raiders never had a losing season. They won seven division titles and played eight times in the playoffs. His post-season record stands at 9-7 and his career win-loss totals read 112-39-7. Under Madden's leadership, the Raiders posted a .731 winning percentage. Madden's 1976 team went 13-1 during the regular season and beat the Minnesota Vikings in Super

Bowl XI, 32-14. At the end of Super Bowl XI, John didn't see the last Vikings' touchdown, because he was celebrating the Raiders 32-14 victory on the sideline. Madden's three tallest players, John Matuszak, Ted Hendricks and Charles Philyaw picked him up and carried him off the field on their shoulders, until one of them tripped over a photographer in front of them. One by one, down they went in a heap, including Madden. No one was hurt. That was the photo used on the front page of the *New York Times* the next day.

"The road to easy street goes through the sewer," said Madden. John's Raiders lost five AFL Championships in their first seven seasons to some of the greatest teams in NFL history and all Super Bowl winners. Still, he was the first and only coach to win 100 games in ten seasons with the same team. Madden still owns the greatest winning percentage of any coach with at least 100 wins; and he also won 75% of all his regular season games.

In 1977, at that time, Madden was the youngest coach to ever win a Super Bowl. Two years later he retired from coaching football at the age of 42. Mike Tomlin of the Pittsburgh Steelers is now the current youngest at 36.

There is no doubt that football was his life, but it was complicated. He hated losing and eventually got burned out. Madden hated holding penalties. "Your team is moving, then, BOOM, fifteen yards for holding," said John. "Now you're second and 25, the biggest stopper in football."

He really didn't have time to enjoy winning, because he was so busy trying to do it again. In 1978, John developed pain in his stomach from ulcers and had to take medication four times a day. Then, in an exhibition games played on August 12th, 1978, Darryl Stingley, a wide receiver for New England Patriots, was hit hard by Raiders Jack Tatum. It wasn't until Madden entered the locker-room after the game that John learned that Stingley had been paralyzed from the neck down from a broken neck. Madden went to the Bay Area Hospital after the game. John and Virginia invited Darryl's wife Tina to stay with them, but she declined. Tina did eventually eat supper with them on a few occasions. Jack Tatum also tried to visit Stingley in hospital, but was turned away by the family. Madden always blamed himself for not taking Tatum with him to the hospital. John Madden visited Stingley every day until he was able to travel. By the end of the 1978 season, Madden had won 103 regular season games in ten years and he was ready to retire. He just never had enough time to enjoy his success. "Coaching is a constant daily mental strain," said John. "It takes so much time from your family and just having a normal life. You live and die with every play. The game was fun and to win was frosting on the cake. I gave it everything I had, but I don't have it anymore. I wasn't enjoying life," said Madden.

Then the phone rang. Barry Franks, president of Trans World International asked John if he was interested in working for CBS Television as an analyst. Retirement was to slow for John, he needed some action. He was a teacher. John was not very impressed with most broadcasters. After some deliberation, John said "Yes." Madden signed his first TV contract with CBS in 1979. Madden joined Bob Costas on CBS for his first broadcast. Interestingly, John Madden was one of the first broadcasters to pay attention to offensive linemen. John was happy; he was teaching and learning again. John Madden is still the only broadcaster to work for all four major networks: CBS (1979-1993), Fox (1994-2001), ABC (2002-2005), and NBC (2006-2008). John worked with everybody: Gary Bender, Jack Buck, Lindsey Nelson, Dick Stockton, Vin Scully, Vern Lundquist, Al Michael and Pat Summerall. John Madden and Pat Summerall were a pair, these two clicked right away. It was like the first time peanut butter met jelly. All we needed for Thanksgiving was turkey to eat, a football to throw and John Madden on TV with a telestrator, a device which allowed him to diagram football plays over video footage. Most broadcasters sit down in the broadcast booth. Not John. He wanted to stand up so he could move around and use his arms, like he did on the sidelines. He considered himself a coach in the booth. He once knocked Gary Bender's glasses off during a broadcast. After more than 500 NFL games, Madden broadcast his final NFL game on February 1, 2009. He announced his retirement on April 16, 2009.

In 1984, in the dining car of an Amtrak train traveling from Denver to Oakland, California, John Madden met Trip Hawkins, the founder of a gaming company known as Electronic Arts (E.A. Sports). Hawkins has floated an idea by John two years earlier and John had agreed to lend his name to a video game, but John had some issues. The original video game was named John Madden Football and had been designed for seven-on-seven football. "That isn't really football," said John. "If it was going to be my name and going to be football, it had to have 22 guys on the screen. If we can't have that, we couldn't have a game." Hawkins quickly learned who would be calling the shots. Trip agreed with Madden. John insisted on realism. Madden's desire was to make the game as accurate as possible. John had envisioned this video game as a tool for teaching the game. It took Hawkins until 1988 to make the changes John wanted. John Madden was now everywhere. His Madden NFL series, the Miller Lite commercials and his 1982 "Saturday Night Live" appearance made him more famous than he ever was as a coach.

The Madden NFL series of video games continues to sell millions of copies annually and has helped turn E.A. Sports into the world's most prominent gaming company. Longtime sports broadcaster Scott Cole declared, "In every dorm room right now, every basement, on every couch, there's people sitting down playing Madden." Through 2018, the games first 30 years, over 130 million copies had been sold. Beginning in the year 2000, NFL stars were chosen for each year's cover. Eddie George graced the first cover. As of 2020, more than 7 billion dollars in revenue has been received.

His All-Madden Teams were made up of the best of the best. There was a lot of pride being a part of that team, because that meant you were tough. "Of all those players, I think Jack Youngblood personified the All-Madden Team spirit," said Madden. John Madden once said to the players chosen for the All-Madden Team, "A lot of people dream about things they have never done. You guys have done it. Everyone who's watching, everyone who's playing or coaching should say 'thank you,' because you guys established the NFL and the Super Bowl."

Looking back, John remembers his days coaching the Raiders. "One of the toughest things I ever had to do was cut George Blanda during the 1976 training camp," said John. "He had played for 26 years and was about to turn 49 and his leg just wasn't strong enough. He had kicked 335 field goals, an NFL record. He had scored 2,002 points, an NFL record. As a quarterback, he had passed for 26,920 yards and 236 touchdowns." In 1981, George Blanda was inducted into the Pro Football Hall of Fame. After the induction, the entire Madden family was invited to George's mother's home for a party. John witnessed George offering to help his 85-year-old mother walk to her bedroom that night to go to bed. She refused the help and insisted that she would be perfectly fine and could take care of herself. "It was then that I understood where George got his stamina from," said John.

John Madden once sat next to Jack Nicklaus on a flight from San Francisco to New Orleans. "What makes the difference in golfers?" asked Madden. "You are all so good, why do you and a few other golfers win all the tournaments?" "Practice," said Jack. "Most people think I'm practicing before I play, but I'm not, I'm just warming up. I practice after the round. The first thing I practice is every shot that I hit poorly that day. Then I practice all the shots I didn't have to hit that day. All golfers like to practice the shots they hit well. Conversely, not enough practice the shots they don't hit well. As a result, they don't get any better. Ever since I learned that, not only have I become a better player, but I have slept better," said Jack.

Under Madden, the Raiders had many of their games remembered in NFL lore. The "Sea of Hands" play was given the NFL Most Significant Play Award in 1974. The "Ghost to the Post" game received the NFL's Most Significant Play Award in 1977. The "Holy Roller" play received the 1978 NFL's Most Controversial Play Award. "We worked on that play for years," laughed Madden. The play known as the "Immaculate Reception" against Pittsburgh will be talked about forever.

A few of John's favorite coaches included Don Shula, Tom Landry, Chuck Noll and Bud Grant. "Grant was the best coach no one ever talked about," said Madden. He considered Hank Stram his biggest nemesis. "Stram was always trying to give me something negative to think about before the game," said Madden. John was always disappointed that he never got to coach against Vince Lombardi. Madden's first year with the Raiders as their head coach was 1969, Lombardi's first and only year with the Washington Redskins. Lombardi died from cancer before the 1970 season began.

Madden insisted that the best quarterbacks he ever coached against were Joe Namath and Terry Bradshaw, in that order. "Namath could throw the eyes out of a football," said John.

Some of his players John liked the most were Ted "Kick'em-in-the-head" Hendricks, Gene Upshaw, Dave Casper, Henry

Lawrence and Ben Davidson. "They were my renegades," said John Madden. Here are a few of the comments he made about Ben Davidson, Gene Upshaw and Art Shell.

Big Ben Davidson stood 6'8" tall and carried 280 pounds into each game. He was huge. He was so tall he had to line up two yards behind the line of scrimmage to get into a three-point stance or he'd be off sides. If you saw his footprints in the sand, you'd call 911. Crowds of people would part when he walked through. Kids put their autograph books away and stared. This Hall-of-Fame defensive end for the Oakland Raiders didn't invent spearing; it just seemed that way. "That's just the way I was taught to play football," said Ben. He was a force in the clubhouse. Half the guys loved him and the other half were afraid of him. I was always glad to see him play on television because that meant he wasn't hiding in the back seat of my car with a knife and masking tape. When asked why he played so viciously, he answered, "If you come to my side of the field, you have to pay."

Oakland Raiders' and Robstown Hall-of-Fame offensive guard, Gene Upshaw, wore uniform #63. At 6'5" inches tall and weighing 280 pounds, he played in three Super Bowls and his nickname was "Highway 63." Why? Because when Upshaw pulled out leading a sweep, there was no rest stop on Highway 63, you either got out of the way or you just got run over.

But his favorite may have been Art Shell. Here are some of his thoughts on Art Shell. Oakland Raiders' Hall-of-Fame offensive tackle, Art Shell, was a monster. At 6' 5"tall and weighing 300 plus pounds before dinner, he owned one of the fastest first steps in the game. What he lacked in speed, he made up for with quickness. Shell played mean. He was the kind of guy who would push you down a flight of stairs. Raiders' coach, John Madden, once said, "We used to estimate how much Art Shell weighed by how much sunlight shined between his legs." John continued, "Left tackle is the toughest position to play in football. Most teams put their tight end next to the right tackle, which means the left tackle doesn't have the tight end to help him block. For that reason, most defensive teams put their best pass rusher at the right end against the offensive left tackle." John Madden later said about Shell after Art had become the Raiders' head coach, "There are three types of players: Players who make things happen, players who watch things happen, and players who don't know what's happening. Art Shell made things happen. No one ever wanted to talk to Art Shell about another player. They wanted to talk about Art Shell."

Madden's fear of flying was well-known. He had lost several friends in an airplane accident in 1960. In 1979, he took his last airplane ride. Why? During a flight from Tampa, Florida, John experienced a panic attack. John explained later that it was not the feeling of turbulence or fear of heights that bothered him, but primarily because he was claustrophobic. Madden then chose to ride a train until he got the Madden Cruiser. Madden rode over 100,000 miles a year on a train, and at that time it took 72 hours to go from coast to coast. Madden initially used Dolly Parton's Tour Bus to get around. In 1987, Madden was supplied a custom bus with drivers by Greyhound Lines in exchange for advertising and speaking engagements. It would be christened the Madden Cruiser. For 23 years, Willie Yarbrough became his longtime bus driver.

During his time in professional football, John Madden was the Head Coach of the Oakland Raiders and winner of Super Bowl XI. As a broadcaster, Madden won 16 Sports Emmy Awards. John was also chosen the 1984 NSMA National Sportscaster of the Year. Madden is also included in the Yahoo! Sports' Top 50 All-Time Network Television Sports Announcers. Madden was inducted into the California Bay Area Sports Hall of Fame in 1991. In 2002, Madden became the Pete Rozelle Radio-Television Award winner. Madden also wrote three best-selling books entitled, <u>Hey, Wait A Minute? I Wrote A Book</u>, <u>One Knee Equals Two feet</u>, and <u>All Madden</u>.

On February 4, 2006, 28 years after he had stopped coaching, John Madden was inducted into the Pro Football Hall of Fame and what a class it was. This class also included Warren Moon, Reggie White, Rayfield Wright, Troy Aikman, and Harry Carson. Madden will always be a football coach. John has the highest winning percentage of any NFL coach in the Pro Football Hall of Fame. He had waited almost three decades to be voted in. "I was emotional for 24 hours," said John. Three hundred people flew to Canton, Ohio, to see him inducted. "The busts in the Hall of Fame talk to each other at night and I can't wait to be a part of that," said John. In 2009, Madden joined the California Hall of Fame and was chosen a 2010 NSMA Hall-of-Fame inductee.

John Madden died unexpectedly at his home in Pleasanton, California, on December 28, 2021, at the age of 85. John and his wife, Virginia, celebrated their 62nd wedding anniversary two days before his death. John loved Virginia more than Banana Cream Pie. Madden is survived by Virginia; their two boys, Joseph and Michael, and five grandkids.

Life is not necessarily a longevity contest. It's a contest of quality. What good you can get from life and what good you could give back. For me, John Madden will always be the head coach of the Oakland Raiders. He was one of the most respected men in football and the most popular broadcaster in NFL history, but he never stopped being a coach. "I talked like I coached, not like a broadcaster," said Madden. NFL Commissioner Roger Goodell said, "Madden was to the NFL what Elvis Presley was to Rock and Roll, King!"

The game feels a little smaller now that John Madden has left us. What I will remember the most is how magnetic he was to the general public and athletes.

SHARPSHOOTER

This guy had more range than Whitney Houston. He helped give the game of basketball pace and speed. You had to be at the game to see his entire shot because the ball was shot with such a high arc it sometimes left your television screen. This fellow was to basketball what jazz was to music, and his bank shot was as pure as a summer rain. There was no ceiling on what this kid could do with a basketball. He was a bit high strung, confrontational and talented. Like most athletes, the fear of failure pushed him. The man was a red-light player. When the red light on the camera came on, he was ready to go. This fellow may have owned two of the greatest hands in the game, and he could get hotter than Texas asphalt on the 4th of July. With a silky-smooth bank shot, you got the feeling he could have scored on crutches.

He was a catch-and-release guy and I'm not talking about fishing. I'm talking about shooting a basketball. This kid was all about hoops. It was simple, he got game. He was all for trash talking. It was the way he grew up, and it sometimes seemed like he lived just a block away from the Twilight Zone. He just played the game a little bit differently than everyone else. He understood that in the game of basketball you have to find your rhythm, not someone else's, but yours. This guy wasn't just a point guard, he was an artist; and he could jump higher than giraffe ears. He had always been a star. The man could read a defense with a blindfold on, and he never flinched when the ball came his way. He was always in motion, only the lens of a camera could stop him. A straight-away bank shot was like a lay-up for him. Sam

Jones was not just a Hall-of-Fame basketball player, he was a ball club. Jones had always wanted to be on the team no one else wanted to play. The Boston Celtics believed that teamwork makes the dream work. When the going got hot, Jones played cool. I get chills just writing about him. Sam Jones, you were ridiculous.

Memories are photos of our mind. They can be more valuable than feelings. Bill Russell was once asked by his friend, Dusty Baker, why the Celtics were so good for so long. "Because we loved each other," answered Russell, the 11 time NBA Champion. There are always moments in time when something happens on the court, and you think to yourself that play just pushed this game forward. So, sit back and let me tell you about Sam Jones.

Samuel Jones was born on June 24, 1933, in Wilmington, North Carolina, the home of "Meadowlark" Lemon and Michael Jordan. Basketball may have been in his blood. Sam attended high school at Laurinburg Institute located in Laurinburg, North Carolina, and graduated in 1951. A fine rebounder and sharpshooter, Sam made his way to North Carolina Central University (HBCU), to play college basketball from 1951-1954, for Hall-of-Fame Coach John B. McLendon and Coach Floyd Brown. Sam then served two years in the U. S. Army (1954-1956). Jones was originally drafted on April 30, 1956 by the Minneapolis Lakers, with the 3rd pick in the 8th round (59th overall) of the 1956 NBA Draft, but he chose to return during the 1956-1957 season, to North Carolina Central, to play his senior year and earn his degree. Jones played in 100 college games, scoring 1,770 points (17.7ppg) and pulled down 909 rebounds (9.1 rpg). N.C. Central was a Division II school at the time and Celtics' Hall of Fame Coach, "Red" Auerbach, visited the 1957 NCAA Champion Tar Heels from the University of North Carolina (UNC) at Chapel Hill. The Tar Heels, with a season record of 31-0, had just won the 1957 NCAA Championship by beating Wilt Chamberlain and the Kansas Jayhawks 54-53, for the title. Red scouted the UNC team and the NCAA Player of the Year, Lennie Rosenbluth.

It's true that Red had "bird dogs" (friends) all over the country to help him look for talent. Wake Forrest basketball coach "Bones" McKinney had played college basketball at N.C. State and UNC, after a tour in the U.S. Army. Bones had also played professionally for the Celtics. Bones told Red that he should visit UNC, but the best player in the state was a few miles away in Durham, N.C., and his name was Sam Jones. Bones had seen Sam Jones play and raved about his talent. McKinney's word was good enough for Red. Jones was 6-foot-4, tall for a guard at that time, but he was much quicker than many smaller guards. Sam also had something else, a bank shot. At a time when two-handed set shots were the norm, Jones showed others how to use the bank shot. Auerbach said, "Jones made it popular, and he made it an art." Jones had scored 1,770 points (17.7 ppg) during his college career and was a three-time All-CIAA League selection. His #41 was later retired by the Eagles. Jones had planned on becoming a teacher until Red Auerbach of the Boston Celtics called, after the draft. On April 17, 1957, Sam Jones was taken with the 8th pick of the first round in the 1957 NBA Draft, by the Boston Celtics. Red Aurbach had left the state of North Carolina without ever seeing Sam Jones play the game of basketball. Lennie Rosenbluth of UNC was taken by the Philadelphia Warriors with the 6th pick of the 1957 NBA Draft.

In Bill Russell's book entitled <u>Red and Me</u>, Bill talks about the drafting of Sam Jones. In 1957, Russell was the only black man on the Celtics team and had just helped Boston win their first NBA title in his second season. After the draft, Red called Bill and said, "I drafted Sam Jones out of North

338

Carolina Central University. How about this guy, Russ? You think he can do good for us?" Bill responded, "Who the hell is Sam Jones? "He's a black kid; I thought you would know about him," said Red. "Listen, Red. I don't know all of them," said Bill. Red laughed, but the question stayed with Russell for awhile. Of course, Sam and Bill would later become roommates.

Jones didn't start right away. Sam averaged 4.6 points per game his rookie year. He and teammate K. C. Jones had to wait behind Hall-of-Fame guards, Bob Cousy and Bill Sharman. Early in the 1960 season, Bill Sharman was injured and Sam Jones got his first start, but he did play the next 11 seasons with Bill Russell, winning 10 championship rings, which was the second most in NBA history. Sam Jones and Bill Russell retired the same year after the Celtics beat Chamberlain and the Lakers in 1969. Wearing #24, this 198-pound right-handed point guard made his NBA debut on October 22, 1957, against the St. Louis Hawks. Sam recorded one rebound in three minutes of play. In his 11th career game, Sam recorded 15 points and five rebounds in a 109-118 loss to the Syracuse Nationals.

During the 1965-66 season, two teams, the Boston Celtics and the Philadelphia 76ers, became the first teams to start five black players. Boston started Bill Russell, Sam Jones, K.C. Jones, Willie Naulls and Tom "Satch" Sanders. The Celtics also hired Russell to succeed Auerbach as the head coach, in 1966. Sam Jones was on the way to a Hall-of-Fame career.

Here's a funny story that you might enjoy. Celtics Hall-of-Fame coach, Red Auerbach had only one ironclad team rule. Why? Because he thought lots of rules would take away his flexibility with the team and hurt the other members who did nothing wrong. Can you guess what his one rule was? Never in a million years! Here goes...no one was allowed to eat pancakes on game day. Red thought the pancakes would sit in their stomach and slow them down on the court. One night after a game, the team flew to Rochester, New York, and arrived at the hotel at 1 a.m. in the morning. Sam Jones and Bill Russell were hungry and decided to get something to eat at a nearby IHOP restaurant. They both ordered a stack of pancakes. Just as their food was served, and they took their first bite, Red walked in. Red said, "That bite just cost you $5 and if you take another bite, it will cost you $5 more." Russell responded, "What are you talking about, we just played, Red; it's 1 a.m. and we were playing at 8 o'clock tonight." Upset, Red said, "I've got one damn rule and you two can't even follow it." Sam and Bill sent their pancakes back and ordered eggs.

Sam knew that to become a legend you have to beat a legend. That's how Jones felt about beating Wilt Chamberlain and the 76ers. "Sam used to taunt Wilt something terrible," said Bob Cousy. "Sam would set up 20 feet from the basket and wave to Chamberlain to come out and guard him." "Come on out big fella," hollered Sam. "As soon as Wilt would take a few steps, Sam would drill that backboard shot and holler 'Too late,' as he ran down the court. Sam never missed," said Cousy.

In Game 7 during the 1962 Eastern Conference Finals against Philadelphia, Jones hit the winning shot over Wilt Chamberlain with 2 seconds left to go in the game. During Game 7 of the 1962 NBA Finals, Jones scored 5 of the last 10 points in overtime, to beat the Lakers for the Celtics' fourth consecutive NBA title. Sam Jones played in five All-Star Games, scoring 41 points, and grabbed 14 rebounds, along with 15 assists in limited play.

Sam Jones played in 871 career regular season games and another 154 playoff games during his 12 seasons with the Boston Celtics (1957-1969). He scored 15,411 points (17.7

ppg) during regular season games and 2,909 (18.9 ppg) during the playoffs. Sam also pulled down 4,305 rebounds (4.9 rpg) and dished out 2,209 assists (2.5 apg). From 1962 to 1968, Jones led the Celtics in scoring three times. At the time of his retirement, Sam was 36 years old and owned the Celtics team record for most points scored in a single game, with 51 against the Detroit Pistons on October 29, 1965. That record has since been broken by several players. When he stepped away from the game, Sam also held the team record for most points scored, with 15,411. Jones won 10 NBA titles, second only to Bill Russell's 11.

Sam Jones was inducted into the NAIA Basketball Hall of Fame in 1962. In 1969, Jones became the first African-American to be inducted into the North Carolina Sports Hall of Fame. An HBCU legend, Jones was selected to the CIAA Basketball Hall of Fame in 1981. He was named to the Naismith Memorial Basketball Hall of Fame in 1984 along with John Havlicek. Jones was also named to the NBA 25th Anniversary Team (1971), as one of the 50 Greatest Players in NBA History (1996), and the NBA 75th Anniversary Team (2021). Jones was also selected to be a part of the inaugural class inducted into the American Basketball Hall of Fame.

Sam Jones made his last bank shot on Thursday night, December 30, 2021. He was 88 and living in Boca Raton, Florida. Jones had been hospitalized for failing health. Sam was married to Gladys Chavis, until her death in 2018. Together, they had five children. The Celtics honored Sam Jones with a moment of silence Friday night, December 31st, before their game with the Phoenix Suns. Jones' #24 had been retired back in 1969, while he was still playing, and now hangs in the rafters at the Boston Garden. Jones coached basketball at Federal City College from 1969-1973 and returned to North Carolina Central University in 1973 to coach one season. He became the assistant coach for the

New Orleans Jazz, in 1974. Afterwards, he retired to Silver Springs, Maryland, where he served as a substitute teacher in the Montgomery County public school system.

Ninety-three-year-old Bob Cousy was beside himself. He had just heard from Satch Sanders of Sam Jones' death. "Now we're down to just three, Satch Sanders, Bill Russell and I are holding up the float, I guess," said Cousy. The Celtics family lost John Havlicek in April of 2019, Tommy Heinsohn in November of 2020, and K.C. Jones on Christmas Day, 2020.

"Celtic teammates don't say goodbye; they say 'See you later,'" said Cousy.

EPILOGUE

THIRTY-TWO

There has always been something special about the #32. I can't explain what it is but I can tell you that it has been worn by many of the very best athletes in all of sports. The first time I noticed the #32 was as a kid watching the great Jim Brown run for the Cleveland Browns. Then Billy Cunningham made the #32 popular at the University of North Carolina before playing for the Philadelphia 76ers. Sandy Koufax and Steve Carlton, both Hall-of-Fame pitchers, wore #32; while "Magic" Johnson, Kevin McHale, Bill Walton, Scottie Pippin, and Karl Malone also earned Hall-of-Fame status in the NBA, wearing that number. Don't forget O.J. Simpson, who also wore #32. Buck Leonard of the Negro Leagues made the #32 famous, and he has also been inducted into the Baseball Hall of Fame. Dale Hunter of the Washington Capitols, Jason Kidd with the Phoenix Suns, and Sean Elliot of the San Antonio Spurs all wore #32. Edgerrin James and Ricky Watters are also on the list. But there is one fellow who slides under the radar when speaking about the #32. His name is Elston Gene Howard, the first African-American to play for the New York Yankees.

Elston Howard was born in St. Louis, Missouri. "Ellie" was a big strong guy who usually played the part of peacemaker. He owned a great smile that displayed the gap between his two front teeth. A four-sport letterman in high school, he is now in the Missouri Hall of Fame. Howard tried out for the

Cardinals in 1948, as an outfielder. He was never called back. Ellie later joined the Negro Leagues, the K.C. Monarchs. His manager was Buck O'Neil, and he roomed with Ernie Banks. "If I had a boy, I would want him to be like Elston," said O'Neil. Howard later signed with the Yankees and was sent to their Minor League team known as the Kansas City Blues. He spent three years being converted to a catcher, by Bill Dickey. The Yankees already had an African-American power hitter by the name of Vic Power in the Minors, but felt that Power was too flashy to fit the Yankee mold. Power was traded in 1953, leaving Howard on deck. Howard was sent to the International Leagues, where he not only hit .331, but was also voted the MVP of the league. He was ready but the American League integrated much slower than the National League. In 1954, New York did not win the American League pennant, which may have helped Ellie. In 1955, there were still four teams that did not have an African-American player. One of those teams was the Yankees, who brought Howard up in 1955. Yes, New York needed an African-American player but they also needed a Yankee. His first game was April 14, 1955, and he did not disappoint. Ellie hit .290, with 10 home runs and 43 RBI's, while he platooned with Yogi Berra and Johnny Blanchard. He also became the sixth player in MLB history to hit a home run in his first World Series at-bat, against the Brooklyn Dodgers. Howard played about 100 games in 1956 and 1957. In 1958, Elston Howard became the first African-American to be named a World Series MVP, as the Yankees beat the Milwaukee Braves.

In 1960, Howard started more games at catcher as Yogi played in left field. Ellie would knock a pinch-hit home run in Game One and hit a smoking .462 in the World Series, against the winning Pittsburgh Pirates club. Casey Stengel was fired after the Series, and Ralph Houk took his place. The first move Houk made in 1961 was to designate Elston

Howard as the Yankees' starting catcher. Howard swatted .348, and the Bombers never looked back. "I'm very fortunate to be with the Yankees," said Howard. "This is the greatest thing in my life."

The year 1963 was huge for Ellie. Not only did he win the Gold Glove Award for the catcher's position, but he basically carried the team as Maris and Mantle were hurt most of the year. For his contributions, Elston Howard would become the first African-American to win the American League MVP Award.

In August of 1964, the Yankees held an Elston Howard night at the stadium. Words like pioneer and "instrument of change" were used. The newspapers wrote, "He may be one of the most important Yankees ever." Teammate Bobby Richardson said, "Ballplayers know who the greatest players are, and they all knew Ellie Howard."

It was during the 1964 season that I won a trip to New York City to visit the World's Fair. I was 13 and we stayed at the Manhattan Hotel. We even ate at Momma Leone's, a world renowned Italian Restaurant. We also got to go see a Yankees Game at old Yankee Stadium. It was on this night that I got to see my sports hero, Mickey Mantle, and watch Whitey Ford pitch to catcher, Elston Howard. I did not realize the significance of this until recently, but Howard would become the first African-American I ever saw play in the Major Leagues in person. Jackie Robinson had already retired.

Howard injured his elbow later on, which required surgery. Unfortunately, he was still unable to straighten out his arm. He would never be the same. To his dismay, Howard was traded to the Boston Red Sox in the middle of the 1967 season. There he led the Boston Red Sox to the World Series against the St. Louis Cardinals and helped Jim Lonborg win the American League Cy Young Award. After fourteen years, Howard retired from playing, at the end of the 1968 season. In 1969, Howard became the first African-American Coach in the American League with the Yankees and should have been the first African-American Manager in 1973, but the Yanks chose Bill Virdon. "If Elston had played for any other club, he would be in the Hall of Fame," said Bobby Richardson.

In 1978, Ellie was diagnosed with a rare heart disorder and suffered from inflammation of the heart muscle. He joined Phil Rizzuto in the broadcast booth as he was unable to fulfill his coaching duties. "I never felt like I had it made. I always played like I hadn't got there yet. It's been a long battle for me. When I look back on the years I can see where I earned whatever I got. Nobody walked up to me and gave me anything. I'm really proud of that. I'm really more proud of trying than I am of anything," said Howard. Elston Howard died at the young age of 51 on December 14, 1980.

The New York Yankees retired Howard's #32. He had played in a total of ten World Series'. "He is the one person I really miss today," said the late Ernie Banks. It has been said, there are no footprints too small to leave an imprint on the world. History will remember #32, Elston Howard.

CPSIA information can be obtained
at www.ICGtesting.com
Printed in the USA
LVHW020733021222
734416LV00001B/86